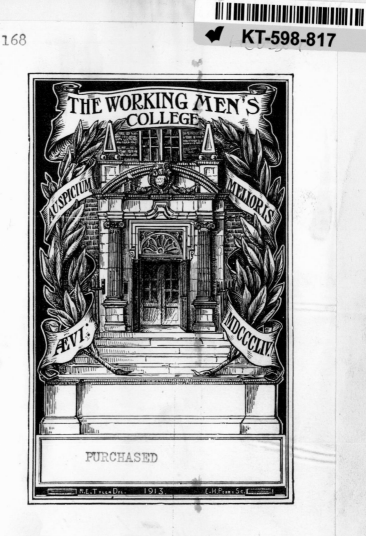

THE WORKING MEN'S COLLEGE

AUSPICIUM

MELIORIS

ÆVI.

MDCCCLIV

PURCHASED

R.E.Tyler Del. 1913. C.H.Perry Sc.

WORKING MEN'S COLLEGE

LIBRARY REGULATIONS

The Library is open every week-day evening (except Saturday), from 6 30 to 10 o'clock.

This book may be kept for three weeks. If not returned within that period, the borrower will be liable to a fine of one penny per week.

If lost or damaged, the borrower will be required to make good such loss or damage.

Only one book may be borrowed at a time.

# YOUNG VICTORIANS

MARION LOCHHEAD

# *Young Victorians*

JOHN MURRAY

ALBEMARLE STREET LONDON

Printed in Great Britain by
Wyman & Sons, Ltd., London, Fakenham and Reading and
published by John Murray (Publishers) Ltd.

To
SIR  JOHN  MURRAY,  K.C.V.O.,  D.S.O.
Gratias debeo;
Gratias plena corde reddo

# CONTENTS

# CONTENTS

## Part Three
## LATE VICTORIAN
### 1870–1900

# ILLUSTRATIONS

# FOREWORD

HAVING written of Victorian Childhood in *Their First Ten Years* I found the temptation to continue the tale of youth irresistible, and the next ten years of girlhood and boyhood, at home and abroad, at school and at college, offered an almost inevitable subject. In this sequel the material has been even richer than in the volume about childhood. I am aware of many omissions, of necessary excisions, of what may appear an arbitrary selection of matter, particularly in regard to schools. For this I beg the indulgence of readers who may look in vain for mention of some favourite memoirs or of their own school. Each chapter has its hero or heroine, and I have tried to make my portrait gallery representative, and to present a cross-section of youthful Victorian society. My self-imposed age limit of twenty has closed the door on the career and marriage of most of my characters.

I gladly and gratefully acknowledge my debts for help and stimulus in many forms to:

Sir John Murray, Mrs. Osyth Leeston (most patient and constructive of critics), Dr. William Beattie of the National Library of Scotland, and his staff for their apparently unlimited resources, including all the delights of *The Monthly Packet*, the London Library, and those who have kindly lent photographs for illustrations.

I am grateful to the following for their permission to quote extracts from the works listed:

The Lady Baden-Powell and Messrs. Arthur Pearson for *Lessons from the 'Varsity of Life*, by the late Lord Baden-Powell.

The Executrix of the late Maurice Baring, Messrs. William Heinemann and Messrs. A. P. Watt for *The Puppet Show of Memory*, by Maurice Baring.

Messrs. Jonathan Cape for *A Child in the Crystal*, by Lady Sybil Lubbock.

Sir Winston Churchill and Odhams Press for *My Early Life*.

Messrs. John Farquharson for *Irish Memories*, by E. OE. Somerville and Martin Ross.

Messrs. William Heinemann for *Recollected in Tranquillity*, by Janet Courtenay.

Messrs. Longmans, Green & Co. for *Impressions That Remained*, by Ethel Smyth, and *Edward Bowen*, by W. E. Bowen.

Mr. Denis Mackail, Messrs. Peter Davies and Messrs. A. P. Watt for *The Story of J. M. B.*

Messrs. Macmillan & Co. for *This Was My World*, by Viscountess Rhondda.

Messrs. John Murray for *The Training of a Sovereign*, edited by Lord Esher.

Sir Harold Nicolson for *King George V.*

The Oxford University Press for *A London Family*, by M. Vivian Hughes.

Susan, Lady Tweedsmuir for *The Lilac and the Rose.*

Mrs. Vachell, Messrs. Cassell and Messrs. A. P. Watt for *Distant Fields*, by the late H. A. Vachell.

# PROLOGUE
## MAJESTIC GIRLHOOD

'TODAY is my birthday. I am today fourteen years old! How very old!' Many a girl has felt the burden of years on such an anniversary. The particular girl who recorded the sentiment in her *Journal* on 24th May, 1833, was the most exalted in England. On this festive day the Princess Victoria rose as usual at half past seven and received her presents: 'From Mamma a lovely hyacinth brooch and a china pen-tray.' In this royal home birthday gifts were both given and received, so: 'I gave Mamma a little ring. From Lehzen I got a pretty little china figure and a lovely little china basket. I gave her a golden chain and Mamma gave her a pair of earrings to match.'

Other gifts came from the royal family and from the Duchess of Kent's household: entrancing trinkets, for the age of elegance was not ended. King William, who cherished his niece and heiress while detesting her mother, sent diamond earrings, and Queen Adelaide a turquoise brooch which the Duke and Duchess of Cumberland matched with a bracelet. From 'Aunt Gloucester, Aunt Sophia and Uncle Sussex' came a *ferronnière* of pearls, from Aunt Augusta a sandalwood box. The Duchess of Gordon presented a china basket along with 'a lovely little crown of precious stones which plays *God Save the King*'. Another basket from the Duchess of Northumberland was of ivory and was 'filled with the work of her nieces', and a host of other delights—a brooch in the form of a lily-of-the-valley, a gold inkstand, a scent-bottle, an album of paintings, boxes, handkerchief sachets and embroidered handkerchiefs were piled on the gift-table. Few girls could have one so costly, but many might be equally delighted by more modest but still exquisite trinkets, such as English craftsmanship still created: a set of corals, a locket of seed pearls and turquoise, beads and embroideries, boxes of carved wood or papier mâché.

The Princess had always had rich gifts but her childhood had not, for all that, been happy. Like her humbler contemporaries she had led a strictly disciplined life under the severe eye of Mamma and the no less vigilant if more benign gaze of her governess Lehzen. Life in a palace was no easier than in any schoolroom in England, but the royal pupil was aware of her position as heiress presumptive and this awareness strengthened her naturally resolute will. She obeyed because she must, a day would come when she could command.

Two years later came the event of her confirmation. There were more presents: 'I gave Mamma a drawing done by me, in recollection of today. I gave Lehzen a ring, also in recollection of today.' The King sent her a set of emeralds. Dressed in white lace with a bonnet of white crape, she drove to the Chapel Royal with her mother, Lehzen, and Lady Flora Hastings, and there in the presence of the King and Queen, received the laying-on of hands by the Archbishop of Canterbury. Her thoughts were not entirely upon lace and emeralds; she realized at least a little of what the sacrament meant: 'I felt that my confirmation was one of the most solemn and important events in my life. . . . I went, with the firm determination to become a true Christian, to try and comfort my dear Mamma in all her griefs, trials and anxieties, and to become a dutiful and affectionate daughter to her. Also to be obedient to dear Lehzen who has done so much for me.'

She was out of her childhood now, and although still under discipline, allowed a little gaiety. Her formidable Mamma realized that the future Queen must be adorned with graces and accomplishments and be given at least a glimpse of the great world. Victoria's love of the theatre and opera was indulged. She loved Italian opera, and did not care for the grave harmonies of Handel. On a visit to York she found *The Messiah* performed in the Minster 'very heavy and tiresome'.

Now she heard Grisi and Lablache sing and saw Joanna Baillie's tragedy *The Separation* performed with Kemble and Helen Faucit in the leading parts: 'Though well written it is rather unnatural and very heavy in parts. I must say I greatly prefer *The Provost of Bruges*.' Lighter entertainment was offered by Madame Vestris and her husband Charles Matthews in a *Birletta: One Hour, or The Carnival Ball.*

She had singing lessons from Lablache whom she found 'not only a most delightful, patient and agreeable master, but a most good-humoured, pleasing, agreeable and honest man. His manners are very gentlemanly and quiet, and he had something very frank, free and honest in his countenance'. She was impressed by his 'volubility of tongue'—the Latin swiftness after so much lumbering German. 'He can sing such quantities of words at such a rate' was her artless comment. Her own volubility in the written word was even more remarkable; she never used one word where six would do.

It was the beginning of her worldly and enjoyable education with the faintest hint of a *schwärmerei* such as might be felt by any schoolgirl, and the irruption of a delicious masculine, even possibly Bohemian, element into her schoolroom.

And so she came to her eighteenth birthday and was of age. 'How old! Yet how far am I from being what I should be. I shall from this day take the firm resolution to study with renewed assiduity, to keep my attention always well-fixed on what I am about and to strive to become every day less trifling and more fit for what, if Heaven will it, I am some day to be.'

If Heaven had not willed it she would have been extremely displeased, but already, with the King gravely ill, the London populace were preparing to shout: 'God Save the Queen.' They crowded the streets to see the Princess drive to a Court ball:

'The anxiety of the people to see poor, stupid me was very great, and I must say I was very touched by it, and feel proud, which I have always done of my country and of the English nation.'

The ball was shadowed by the absence of the King and his gentle Consort, but youth could not but enjoy it, for all that. Victoria danced a great deal, but no waltzes: 'In my station I unfortunately cannot valse or gallop.'

During the quiet days that followed she had kind thoughts of
the dying King: 'Poor man! He was always kind to me and he
meant it well, I know. He was odd, very odd and singular, but
his intentions were often ill-interpreted.' ('Odd' is a meiosis, but
this quality had, if anything, endeared him to a people who enjoy
eccentricity.)

On 15th June, 1837, Lord Liverpool came to Kensington
Palace and Victoria 'had a highly important conversation with
him—alone'. It is the first entrance of that *motif* 'alone'. Heaven
played its part. On Tuesday, 20th June: 'I was awakened at
6 o'clock by Mamma who told me that the Archbishop of Canterbury and Lord Conyngham were here and wished to see me.
I got out of bed and went into my sitting-room (only in my
dressing-gown) and *alone* and saw them.' They brought the
news she had expected: Lord Conyngham making the formal
announcement of the King's death, the Archbishop assuring her
that the end had been peace. The young Queen charged them
with a message of sympathy to the widowed Queen Adelaide,
and withdrew to dress. Her traditional vow: 'I will be good'
was thus set down and amplified:

'Since it has pleased Providence to place me in this station, I
shall do my utmost to fulfil my duty towards my country. I
am very young, and perhaps in many though not in all things
inexperienced, but I am sure that very few have more real good
will and more real desire to do what is fit and right than I have.'

After breakfast she received her Prime Minister Lord Melbourne 'in my room, and OF COURSE QUITE ALONE as I shall
always do my ministers' and held her first Council—'I went in,
of course, quite alone.' The *motif* recurred: she ordered her bed
to be removed from her mother's room to one of her own. In
one morning she passed completely out of her mother's power
and influence.

Until the end of her long life she was to be alone in majesty;
she gloried in her unique queenhood; it was as essentially part
of her as her present girlhood or as the womanhood, wifehood
and motherhood that awaited her. She was Queen first, last and

all the time, Queen more than daughter, more than wife until love so subjugated her that she announced herself 'Your wife, Albert', and most certainly Queen more than mother. Much of the fascination of her *Journal*, so artless by any literary standard, so enthralling by the psychological, lies in its revelation of the gradual possession of the girl by the Queen, for it *was* possession.

Did she ever, for all her volubility of self-expression, see herself alone, untenanted by majesty? She became Queen as another girl might become a nun, fulfilling a vocation, wholly absorbed into the new life.

For thousands of her girlish subjects this must have seemed like a fairy-tale, this passing from schoolroom to throne-room, a girl not unlike themselves laying aside lesson-books for a sceptre, the simple dresses ordered by Mamma for robes of velvet and ermine. Young ladyhood was exalted in the Queen and the sentimental heart of the public throbbed to the appeal of innocent majesty after reigns which, though never lacking elegance, had attained innocence only through witlessness. Victoria had no fairy princess beauty, but she walked in enchantment. Royalty enveloped her dumpy little figure and was never laid aside.

It invested her all that day of her proclamation, while she gave audiences and considered the affairs of her realm. At the end: 'I went down and said good-night to Mamma,' who could no longer dismiss her daughter to bed. As for the other, gentler guide: 'My *dear* Lehzen will ALWAYS remain with me as my friend, but will take no place about me.' There would be no grey eminence behind this throne. The door of the schoolroom was firmly shut, and the royal feet walked quickly out of girlhood as the Queen moved to Buckingham Palace from Kensington:

'I have had pleasant balls and delicious concerts here. *Enfin*, I like this poor old Palace. . . . I have gone through many painful and disagreeable scenes here, 'tis true, but still I am fond of the poor old Palace.'

It had not been a happy girlhood; she had been guarded but

B

not cherished. Twenty-four years later when the Duchess of Kent died, the Queen wrote sadly of that lack of tenderness:

'To miss a mother's friendship—not to be able to have her to confide in—when a girl most needs it, was fearful. I dare not think of it—it drives me wild now.'

Her golden years had begun; she had freedom and power, all the splendour she loved and popularity too: the London crowds cheered her every appearance. She found, too, in one man the love, admiration and stimulus she craved, and they were all offered her with the utmost decorum.

Melbourne gave her all she had missed through her father's early death, though how much the Duke of Kent could have given is matter for debate. The old King had been kind and she had loved him, but not with any veneration. No one had given her a truly fatherly and protective devotion until now. For Melbourne, the relation was completely satisfying. He was a *père manqué*, and all his pent-up tenderness was evoked by this royal girl, his Queen to whom he paid homage of the heart as well as of duty. He was, as even the cynical Greville admitted, utterly discreet, always the subject and Minister; the Queen was set apart from him as from all her subjects by her very queen-hood, yet she was to him the daughter he had never begotten, perhaps as well so, for Lady Caroline's child would have had a wretched heritage. Melbourne did more to form the Queen for the world than any other influence. 'He has such an honest, frank yet gentle manner. . . . I always feel so satisfied when I have talked with him.'

Her *Journal* from this point becomes more intricate in pattern. There is still the volubility, still the rapture, sometimes the silliness though a hard core of sense is never lacking; but when Melbourne's talk is recorded, as it is so often and so fully, we are aware of a new spirit, a mellow wisdom, a ripe and delectable worldliness, a depth of civilization alien to the royal mind and all the more fascinating.

This talk was her chief delight but there were other pleasures: music, to which her German blood responded even if her taste

were sentimental. Thalberg played to her his own fantasias on
*God Save the Queen* and on airs from *Norma* and *Les Huguenots*:
'Never, never did I hear anything at all like him. He combines
the most *exquisite, delicate,* touching feeling with the most wonderful execution. He is quite unique and I am quite in ecstasies
and raptures with him.'

There are moments when we see through the clear glass of
her *Journal* the Queen as she could not see herself: as extremely
and endearingly young, especially in her delight at being grown-
up and 'a regular royal Queen'.

She revelled in playing hostess to her first guests, 'Uncle
Leopold and Aunt Louise' (of Belgium) at Windsor: 'an in-
expressible happiness and joy to me to have these dearest, beloved
relatives with me in my own house' and in being a fellow-
monarch not merely a niece. She enjoyed a levée: 'I had my hand
kissed nearly 3,000 times.' Even more, she enjoyed a review:
'I felt for the first time like a man and as if I could fight myself
at the head of my troops.'

Her first summer at Windsor passed quickly. She rode with
Melbourne and with members of her household, held councils,
received guests, and gave dinners with something of a child's
delight in playing hostess. Greville, bidden to Windsor in the
following year found in the atmosphere the dullness rather than
the sparkle of youth: 'It is perhaps impossible that any court
should be gay where there is no social equality. . . . Without that
ease there can be no real pleasure.'

Victoria was gracious and cheerful but she was always the
Queen, and she was too young and socially inept to make her
guests feel comfortable or to direct the talk towards entertainment or brilliance. This was partly due to temperament; she
never cared for things of the mind, for abstract discussion, for
the thrust of wit. It was enough for her subjects to be guests at
her table; there was no need to make them comfortable or to
entertain them.

They all sat, after dinner, at a round table where 'two mortal
hours are consumed in such conversation as can be found which

is very uphill work'. Fortunately for Greville only the evenings were spent like that; the rest of the day was free if little more amusing: 'There is none of the sociability which makes the agreeability of an English country house'—no hall or library or billiard-room where guests could gather as they chose, to talk, play games, write letters, read new magazines and reviews. There *was* a billiard-room but in such a remote corner of the Castle that it 'might as well be in the town of Windsor'; the library was 'a mere library offering none of the comforts and luxuries of a habitable room' and a smoking-room was beyond contemplation. The Queen never made up the defects of her solitary and over-feminine childhood.

She herself was never bored: 'The pleasantest summer I ever passed *in my life*' she wrote of this first season, and returned to London with something of the regret of a schoolgirl at the end of a blissful holiday; a girl, however, who is returning to new importance in her world as Head Girl. The new term, if we may continue the metaphor, proved as delightful as the vacation and far more exciting. The Queen drove, one November day, to the Lord Mayor's banquet, 'dressed in all my finery', attended by lords and ladies and drawn in a state coach by eight horses. Cheering crowds lined the streets: 'I cannot say HOW *touched* I am by the very brilliant, affectionate, cordial, enthusiastic and unanimous reception I met with in this the greatest metropolis in the world. There was not a discontented look, not a sign of displeasure—all loyalty, affection and loud greeting. . . . I felt deeply grateful for this display of affection and unfeigned loyalty and *attachment* from my good people. It is much more than I deserve.'

In the following May (1838) she noted: 'I this day enter my 20th year which I think very old'—and indeed it does sound older than being merely nineteen. About six weeks later, on 28th June, she went to her crowning in Westminster, through 'millions of my loyal subjects whose good humour and excessive loyalty was beyond everything. I really cannot say how proud I feel to be the Queen of such a nation'. 'Millions' is a pardonable and by no means gross exaggeration. Greville reports one million, made up almost equally of Londoners and of country people who flocked into town.

The sentiment of loyalty was temporarily revived but it was not universal or long-lasting. At Ascot, that summer, the Queen was, according to Greville 'only tolerably received' with very little cheering and 'few hats taken off. This mark of respect is quite gone out of use, and neither her station nor her sex procures it; we are not nearer a revolution for this, but it is ugly', and indeed revolution was no remote possibility.

Her coronation was more seemly than that of George IV which had had a *succès de scandale,* but it was far from reaching the solemnity and spiritual beauty of those that this century has witnessed. That it was a sacramental rite, the anointing, enthroning and crowning of the Lord's anointed whose authority was from God occurred to very few of her subjects and did not greatly impress even the prelates who performed the actions. Even Greville who was no ardent churchman was shocked by their bungling and ineptitude. The Queen did not know what to do with the orb, and the Archbishop could not direct her. She herself was a little startled to find St. Edward's Chapel turned into a buffet with 'what was called the altar . . . covered with sandwiches and bottles of wine'.

Yet there were moments of beauty. The royal girl bore herself with dignity; her eight train-bearers, daughters of the peerage, were exquisite 'in white satin and silver tissue with wreaths of silver corn-ears in front, and a small one of pink roses round the plait behind, and pink roses in the trimming of the dresses'.

Youth cannot but be touching at moments of high ceremonial, and youth itself is touched. The Queen was deeply moved by the act of crowning. Melbourne, standing close behind her, 'was completely overcome. . . . He gave me such a kind, and I must say fatherly look'. When he paid homage 'he kissed my hand and I grasped his with all my heart, at which he looked up with his eyes filled with tears'.

The golden days continued, the new duties were still a delight.

Everything, from affairs of state to domestic matters, from questions of taste, fashion and morals even to art and literature could be discussed with her Prime Minister who was also her beloved friend.

The very artlessness of her *Journal* is more effective than any art in conveying the flavour of their talk. They exchanged opinions on education. When the Queen confessed her dislike of ancient history, of learning generally 'and particularly Latin, and being naughty at this and at my Bible lessons', Melbourne defended Latin. A little of it was excellent, even for young ladies 'on account of the construction of English', and a little more might have disciplined the royal style. Greek he thought unnecessary.

It was a masculine age, and Melbourne was probably not alone in asserting that 'No woman ever wrote a really good book', though he conceded some merit to Hannah More, Maria Edgeworth, and Madame de Sévigné. Jane Austen was not mentioned; her delicate irony would be beyond the royal comprehension, but it might have been expected to appeal to Lord M. They had both read Dickens and the Queen found *Oliver Twist* 'excessively interesting'.

They discussed religion as all Victorians were to do. Neither of them leaned towards the new Tractarian devotion. Melbourne 'spoke of not liking the Cathedral service—all that singing', which he found 'inconsistent with a calm and right devotion' and 'somewhat papistical and theatrical'. Thus was sounded the first blast of the trumpet against ritualism which was to peal so lustily and with royal approval throughout the century. Dogma was no more attractive than ritual: 'I said one could get oneself quite puzzled by thinking too much about these matters' and Lord M. agreed that 'The Trinity isn't comprehensible' and was better left beyond speculation. 'This is all just as I feel.' She was enjoying the illusion of intellectual discussion.

They talked of education. 'It does not much signify what is taught,' Melbourne declared, 'if what is taught is well taught.' He approved of the classics but deplored the absence of French from boys' education.

Melbourne recalled his own boyhood at Eton and the Queen
visited the school for 'Montem'—that peculiar feast when the
boys ruled for a day, wore fancy dress, and levied 'salt' or toll
on travellers and visitors. The Queen gave £100, and far from
grudging the gift, was much opposed to the reforms of the new
headmaster, Dr. Hawtrey, who shortly afterwards put down the
feast.

After one of their talks she thought much of 'dear Lord M.'
and his marriage to Lady Caroline—'really quite crazy'—and his
horror now 'of any woman who is in any way eccentric or
extravagant'.

This explains part of his devotion to this royal girl, who might
well have appeared insipid to him as she did to Greville and other
critics. Her simplicity was like a draught of spring water to his
thirst. Did he guess the depth of passion, the sensuality beneath
that limpidity? If he did, he may knowingly have diverted it
into the channel of friendship with himself until it could sweep
into the river of married love.

The complexity of his character was beyond her grasp but she
could appreciate his strength: 'I feel so safe when he speaks to
me and is with me.' Even Greville was impressed by Melbourne's restraint: 'His free and easy language interlarded with
"damns" is carefully guarded and regulated with the strictest
propriety, and he has exchanged the good talk of Holland House'
—with its brilliant, arrogant and divorcée hostess—'for the
trivial, laboured and wearisome inanities of the Royal circle.'

The populace in its usual ribald way called her 'Mrs. Melbourne', but he, more than any other, prepared her for both
queenship and marriage. He gave her more than he received
even from her whole-hearted affection and gratitude. Emotion-
ally she was ripe for marriage, but a little more of Melbourne's
influence might have made her a woman of the world agreeably
tinged with culture. Prince Albert was indeed bookish, but in
the pedantic German manner. Had Victoria been further formed
by Melbourne her Court might have retained something of the
elegance of the Georgian era while repudiating its immorality.

Fate and her heart ruled otherwise. In October, 1839, the two Princes of Saxe-Coburg, Ernest and Albert, came to visit her, Albert as her approved suitor. She found him 'Beautiful . . . really quite charming and excessively handsome'. On 15th of October she proposed to him telling him she was quite unworthy of him, a statement he did not contradict. A week later she announced her forthcoming marriage, addressing her Council in the clear, sweet voice which was one of her charms. She was composed, only her hands trembled a little. 'I did a much more nervous thing a little while ago,' she told the Duchess of Gloucester. 'I proposed to Prince Albert.'

As she walked out of the Council Chamber the gates of girlhood imperceptibly but finally closed behind her, and there was no backward glance.

*Part One*

# Early Victorian

## 1837–1850

# I

## YOUTH IN THE YOUNG QUEEN'S REIGN: BACKGROUND WITH FIGURES

THE Victorian girl awaited creation in literature. In real life she was still in the schoolroom or only just about to emerge into society; into one of strict conventions and of rapidly improving morals. A girl newly 'out' was closely guarded and simply dressed, her muslin and ribbons symbolical of an attitude. Grandeur was attained only after marriage.

The clothes though simple were charming. Their mere delicacy of fabric and colour was as clear a token of luxury as any splendour of silk or velvet or brocade. These muslins, tarlatans, gauze and silks were intended for wearers who lived delicately if sometimes austerely without exposure to rough weather or to the demands of toil. Even in winter they wore soft garments; of cashmere or poplin, merino or velvet, with a pelisse trimmed with fur and lined with quilted silk, and a muff. Shoes were of fine kid. Bonnets were replacing hats. The fashion was elegant and graceful with a plain bodice above a long, full skirt, but with no complication of draperies or trimming. The bodice for day wear might be cut low over a chemisette of white lawn or muslin, or might be worn with a fichu or collar or cape. The brooch was an almost necessary ornament, to fasten collar or fichu, and a girl who was too young to possess any important jewellery might have a number of very pretty brooches in gold and silver filigree, coral, turquoise, pearl and garnet, perhaps a parure or set of necklace, bracelet, brooch and earrings in one of those charming gems which Victorian craftsmen handled so exquisitely.

Every period has its own particular fabric and the Victorian cultivated muslin above all for girls. Muslins were various: the finest of all was Indian, very soft and silky, of a fine but opaque texture, and mull and organdy resembled it; Swiss and book muslin were semi-transparent and stiff. Tarlatan was like a stiff gauze, and a soft gauze with the alluring name of 'illusion' was worn in clouds of drapery over a silk muslin gown. If one could not afford a new dress some fresh illusion would transform the old, and with blue ribbons changed for pink, or cherry for yellow, and a wreath and nosegay of flowers, one could achieve a new and most charming look. Amy March (born, in fiction, long after this decade) knew exactly what to do.

While the grown-up girls sat with Mamma in the drawing-room or drove out with her and went to parties, their sisters in the schoolroom were learning history, French and perhaps Italian; were sewing a fine seam (more or less), sketching picturesque ruins or cottages, copying flowers or prints, practising the piano and possibly the harp. A few went to school, to a Miss Pinkerton's Academy. Some trifled with learning and 'accomplishments', preparing only for a genteel appearance in the drawing-room; others read a great deal and very solidly, especially in history. There was no norm of female education as there was and had long been of masculine schooling. Boys of the professional and upper classes went to grammar or public school, then to Oxford or Cambridge; their education was exclusively classical and at least a residuum of Latin or Greek could be found in them in after life. A girl's achievement depended on her individual intelligence and on her governess or her parents.

The young Queen admitted the defects in her education and her own resistance to learning. Melbourne reassured her; she was aware of learning if not herself learned. His opinion had value, for although he abhorred a bluestocking he did not like a girl to be silly and ignorant, and deplored the standards of the average schoolroom. His own nieces, the Ladies Emily and Fanny Cowper were 'the best-brought up girls in England, but their education was shocking'.

Too much was left to chance, and too often a governess was only a poor gentlewoman, anxious about her gentility, insisting on ultra-genteel standards of speech and conduct, herself untrained and half-educated but acceptable as governess because she *was* a gentlewoman, would keep the girls occupied and out of the way, and if she did them little good would do them no harm.

It was a period of transition. The old domestic culture was almost lost, for it was no longer held necessary or even desirable for a young gentlewoman to learn the lore of the still-room, to spin, or to work tapestry.

Even a modest household was well staffed. The higher education of girls lay in the future; professional careers were not contemplated except in the pale shadow of them found in governessing or in keeping a select boarding-school.

All the same a girl of intelligence could fulfil herself intellectually, given wise parents and a good background. In an upper-middle-class or aristocratic family she was born into security and dignity; a good governess, if she were so fortunate as to have one, laid a solid foundation of learning and taught her to read, really to read, for reading was itself an art, a mental discipline of a type hardly known nowadays. A girl's reading was, of course, guided and censored and not without reason. Two of the greatest novelists were available for her delight and were as impeccable in morals as they were superb in genius: Scott and Jane Austen; but there was a flood of contemporary fiction of the utmost silliness against which it was only sensible to raise some dykes. Even the best novels were permitted as a treat and indulgence after lessons were done. Charlotte Yonge remembered being allowed to read a Waverley novel after finishing her stint of history. Scott was for the Victorian young an enchanter, never a taskmaster. The habit of reading formed in the schoolroom could make a girl intellectually rich for life.

For good or ill most girls were educated at home: some were sent to school; it might be to a kind, sensible if not intellectual Mrs. Goddard, it might be to Miss Pinkerton. The latter's Academy existed in many places; one was in Brighton and it was entered in 1836 by a lively young Irishwoman of fourteen, Frances Power Cobbe. Her childhood had been spent at Newbridge, near Dublin; she was a daughter of the Irish Protestant gentry and grew up in the Big House, the youngest of five and the only daughter of middle-aged parents; her mother was forty-seven when Frances was born. The background of such families had still much of the spaciousness and elegance of the eighteenth century, and France's childhood in the country had a healthy and, by contemporary standards, unfeminine freedom.

'You bould Puckhaun,' her nurse called her. One of her earliest exploits was deliberately to fall in the mud in order to spoil a new silk pelisse; she detested finery and was born to wear tweeds. She was not, however, rebellious for mere love of rebellion, and made a compact with her governess that she would do all her tasks in return for having plenty of time out-of-doors. When indoors she read voraciously in her father's library, learned astronomy, made a map of the stars out of peacock's feathers, collected shells, practised carpentry and wrote poetry.

Altogether a lively, healthy and most intelligent girl, she was by no means a Miss Pinkerton's ideal and it is difficult to understand how her intelligent and sympathetic parents chose this particular Academy for her. She wrote of it in retrospect: 'The education of women was probably at its lowest ebb . . . more pretentious than it had ever been, and infinitely more costly than it is now.' The fees were nominally from £120–£130 a year, but were actually higher, and in Frances' case came to £1,000 for two years of 'education . . . carried out to the extreme of expenditure and high pressure'.

Perhaps the greatest ordeal was noise. The school was nicknamed by 'profane persons' The Convent, but there was no conventual silence about it. 'The din of our large double classroom was something frightful'—with girls reciting their lessons aloud to governesses at separate tables, in a babel of English, French, German and Italian, with four pianos next door or upstairs being played at one time but not to one tune, and in the midst of this uproar other pupils trying to write their themes and exercises and to learn pages of prose by heart.

There was no exercise or recreation beyond dreary walks during which lists of French verbs must be recited; and on

Saturday afternoon occurred the ordeal of 'Judgment Day'. The two headmistresses sat at a table with the governesses ranged behind them as 'assessors', and the report-books laid out in front of them while 'round the room against the wall, seated on stools of penitential discomfort, we sat, five-and-twenty damosels anything but blessed'. Penalties were inflicted for not having finished lessons or piano practice by bedtime, for stooping, for having shoestrings untied, for being impertinent and for telling lies. Each offence was punished by the loss of a mythical card; the loss of three cards meant a solemn public scolding and being put in the corner for the rest of the evening. Sometimes three rooms were occupied by 'no less than nine young ladies . . . like naughty babies . . . half of them of marriageable age, and all dressed, as was *de rigueur* with us every day, in full evening attire of silk or muslin with gloves and kid slippers'. The pupils ranged in age from nine to nineteen. Letters home were written on Saturday evening, all of them censored, so that there could be no relief to pent-up feelings.

The girls were all of good family, some of them heiresses, and they were in every sense 'nice'; well-disposed, intelligent, some of them full of talents and capability which their schooling ignored. There was very little of the silliness, snobbery and petty cruelty so often ascribed to schoolgirls. Frances repudiated the description of a similar school in G. H. Lewis's novel, *Rose, Blanche and Violet,* as utterly false regarding the girls. Rose and Blanche were sent to school with very little pocket-money and were despised by their purse-proud companions. The real girls of Frances' recollection had no such fault. They were all of the same class and made no pretensions; indeed they would appear to have escaped, by nature or by grace, from being perverted into malignant nitwits, for everything was done that could repress or distort intelligence. 'Everything was taught us in the inverse ratio to its true importance'—morals and religion coming lowest and last, in spite of severe Sunday discipline when only religious books, most of them dull, might be read. Church-going was obligatory, and the collects and catechism must be learned along with a daily text of Scripture. Most of the girls learned this while brushing their hair, or had it read to them by a friend while they had a bath behind a screen. The school was High Church in a dim way, and salt fish used to be served on Ash Wednesday along with roast mutton. In theory the girls might make their own choice, but 'the merits of the Lenten fast' having been expounded they were reminded that 'it was good for our souls and our figures' to choose the 'maigre' diet.

Music, of a sort, was important for these young ladies were destined to be ornaments of society and as such to display virtuosity on the pianoforte. 'To be marked P (or Pretty Well) for music meant the loss of a card and was a grave misdemeanour' and on one occasion a girl found guilty of lying was told: 'We had almost rather find you have a P in your music than tell such falsehoods.'

Dancing was well taught, by a famous old dancer Madame Michaud, and included not only the English dances of the pre-polka period but many European national dances. There was also a class in calisthenics when a 'Capitaine Somebody' drilled the girls with poles and dumb-bells; but 'how much better a few good country scrambles would have been'.

Drawing was badly taught: the girls made copies of the master's drawings and he 'touched them up'. Languages were compulsory: French or German or Italian must be talked all day until six o'clock. There were masters for English, writing and arithmetic; history and geography were taught in alternate weeks; and nearly everything was taught by rote and learned by heart. In one week Frances thus learned thirteen pages of Wood-houselee's *Universal History*.

There was no solid instruction, no real mental training, no awakening of the mind. 'What a delightful thing it is to have done with study! Now I shall really enjoy myself' was the usual reflection of those leaving school; in Frances it was modified by dismay at her own ignorance.

Returning home she set about educating herself. Her early habit of reading was easily resumed; she learned Greek and geo-

THE HEAD MASTER AND YOUNG BROOKE

From *Tom Brown's Schooldays*

CHAIRING TOM BROWN AT RUGBY

metry from the Rector of the parish to her great satisfaction. Of geometry she said: 'I have ever since recommended this study to women as specially fitted to counteract our habits of hasty judgment and slovenly statement.'

Her reading was both wide and thorough, including a great deal of history, and some of the Italian as well as the English classics. Her father had a good library, her mother her own collection of books, and Frances bought new publications out of her pocket-money. Her intellectual curiosity was insatiable; between the ages of sixteen and twenty, when most girls of her class were expected to be content with light domestic duties and small gaieties, she learned something of heraldry, astronomy, architecture and philosophy; above all she studied comparative religion.

'I had neither cares of love nor cares of money to occupy my mind or my heart'; there was ample leisure for her development. She consented to attend a few balls and parties in Dublin but society bored her, except that she loved entertaining guests at home and was a most capable hostess. Her mother was delicate and Frances gladly took over the housekeeping. The mind that appreciated the order of geometry and the perfection of Greek prose and poetry loved also the seemliness of a well-appointed house. The china closet was her particular pride. On a visit to a neighbour she was snubbed by her hostess for venturing to talk about her beloved geometry and Greek; a lady's duty, she was told, was to attend to the house. Presently she was invited to inspect some heirloom china and was conducted to the basement and to a 'shocking china-closet all higgledy-piggledy, exquisite china with coarse dishes' mixed together, and a fine desssert service 'with the dessert of the previous summer rotting on the plates'.

Frances savoured her revenge: 'Indeed, this is a splendid service; *Style de l'Empire* I should call it. We have nothing like it, but when next you do us the pleasure to come to Newbridge, I shall like to show you our Indian and Worcester services. Do you know, I always take up all the plates and dishes myself,

c

when they have been washed the day after a party, and put them in their proper shelves with my own hands.' And the devil in her added: 'though I do know a little Greek and geometry.'

Frances was of extraordinary force of character as well as of intellect and ahead of her generation in learning; she was to be a pioneer in journalism for women in her maturity and also in social work. She was already interested in people and their way of life outside her own class, and her own village and country-side gave her variety of outlook. Her father, and her brother after him were good landlords who kept their cottages in good repair, built a school and encouraged Frances to play Lady Bountiful as girls of the Big House or the manor and vicarage on both sides of St. George's Channel were beginning to do.

The Ireland of her youth was comparatively prosperous, be-tween the troubles of the late eighteenth century and the famine of the forties. The people lived frugally but healthily enough on a diet of porridge or stirabout, milk, griddle-bread and potatoes; the latter were delicious, 'smiling' or bursting from their jackets. Little girls used to carry dinner to their fathers in the fields: potatoes and butter, a hunch of griddle-bread, a jug of milk. At Christmas an ox was killed and distributed in joints and cuts. The cottages or cabins were rough, they lacked the adornment of flowers, a patch of garden or even a row of geranium-pots such as made an English cottage gay and pretty. 'Nothing seems to be more absurd and unhistoric,' Frances remarked, 'than the com-mon idea that the Celt is a beauty-loving creature, aesthetically far above the Saxon.'

Like many of her contemporaries and successors over the water she taught in the school but was hindered, as no English girl would be, by the priests. In England manor and vicarage worked together; in Ireland the quality were suspect as heretics.

Frances began to write again but no longer the poetry of her childhood. Her mind was analytical rather than creative; she wrote essays and studies, a few stories, 'played the sedulous ape' to Gibbon and other models, and prepared herself unknowingly for her future career in journalism.

It is disappointing that the scenes and people she knew so well did not touch a spark of the creative fire in her, for she might have left pictures of Irish life in fiction to fill the gap between Maria Edgeworth and E. OE. Somerville and Martin Ross.

Beyond the Big House lay a world foreign to that of the English village; but the domestic background hardly differed from that of contemporary England. The atmosphere and standards of both were domestic. A young lady was educated to take her place in parental society and then, it was hoped, in her husband's home. Accomplishments were desirable, and if she understood housekeeping and the household arts, as Frances did, so much the better. This might come in time with experience, but there were always maids in plenty.

The young lady was prepared to be mistress of a large and comfortable house, the young person from the village to be housemaid or kitchenmaid, rising perhaps to be cook or even housekeeper. Where the lady of the manor was benevolent a career was ensured for any girl who would go into service; she was fed and sheltered, trained—rigorously or kindly according to the nature of her mistress and the upper servants, and then, like the maids trained by Madam Brown in *Tom Brown's Schooldays*, 'started in life amongst the neighbouring families with good principles and wardrobes.'

For the majority in both classes life might be secure. There was, for the village girl, the risk of finding herself in a bad place; for the young lady, that of a paternal loss of fortune. Breeding without money was possibly the hardest lot of all.

## II

# THE WORLD OF BOYHOOD

### I

ON the masculine side the public schools were far from being homes of kindly nurture. Discipline was stern, conditions were Spartan and there was an appalling amount of cruelty and of bullying. Most boys were miserable in their first years at school, yet these foundations won and held the loyalty of their sons, and this retrospective sentiment helped to form the Victorian man.

Tom Brown going up to Rugby at the end of the old King's reign was unconsciously crossing the bridge between the old Georgian and the new Victorian world. His childhood had been spent in a countryside which kept the traditions of old England, with fairs and 'veasts' and a feudal order of things ruled by Tom's father the Squire and by his mother Madam Brown who trained every girl in the village for domestic service.

It has been Thomas Hughes' own background which he recalled nostalgically when writing in the 1850's: 'Don't let reformers of any sort think they are going really to get hold of the working boys and young men of England by any educational grapnel whatever, which hasn't some *bona fide* equivalent for the games of the old country "veast" in it. . . . In all the new-fangled comprehensive plans which I see this is all left out; and the consequence is that your great Mechanics' Institutes end in intellectual priggism and your Christian Young Men's Societies in religious pharisaism. Life isn't all beer and skittles, but beer and skittles or something better of the same sort must form a good part of every Englishman's education.'

Beer and skittles were translated into cricket and football played with deadly seriousness and an almost artistic standard. Hughes was probably too close to Arnold to realize how much he and his Rugby made the new type of young Englishman that would outlive the century: a lover of games rather than books though by no means lacking in scholarship; a Stoic more than a Christian and in his Christianity interested in ethics rather than dogma and untouched by mysticism. It must be his own kind of Christianity, not one suitable for women or foreigners or New Testament characters. This new type was a youth of utter integrity and courage, complacent, a little priggish, kind but insensitive and inexpressive: in fact, 'the Englishman with his habitual bloody cold', as the French schoolboy put it in an inspired mistranslation.

Squire Brown's reflections on the eve of Tom's departure were those of many parents: 'If only he'll turn out a brave, helpful, truth-telling Englishman and a Christian that's all I want.' Were these virtues given in an ascending or descending scale of values? Dr. Arnold and many other headmasters were to inculcate them.

Tom was only ten but he had left childhood behind him and acquired a new spirit along with his new hat. He 'would have liked to hug his father well' on this last evening, but as a public schoolboy he must not be demonstrative, and so had stipulated that kissing should now cease between them. This laconic attitude was for boys what primness and gentility became for their sisters, the exaggeration of a virtue. One was based on fortitude the other on chastity but both grew crookedly.

Tom was introduced to the new rule by his new friend East: 'This'll never do'—this being Tom's cap. 'We never wear caps here. Only the louts wear caps. Bless you, if you were to go into the quadrangle with that thing on, you don't know what would happen.'

The new hat was too fine and shiny for any but Sunday wear, he must buy another 'regulation catskin at seven-and-sixpence'; already there was a code of dress as of behaviour: 'You see, a great deal depends on how a fellow cuts up at first. If he's got nothing odd about him and answers straight-forward and holds his head up he gets on.'

Tom did all that and more: in his first rugby game he was

knocked down in the scrum and picked up 'a motionless body' by that demigod, Old Brooke, head of the school. To the query: 'How do you feel, young 'un?' he answered, 'Pretty well, thank you' and received the accolade: 'Well, he's a plucky youngster and will make a player.'

Old Brooke, in his after-supper speech that evening, celebrating the School-house victory over School, developed the ethos more deeply and spoke for generations to come of schoolboys: 'Why did we beat 'em? . . . It's because we've more reliance on one another, more of a home feeling, more fellowship than School can have. . . . We've union, they've division—there's the secret. . . . I take it we're all in earnest about beating the School, whatever else we care about. I know I'd sooner win two School-house matches running than get the Balliol scholarship any day' —at which there were 'frantic cheers'.

The inmost expression was left for the Doctor's sermons: 'What was it that moved us . . . who feared the Doctor with all our hearts, and very little besides in heaven or earth; who thought more of our sets in the school than of the Church of Christ, and put the traditions of Rugby and the public opinion of boys in our daily life above the laws of God? . . . It was not the cool, clear voice of one giving advice from serene heights to those who were struggling and sinning below, but the warm, living voice of one who was fighting for us and by our side. . . . It was the thoroughness and undaunted courage which more than anything else won his way to the hearts of the great mass of those on whom he left his mark.'

Arnold had come to Rugby filled with reforming zeal and there was much need for reform. Tom encountered some evil and bullying. Flashman was a type that infested most schools, and one which needed and justified Dr. Arnold's measures. His prefectorial system was not new. Winchester had long had her prefects. Dr. Arnold called them praepostors and fostered in them the spirit of responsibility with authority, believing that a strong Sixth Form would do more than his own interference in quelling the bullies. In the main, his method worked well, but it had its dangers: Boy the Brute did not always turn, as Arnold hoped, into Boy the Hero; he sometimes became Boy the Prig.

Tom Hughes himself, like Tom Brown, was a happy schoolboy after the pains of initiation had been endured, and like Tom Brown he came only gradually to revere Dr. Arnold. After the Doctor's death, hero-worship became apotheosis. Reflecting on the period from ten to eighteen which he held of supreme importance in forming a boy's character, he declared: 'I passed all those years under the spell of the place and Arnold, and for half a century have never ceased to thank God for it.'

Perhaps the most lasting effect was in the new zeal for social reform, for the translation of Christian ethics into action.

Tom Brown, when he heard of the Doctor's death, came back to Rugby Chapel and knelt there in tears. 'Where better could we leave him than at the altar before which he had first caught a glimpse of the glory of his birthright, and felt the drawing of the bond which links all living souls together in one brotherhood—at the grave beneath the altar of him who had opened his eyes to see that glory, and softened his heart till it could feel that bond?'

The Doctor's son paid a like tribute:

> Through thee I believe
> In the noble and great who are gone;
> Pure souls honour'd and blest
> . . . Souls tempered with fire,
> Fervent, heroic and good,
> Helpers and friends of mankind.

—in short, perfect Rugbeians. Matthew Arnold's *Rugby Chapel* is a poetic expression not only of filial devotion but of the public school religion grown despondent, and it presents one of the most depressing pictures of the hereafter ever set forth: no Paradise but a glorified Rugby where:

> Prompt, unwearied as here,
> Still thou upraisest with zeal

*The humble good from the ground,*
*Sternly repressest the bad.*
*Still like a trumpet dost rouse*
*Those who with half-open eyes*
*Tread the border-land dim*
*'Twixt vice and virtue.*

Dr. Arnold as a celestial headmaster is awful to contemplate.

II

'Please God I will do something for these poor boys.' That resolve was uttered not by the compassionate new master of a reformatory, orphanage or charity school but by Provost Hodgson of Eton on his appointment in 1840. What the poor boys at this, one of the most aristocratic schools in England, suffered in this decade is described by one of them, Arthur Duke Coleridge, in *Eton in the Forties.*

'There is no exaggeration in saying that some of the best men I have ever known ran a considerable risk of becoming the worst, from the ordeal of Long Chamber as I remember the famous dormitory. . . . Ours was a Spartan tradition which required some stoicism to put up with, and one not likely to be forgotten by any who had survived such a purgatory.'

Another Etonian asserted that what the boys endured 'might have broken down a cabin boy and would be thought inhuman if inflicted on a galley-slave'; while yet another, having told a Life Insurance Board that he had survived eight years of Long Chamber, was forthwith accepted as a safely insurable life.

The younger boys slept in close-packed rows in this 'rough barrack which on occasion became a torture-chamber'. There was nearly always at least one Torquemada, and 'cruelty is sadly infectious'. The headmaster, Dr. Hawtrey, deplored it and preached against it but took no active measures. Boyish reticence was in part to blame; no one 'told' at home; a horror of tale-bearing, a stoic pride in endurance both helped to shield the bullies.

Seniority in the school brought an escape from persecution and into a large measure of freedom, even of grandeur; and in retrospect even the horrors were seen in a mellowing light: 'Granted that the Augean stables want cleansing, still some very fine fellows had been stabled there. Hereditary dirt . . . was a savoury legacy we were proud of.' Even the lack of hot water and of baths was not to be lamented: 'We have the College pump, and we can wash overnight if we please.'

It was a tough as well as a luxurious age, and youth knew little of the luxury. Even at home these boys knew Spartan conditions; they had the knack of making themselves snug, and once the horrors of initiation were over school could become paradise enow. Tom Brown at Rugby had thought the studies more interesting 'than Windsor Castle or any other residence in the British Isles', although to a detached observer they might have appeared mere cells, six feet by four, with barred windows, and furnished only with a table, a hard sofa, a wooden chair and some shelves and cupboards. There was no fire, only the one at the end of the passage; but it was 'a Rugby boy's citadel . . . the first place he could call his own'.

So, at Eton, even Long Chamber became cosy in winter evenings with the beds drawn round the fire, and amateur cookery in process: grilled bones and kidneys, toasted cheese and sausages, and an atmosphere of genial fug. Comfort increased with progress in the school and Coleridge was happy at his Dame's, in spite of a surfeit of damson pudding in season, and 'an occasional creeping thing in the salad'.

Dr. Arnold would not have been welcomed at Eton, and although a public school ethos could be recognized at all the great schools throughout the century, the spirit of Eton was very different from that of Rugby. Earnestness and moral uplift were not noticeable. The peculiar spirit or privilege of Eton was liberty.

Reforms did come, under the new Provost Hodgson and his colleague the headmaster, Dr. Hawtrey. The latter abolished Long Chamber and began new buildings which gave the boys

separate rooms, a wash-room and a sick-room. He reformed the
teaching, reducing the size of the classes, and himself wrote new
and better textbooks. His personal influence was good. It was
said that whereas the usual rebuke of his predecessor, Dr. Keate,
had been: 'I'll flog you, boy,' Hawtrey's was: 'Your conduct is
not *quite* that of a gentleman.' He also closed the Christopher Inn
where generations of boys had caroused in a manner hardly bene-
ficial to their health, their manners, or their morals. His reforms
were not always popular; there was a good deal of lament
over the suppression of 'Montem', Eton's own carnival, the
young Queen herself joining in the lament.

This was the Eton she and the Prince Consort saw as they
drove to Windsor on the wedding-day, and young Arthur
Coleridge and his friends ran, cheering, after her carriage. The
Queen was much gratified, and the Prince 'dazed and bewildered
at our Eton ovation'. Coleridge added that 'our great capacity
for noise impressed all foreigners, our Eton French master included'. They could, however, control themselves on occasion,
for one reason or another. When the infant Prince of Wales
appeared in public they refrained from cheering for fear of
waking him; again when the Queen brought that unimpressive
monarch Louis Philippe to visit the school there was no cheer;
it was reserved for the Duke of Wellington.

Hawtrey not only taught well himself but encouraged the
wide reading and private learning which has become a tradition
in the school. A scholar could be formed even before he went
up to Oxford or Cambridge. For the majority, however, the
river was more alluring than the library. Boating was becoming
a cult and a fine art at the two river-schools, Eton and Westminster, as at the universities. Rugby had the new football game,
and Old Brooke, in his many incarnations, was a monarch
'absolute as he of Russia, but wisely and bravely ruling over
willing and worshipping subjects'. At Eton it was the Captain
of the Boats: 'The uninitiated can but faintly appreciate the glory,
ephemeral though dazzling, that radiated from his person and
his high office.' Cricket had its exalted place and its devotees,

but the wet bob was superior to the dry. There was a legend that William the Fourth had died of a broken heart because, on his last public appearance in 1837 he saw the defeat of Eton by Westminster on the river.

Eton had, more distinctly than Rugby, a system of caste. The background of Rugby boys was probably more uniform; most of them the sons of squires, clergy, professional gentlemen rather than of the great, titled families. At Eton, some of the collegers came from the town of Windsor, being the sons of lawyers and doctors, of the royal servants and tradesmen. These were somewhat looked down upon: 'The further away from Eton a boy lived, the more he was respected.' Boys from the north of England and from Scotland were credited with 'long purses and ancestral acres'. Even without such adjuncts, young Scots would not be likely to endure contempt; not so much because they would resent and punish any insult as because mere Sassenach opinion was of no great importance.

III

There might be a few such Scots, of long purse and even longer pedigree at Eton, but those who went to school in their own country knew a very different way of life and learning. The parish school educated laird's son and ploughman's son together; the rudiments once acquired, both might proceed to a grammar school and to college. There was one point of resemblance: Scots education like that of the English public schools was founded and built upon Latin, or Humanity, as it was and is called in the four universities.

A much-loved Professor of English in late-Victorian Edinburgh, David Masson, recalled his schooldays at Aberdeen Grammar, Byron's school, in a pre-Victorian boyhood (1831-5); the pattern, however, did not change for many years to come. He went to the Grammar School at the age of nine and proceeded to Marischal College, Aberdeen at fourteen; he was a young, but not abnormally boyish 'bejan' or freshman.

'It was all but entirely a Latin school,' he wrote in his memoirs, with 'a little history worked in with the Latin, but the business of the school was Latin, Latin, Latin'—and only a little Greek. England, ever since the Renaissance had been Grecian as well as Roman, but Scotland had too little of the lovelier of the classic tongues.

It was assumed at the Grammar School that boys had already been taught the rudiments of English and arithmetic; most of them attended a separate school for mathematics and for writing; the fees were not extortionate: 10s. 6d. a quarter at the Grammar School, 6s. 6d. at the others. Some of the wealthier boys had a tutor at home who was usually a poor student working his way through college. 'Extras such as French, German, fencing, music and other kickshaws were very rare indeed in Aberdeen; they were to be had, I know, but it was as turtle and champagne were to be had.'

At school, the boys did Latin for five hours a day, except in their holiday month of July; only those preparing for college were 'tipped with a little Greek'. Concentration was necessary, for the bursary examination lay between them and the university; few could afford to attend college without a bursary and this was granted only for success in Latin, particularly in Latin prose.

It was a narrow but thorough education and under a great teacher it could have depth and inspiration. In Masson's time the headmaster was Dr. Melvin: 'As a born ruler of boys, Dr. Arnold himself cannot have surpassed Melvin. . . . Even had he taught nothing expressly it would have been a mortal benefit' to be under his influence. He did teach, expressly and effectively. He was the most accurate of scholars and insisted on accuracy in his pupils. Their reading was narrow—Horace and Virgil, Caesar and Livy, and the Latin Psalms of George Buchanan—but it was thorough: 'Every sentence was read and translated, word for word'—then rendered 'more freely and elegantly', finally analysed for syntax, etymology and idiom. This might have killed a feeble love of Latinity, but Melvin could communicate his own passion for his authors, especially for the poets. The severest drill of all was in Latin prose; the boys were trained to note idioms and 'any niceties about *Ut, Quum, Quod* and *Quia, Ille* and *Iste, Uter* and *Quis, Suus* and *Eius, Plerique* and *Plurimi* and the like'. This training in accuracy long outlasted their schooldays and use of the Latin tongue. The Scots mind took readily to such discipline and it helped to shape, among other things, the Scots sermon, that long but ordered exposition of dogma.

These proses were marked according to their 'freedom from faults or illegalities' and in three grades of error: *minimus* or *minie, medius* or *medie, maximus* or *maxie*. The depths were reached with a double *maxie,* the heights, serene and Olympian, with a *sine errore, elegantissimo.* The system became so ingrained in the boys' minds that 'I question whether there is a Melvinian extant in the world now that does not classify sins and social crimes as *minies, medies* and *maxies*'.

David Masson was followed at the Grammar School, at the interval of a few years, by George MacDonald, poet and seer, writer of tales that still hold children from play and of novels in which some admirable pictures of Scottish Victorian life are almost hidden under mists of preaching. He came to Aberdeen from his native Huntly in 1840, aged sixteen. Some of his memories were transmuted into fiction in the experiences of his hero Robert Falconer.

Robert, like MacDonald himself, was not bitterly poor but must live frugally. He brought with him from home a box of provisions—oatmeal, cheese, butter and jam 'which ought to have tasted of roses for it came from the old garden where the roses lived in such sweet companionship with the currant-bushes'.

He worked well and was happy in school, and in the play-ground which was filled 'with the shouts of eager boys kicking the ball about with mad rushings to and fro' with less solemnity and perhaps less style than at Rugby but with no less exuberance. Certainly no boy at the Grammar School would have applauded Old Brooke's desire to win a match rather than a scholarship.

A scholarship or bursary was necessary before any of them could go to college and take a degree. 'If the master was stern and hard, he was true,' MacDonald wrote of Melvin. 'If the pupils feared him they yet cared to please him; if there might be found a few more widely read scholars than he, it would be hard to find a better teacher.'

Robert and his comrades went up for their examination in much fear: 'The black-gowned professors walked into the room . . . and the lads crept to their seats as if for a trial for life before a bench of the incorruptible.' Robert found afterwards, to his horror, that he had made a *maxie*. He was awarded a very small bursary, only £5 a year. MacDonald himself was more fortunate, being twelfth in the list with a bursary of £14 a year.

# COLLEGE DAYS AND COLLEGE WAYS:
# ABERDEEN AND OXFORD

*Poverty has the Gaelic and Greek*
*In my land*

sings the Princess of Scotland in Rachel Annand Taylor's poem.
There was not always a great deal of Greek, though the modicum
acquired at school was increased at college. There was Gaelic at
Aberdeen where most of the Highland students came, and some
at Glasgow, for that too was a Highlanders' city; and those who
had the Gaelic had another way of thought than the Lowlander,
a heritage of ancient beauty and poetry, an enrichment of the
mind.

Poverty in Scotland never starved of learning. 'All who chose
might come and no questions were asked'—so David Masson
wrote—no questions about money or family or social position;
the poorest might come to college if he had but money enough
to pay his fees and a bare lodging, come wearing rough home-
spun, with a box to hold his books and few clothes and another
with meal and a cheese and what other stores could be afforded
him from home.

The session was only from November till March with no
summer term; the long vacation gave time to earn money for
the next session. A poor student might act as tutor or he might
return to the farm or the herding. Only a few were wealthy
enough to enjoy a vacation of study and play, to travel and see
something of men and cities as well as of books.

College was a continuation of school except that it had more
freedom. The student, as undergraduates are usually called in
Scotland, escaped the compulsion of the 'tawse' and of lines and
impositions that compelled him to work. He could, if he chose,
idle his way through three or four years, but that would be

senseless behaviour. A man went to the university to learn as much as he could, to take a degree that would qualify him for one of the professions or for the ministry of the kirk. The idea of college as a preparation for life in the world, as a delightful period between the discipline of school and the responsibilities of a career, occurred to very few Scots; those who had such a notion and the means to gratify it were likely to go over the Border.

Education was dearly bought and dearly valued; it was still, in the main, classical, and still retained the medieval pattern set by the founders of three of the universities, with the mental and moral sciences interwoven with the humane letters. The natural sciences were also taught and the Scots Master of Arts graduated through a well-balanced course of study. What was lacking was the grace of intellectual life: the tradition that can come only from a communal life shared not only with contemporaries in the flesh, but with generations of those who, in the past, have lived and learned, worked and played in the same house. The monastic ideal was almost entirely lost in Scotland at the Reformation; in England it survived, though transformed, in the public schools. Scotland, however, cherished the medieval ideal of the poor scholar.

When the Queen was crowned, young Masson was in his third year at Marischal College; a 'tertian' after his first year as 'bejan' and second as 'semi'; in his fourth year he would become 'magistrand'—one who is about to be a Master of Arts.

At the sister college of King's, George MacDonald followed the same course, broken for a time by his father's poverty; in this interval he found work cataloguing the library of a great house somewhere in the north: an experience he was to use in more than one novel, notably in *Donal Grant*.

'I was in my element. The very outside of a book had charm for me.' This experience gave him not only a temporary livelihood but a glimpse of a new and statelier world than he had ever known. His youth, so far, though not unhappy, had been

LONG CHAMBER, ETON

YOUNG VICTORIANS

From *The Daisy Chain* by Charlotte M. Yonge

narrow, and one passion had been repressed—his love of the theatre. The stage was not altogether well seen in Scotland at this time; but in Scots as well as English mansions there was a vogue for private theatricals, and the young librarian proved an asset in such ventures. He acted well and was adaptable. In one part an old, green coat was produced for him to wear; it lacked buttons, so George asked for a carrot, cut it into neat discs and sewed them on. 'The effect was prodigious.'

MacDonald needed more than book-learning; he would have developed more happily in Oxford, but he understood the passion for pure scholarship that drove so many poor lads through arduous years. His Donal Grant 'had an altogether unappeasable hunger for every form of literature' but no ambition for a career in the kirk: 'Gin I can be a schulemaster an' help the bairnies to be gude as my mither taught mysel', and hae time to read an' a few shillin's to buy buiks about Aigypt and the Holy Land, an' a full an' complete edition of Plato an' a Greek lexicon—a gude ane—an' a Jamieson's Dictionary, haith I'll be a happy man.'

The contrast between poor boy and rich is nowhere more startling than in pictures of the Scots and the English undergraduate. There are many in memoirs and biography and some clear glimpses in fiction. MacDonald's novels contain such glimpses, and on the English side there is vivid portraiture in *Tom Brown at Oxford*. Tom appreciated the beauty of 'St. Ambrose's'; the portraits in hall, the ordered ritual and tradition.

'One got a taste for that work from the Doctor,' he wrote to his friend Arthur, still at Rugby; but the intellectual level was low. There were too many gentlemen-commoners in the college, who sat apart in the hall, wore a silk gown and a velvet cap with the gold tassel or tuft which gave the name of 'tuft-hunters' to snobs and toadies. 'The College was decidedly fast'; the wealthy and fast set giving wine-parties, smoking cigars at two or three guineas the pound, playing billiards and driving tandem which for some reason has always been more rakish than driving

D

a pair or a single horse. They were expected to run up bills; prompt payment was middle-class and even vulgar.

'It's an awfully idle place,' Tom informed Arthur, with his Rugby conscience still alert: 'Twelve lectures a week of an hour each, Greek Testament, first book of Herodotus, second Aeneid, and first book of Euclid . . . two hours a day and all over by twelve or one at the latest, and no extra work at all in the shape of copies of verses, themes and other exercises. I sometimes think I'm back in the Lower Fifth.'

Chapel was compulsory every day and twice on Sunday. (The young Scot was under no such obligation, except that social pressure to say nothing of conscience drove him to kirk twice on Sunday. Attendance on a week-day was a Popish habit.) 'We keep very gentlemanly hours,' proceeded Tom—having to be in college by midnight; and were expected to dine in hall at five o'clock, at least four days a week, wearing cap and gown. Dinners were good and cheap, and bread and cheese for break-fast; lunch and supper could be had at the buttery. Only the wealthy and luxurious indulged in anything elaborate at those meals. There was always plenty of beer 'in one of the silver tankards of which we seem to have an endless supply'.

At the other end of the scale from the gentleman-commoner was the poor scholar who would have been the norm in Scotland but who in Oxford was kept in his peculiar place as servitor. One of the 'gentlemen' explained him to Tom: 'He does the dons' dirty work and gets their broken victuals. I believe he pays no fees.' 'But servitors are gentlemen, I suppose?' asked Tom. 'A good deal of the cocktail,' he was told; the term mean-ing an upstart. 'The thing to be able to do at Oxford is to pay.'

Tom, good fellow, made friends with a servitor, Hardy, who proved a good counsellor. He also found himself, for a time, in a wealthy set, led by one Drysdale: 'No man in St. Ambrose's gave such breakfasts.' Most men were content if not with bread and cheese at least with the college-kitchen fare of 'buttered toast and eggs, with a dish of broiled ham or something of the sort, and marmalade and a little ale to finish with'. Drysdale founded a breakfast club who feasted on 'fresh-caught gudgeon sent in from the town' with now and then 'an eel or a trout which the scouts on the staircase had learned to fry delectably in oil', and on chicken or grilled turkey's leg from the kitchen, on water-cress, plovers' eggs in season, and 'at the worst a dainty ome-lette', while 'a distant baker famed for his light rolls and high charges sent in the bread—the common domestic college loaf being out of the question for anyone with the slightest preten-sions to taste'.

Tom was naturally attracted by this new ease of living and for a time in danger of being led astray; his own good sense, the memory of the Doctor's teaching and the friendship of Hardy kept him safe. Hardy in his counsel speaks for the mature Thomas Hughes recalling his own youthful difficulties: 'About the toughest part of a man's life is the part he has to spend here.' Boyhood was past but the wisdom of manhood was still lacking; beneath all the fun of college days there was a sense of bewilder-ment. 'No amount of physical or mental work can fill the vacuum. It is the empty house swept and garnished . . . which must be filled somehow. It's a pretty good three years' work to learn how to keep the devils out.' There is an echo of St. Augustine's cry: 'Our hearts are restless till they find rest in Thee.'

Tom also found himself, somewhat to his own surprise and very briefly, in a holy-aesthetic group such as began to flourish after the Tractarian Revival: 'A set of waspish, dogmatical, overbearing fellows,' Tom described them to Hardy, meeting in a room with 'a piano in one corner and muslin curtains—I give you my word, muslin curtains beside the stuff ones.' They used scent 'three sorts on the mantelpiece besides Eau-de-Cologne'. (Can there have been a whiff of incense?) Tom might have stood it, however, had it not been for the talk. Some of the men called St. Paul's 'a disgrace to a Christian city'. Tom, having been 'bred up to respect St. Paul's' spoke in defence, and was repaid with a lecture 'about the Middle Ages and the monks'

of whom he, as a stout Protestant thought England was well
rid. 'And then they got on to Protestantism and fasting and
Apostolic Succession and passive obedience and I don't know
what all. . . . They tried to push Mother Church, Mother Church
down my throat at every turn. I'm as fond of the Church as any
other, but I don't want to be jumped on her back every minute
like a sickly chicken getting on the old hen's back to warm its
feet whenever the ground is cold.'

It is one of the pithiest expressions of manly Christianity as
taught by Arnold and practised by generations of Englishmen.
Tom was devoted enough to the Church to be slightly shocked
by the apathy in chapel: 'I don't think the men care a bit about
it. . . . The service is gone through at a great pace'—and some
of the men brought their lecture notes or books to chapel. He
had no use, however, for the other extreme of ritualism—'all
a Gothic moulding and man-millinery business'. This last
phrase remained a label to tie on to the ritualists for the rest of
the century.

St. Ambrose's was presumably Oriel, Thomas Hughes' own
college and that of his brother George. At this time, in the
1840's, it was at a spiritual nadir after the loss of Keble who was
serving his parish of Hursley as a faithful priest and of Newman
who had, in J. G. Lockhart's word, 'Romanized'. Only a decade
earlier, they and their fellow 'apostles' of the Oxford Movement
had raised it to the zenith of spiritual influence, but now under
Hawkins as Provost, Oriel was a college of Laodiceans. The
influence of the Movement, being more than personal, was to
endure, the stability and faithfulness of Keble strengthened the
Church, but in the last years of his Anglican faith Newman was
above all the force, the magnetism of religious Oxford. He won
the title of 'the Chrysostom of the English Church', and a young
Presbyterian Scot (afterwards Principal Shairp of St. Andrews)
who heard his compelling sermons at St. Mary's said: 'It was
almost as if some Ambrose or Augustine of older days had
returned.'

Oxford had no more devoted son than Newman and part of

the agony of his conversion was his exile from the beloved city
of spires. He recalled it in his novel *Loss and Gain* where the
young hero, Charles, also a convert, visits Christ Church Meadows for the last time and plucks some leaves from a tree as
mementoes.

Neither Tom Brown nor Thomas Hughes knew any such
poignancy, but there are passages in the novel that have almost
the magic of poetry in recalling the golden days of youth, and
the enchantment of Oxford in high summer-tide.

The novel holds reflected memory; but a more direct vision
is given in his memoir of George Hughes. When George came
up to Oriel in 1840 his father wrote: 'I do not know that much
loss of time can occur to a person of perfectly sober habits as
you are, if he leaves wine parties with a clear head at chapel
time, and eschews supping and lounging and lunching and gossiping and tooling in the High Street and such matters.' The
catalogue is interesting; a habit of leisurely or luxurious lunches
meant lounging and gossiping and drinking. 'Row, box, fence
and walk with all possible sturdiness,' continued Mr. Hughes,
adding that if George cared to ride, a horse would be sent to
him with an extra allowance of £5 for stabling: 'This is a better
style of things than piaffing about on hired Oxford cocky-
horses.' ('Piaffe: to strut, to make a show; ulterior origin uncertain.'—*Oxford Dictionary*.)

He hoped to see his son take a pass degree but did not urge
excessive study, and George, according to his brother, was of 'a
constitutional indolence which led him to shirk trouble' and so
was unlikely to shine intellectually. Where he did immensely
distinguish himself and create another legend, as he had created
one on the football field, was on the river. He even gave up
cricket for rowing to his brother's dismay; but it was worth
while, for he stroked the Oxford crew to victory against Cambridge in 1843 and in a seven-oar boat. The crowd went wild
with excitement; the toll-gate at Henley was pulled down by
'a mob of young Oxonians headed by a small, decorous, shy man
in spectacles who had probably never pulled an oar in his life,

but who had gone temporarily mad with excitement'. One likes this little man who flashes across the scene like a kingfisher on the river.

Tom Hughes in turn succumbed to the spell of the river, and rowed in the boat, again stroked by George, which won the Gold Cup at Henley Regatta: 'It's the stroke who wins boat races. . . . There are few pleasanter memories in my life than those of the riverside when we were training behind him in our college crew.' George was a good and an easy coach, by strict rules perhaps too easy, but results justified his leniency. 'The rules of training were then barbarous, and I think we were all the better for not being strictly limited even in the matter of a draught of cold water, and being compelled to eat our meat half-cooked.'

George used to come back as umpire to every boat race; and he proved himself gifted in that peculiarly Victorian art, the writing of light verse, in his boating song:

> *The sons of St. Dennis in praise of their tennis*
> *Of chases and volleys may brag to their fill;*
> *To the northward of Stirling, of golf and of curling*
> *Let the chiels wi' no trousers crack on as they will.*

> *Cricket, football and racquets—but hold, I'll not preach,*
> *Every man to his fancy, I'm too old to mend,*
> *So give me a good stretch down to Abingdon Reach,*
> *Six miles every inch, and hard all to the end.*

> *Our maundering critics may prate as they please*
> *Of glory departed, and influence flown,*
> *Row and work, boys of England, on river and sea,*
> *And the old land shall hold, firm as ever, her own.*

The Oxford of George and Thomas Hughes, and of Tom Brown—of many Tom Browns—and his friends still held something of the enchantment of the Middle Ages; the clouds of eighteenth-century lethargy were slowly drifting from her sky; she was soon to enjoy or endure changes and reforms. Essentially Oxford remained as they had known it until the end of the century and beyond until 1914 when the old world ended in war. Life at college was a golden age for English youth through all the Queen's reign.

# IV

## THE FEMININE WORLD: A PERFECT VICTORIAN

IF it is tenable that Dr. Arnold made the Victorian schoolboy, it is still more probable that the Victorian girl was moulded and perfected by Charlotte Yonge, herself a perfect Victorian. She was born in 1823 and so was a girl in the schoolroom when her Queen was crowned. She barely outlived that reign, dying fulfilled and contented, a venerable and beloved personality, some few months after the Queen. Her influence and popularity were a little on the wane; a new type of girlhood was taking possession of 'the weald of youth'. A little longer and she would have been set aside. She died most timely.

Outwardly her life was uneventful, but the inner, creative life was intense. At one time she was writing two novels at once: a contemporary family chronicle and an historical romance, along with a series of historical sketches or 'cameos' and one of instructions on the Catechism and Prayer Book. Her knowledge of history was wide, and the setting and period of her tales ranged through France and Italy, Germany and Palestine, from the Crusades to the Middle Ages, from the Eve of St. Bartholomew to the French Revolution; but her characters, whatever their names and costumes, their dates and local habitation, remain English, Victorian and Anglican. One of her greatest gifts was the creation of individual characters; every member of each of her large families is distinct; but she could not change her own mind or enter that of another age. The boys and girls of her historical tales are young Victorians dressed for private theatricals; they play their part excellently well and then return to their nursery or schoolroom. Charlotte Yonge was possessed by the Victorian and English spirit at its best.

Her career belongs to the middle of the reign, her own girlhood to its early years. 'Looking back it seems that childhood proper ended with me at thirteen,' she wrote in her brief auto-biography; by that time 'I had begun some of the pursuits that have been a stay to me all my life, those of flowers and of shells'.

Botany was one of the few sciences permissible for girls, one indeed more studied by them than by their brothers, and often complemented by a talent for the delicate and precise drawing of flowers and leaves. Charlotte's love of conchology was a more unusual taste but not uncommon. Such pursuits gave point and interest to the country or seaside walks which for many girls was the only available exercise. Some of them rode, and some were expert in archery; later on croquet came into vogue; but girls in the country walked for exercise, and it was more profitable to look for plants on those walks than merely to ramble and gossip. They might also, of course, walk to the village to visit the poor or to teach in the school.

Charlotte's background was the country house—Otterbourne in Hampshire—her family was of the gentry and squirearchy, with scholars and clergy among her forebears and kinsfolk; the Yonges were cousins, in varying degrees, to the Coleridges and Pattesons, with a strong legal tradition and more than a flash of poetry. The Coleridges were descendants or collaterals of Samuel Taylor Coleridge himself, the Pattesons produced the missionary and martyr-Bishop; the background and heritage were of pro-found culture, intelligence and breeding with a solid amount of wealth. There was never ostentation for that was vulgar and un-Christian, but there was no anxiety about money. Charlotte's skill in depicting genteel poverty is one of the miracles of her imagination.

Solid comfort endured all her life but in her girlhood it was tempered by asceticism. Her day began early and was strictly regulated. She did some of her lessons before breakfast, with her father who was a stern tutor. These lessons were by no means without tears; she loved history and learned languages with ease: French, German and Italian. In the last she was far beyond her father and translated for his benefit the *Promesi Sposi* of

Manzoni. In mathematics, however, she was a dullard, and the lessons in arithmetic and Euclid often ended in tears. Her gratitude to her father for his sound teaching, her respect for his rarely given praise, overcame her fears and depressions and submerged them in retrospect.

She read with her mother, too, and under her eye drew copies of the fine engravings collected by her father; those portfolios took the place, for untravelled girls, of visits to art galleries and museums.

In the afternoon she took exercise in moderation, and less than her active young body needed. The rules imposed on her were perhaps stricter than the average, for the real head of the household was her maternal grandmother, a matriarch of imposing authority. Mrs. Yonge herself was delicate and could not walk far; and as a young lady must not walk out alone, Charlotte depended upon her father's escort or that of a maid. When neither was available there remained only the garden which offered 'endless occupation out-of-doors except on the damp days when three times round the gravel walk which bounded what Grandmamma called the premises, was reckoned equivalent to a mile, and made my required exercise, enlivened with many a fancy'.

The fancies concerned imaginary families, so often the comfort of the solitary. They were not altogether creatures of fantasy but had kinship with a real family of cousins in Devonshire and with the Moberlys, the children of the new headmaster of Winchester who were half a generation younger than Charlotte and whom she knew from their babyhood. In that reality her intensely creative imagination took root; her dream-children were never elfin creatures; faery was the one region she never entered.

Her heroines were, many of them, active in good works among the children and the poor of their village, but that interest came to Charlotte after the years of girlhood. In youth she was kept secluded. By her own confession she was 'a great chatterbox' likely to hear and say too much, and so 'all gossip and familiarity with servants, as a rule, and poor people, was decidedly checked'.

She once described herself as 'shatter-brained'; granting this confession and her mother's desire to shield her from any contamination, the rule of seclusion can be understood if not approved. Rural England was then 'much less cultivated than nowadays' and Victorian standards of propriety were long in being acquired by the peasantry. But Charlotte regretted the seclusion: 'The shyness of other classes that was engendered has never left me, and though I have been working for my village neighbours all my life, I have never been able to converse with them with any freedom.'

She was confirmed in Coronation year, after preparation by John Keble her parish priest and for many years to come her chief counsellor in all matters spiritual and intellectual. The preparation 'was done by working through the Catechism and the Communion Service, with the last comparing old liturgies and going into the meaning. It was a great happiness and opened my mind to Christian doctrine, but I well remember the warning at the end against taking these things up in a merely poetical tone for their beauty'.

Religion was not an aesthetic cult, it was a rule of life and way of worship, and this ideal formed her writing as it did her character. Her motto was *Pro Deo et Ecclesia* and the Anglican Church has never had a more serviceable daughter. She was never hampered by the rules of her faith, of her period or of her class; more than any other woman of talent she fulfilled herself completely within the setting they made for her.

Religion strengthened the discipline of her intellectual training by her father. He was severe but thorough: 'He required a diligence and accuracy that were utterly alien to me. He thundered at me so that no one could bear to hear it,' yet—'I believe in spite of all breezes over my innate slovenliness, it would have broken our hearts to leave off working together.'

As she grew older, Charlotte began to teach as well as to learn, her pupil being her brother Julian, six years her junior. She taught him Latin and they read Phaedrus and Cornelius Nepos, proceeding to Virgil and Horace. Her own studies continued, and in the evening there were books for amusement, Papa often reading aloud while mother and daughter sewed. Mr. Yonge had an excellent library, containing all the classics of English poetry and biography, history and fiction. New books were not easily to be had; there was a circulating library in the neighbourhood but the books became so dirty that they were disagreeable to handle, and in any case were hardly worth reading. A private book club was therefore started among the gentry: each subscriber might order a book, and when all the books had been circulated they were sold to members, and new volumes bought. These were carefully chosen and 'the plan prevented an immense amount of mischievous reading'.

There was a flood of trivial fiction; there were the masterpieces of Scott and of Jane Austen; but between these groups lay a deep gulf. There was another gulf between books for children (themselves few, as yet) and those mature classics. There was not much for a girl to read about her own young world and her own kind.

Elizabeth Sewell, sister of one of the early Tractarian clerics and schoolmasters, and herself a schoolmistress, began in the 1840's to publish her edifying and by no means unreadable tales of girlhood: *Amy Herbert, Margaret Percival, Laneton Vicarage, Experience of Life,* and others. They had a vogue in High Church circles and are still valuable as period-pieces, but they were written with a purpose, to inculcate sound Anglican doctrine, and the purpose is too often evident.

Charlotte never lacked purpose, writing as she did *pro Deo et Ecclesia,* but she could not and did not repress the creative force in her which gave life to her characters. As a writer she owed something to her father's training, something to Keble's encouragement, and, more directly, something to her French master, an old *émigré,* Monsieur de Normanville, 'an old man with white hair, powdered and a huge French nose and rimless ears . . . a very good French scholar of the old, idiomatic style'. He set her to write, in French, a series of stories modelled on those in *Les Veillées du Château* by Madame de Genlis: 'My first beginning of composition—an endless story in which Emilie, Rosalie, Henriette and Pauline Melville had endless adventures.'

Her imaginary families of those solitary walks in the garden began to take form. Some time later she revised the stories in her *Château de Melville* and published them for the benefit of the village school. The next stage was the writing of her first schoolroom novels or *romans jeune fille*: *Abbeychurch, The Two Guardians, The Castle Builders,* and *Scenes and Characters.*

Alice Meynell has written, in poetry, *A Letter from a Girl to Her Own Old Age*; Charlotte from her thirties onward, was to look back on her youthful self, and with indulgence and infinite understanding create a succession of heroines who held something of that self and who were, in spite of all differences of temperament and of period, essential girlhood.

In the first novels—*Abbeychurch, The Two Guardians,* and *The Castle Builders*—she was still dominated by her moral purpose and still too close to her own girlhood to give a detached picture of girlish heroines; her own gravest self appears in Elizabeth of *Abbeychurch.* But in *Scenes and Characters* she created a family of real young people, so different from each other that no reader could ever confuse them, so human that every young reader must recognize them as kin. Charlotte was to write better and more famous novels but this is the first good schoolroom novel in literature. Lilias Mohun, who had much of the impetuous, even 'shatter-brained' Charlotte in her, and her sisters Emily, Phyllis and Jane, were the first young girls in fiction to come alive and win the affection (in one or two incidents the disapproval) of contemporaries of their own age. The girl in the schoolroom had, at last, books written for her. Out of that perfect Victorian girlhood in the first years of the Queen's reign came a new form of fiction.

# V

## OTHER GIRLS

SECLUSION might be the rule for girls but there were exceptional girls, one of the most notable being Henrietta Ward the artist, born in 1832. 'I never had a formal "coming out",' she recalled, 'because from my earliest years I was taken everywhere.'

As the daughter of artistic parents she enjoyed the freedom of Bohemia, a most respectable and elegant Bohemia but still much more spacious than the country house or vicarage which sheltered most young ladies. A precocious child, she went to her first ball at the age of eleven, dressed in white tarlatan trimmed with white satin ribbon, the wide skirt looped up with a rose; she looked not merely pretty but what mattered more, so grownup that one admirer asked if he might call. He took her for eighteen, and his intentions were strictly honourable. In return for this ball given by a friend she was allowed to give one at home, and spent most of the time playing the piano for the others' dancing, not because she disliked dancing but because she 'loved to see the *joie de vivre* of the guests in the full sway of movement'.

Always as a child she had disliked children's parties, preferring adult company, though childish enough to relish the delicacies left over from grown-up parties: barley-sugar baskets filled with meringues and other delights. The Victorians had a culinary genius for pretty delicacies, and for parties that were (to quote from a child's rhyming story of much later date):

> *So sumptuous and yet so neat,*
> *Refined yet hearty.*

The austerity of the average nursery and schoolroom diet made

such treats all the more delectable. Henrietta remembered other
delicacies, such as oranges in syrup and pink castor sugar.

Even without parties her life was by no means dull, and it
became sparkling when she presently fell in love, at an age even
younger than Juliet's, with all Juliet's ardour and certainty but
happily without Juliet's fate. Her Romeo was Edward Ward,
the son of some neighbours in Fitzroy Square, namesakes but not
kindred. An inevitable confusion of letters led to an acquaintance
which developed into friendship. Edward, being an artist like
Henrietta's father, was *sympathique*. Henrietta was already showing talent and he was invited to help her with her drawing and
give criticism and advice. With parental approval she sat to
him as model; he (being twenty-seven) was so much older than
she that it was perfectly proper.

'I took a fancy to him at once' for he was tall, dark and handsome besides being extremely charming in manner; and he took
a fancy to her. It proved more than fancy; it was first and last
and lifelong love for both. They became engaged when the
young lady was fourteen: an *annus mirabilis* for her for that
spring she had a picture—a drawing of *Elizabeth Woodville
Parting From the Duke of York* hung in the Royal Academy.
Edward too was successful with his *South Sea Bubble* and *Dr.
Johnson's Audience With Lord Chesterfield*. The engagement was
permitted, or tolerated by her parents, but there must be no talk
of marriage for a while yet. That was reasonable enough and
parental conditions would have been accepted had not Henrietta's
mother begun to show jealousy and resentment about the affair.
She was exacting, fretful and interfering and made things un-
bearable for the lovers for the next two years, until they met one
day, at the Academy, and planned a secret wedding.

Edward's sister-in-law entered the conspiracy. Having invited
Henrietta to lunch at her house, Grove End House, St. John's
Wood, she called, as was proper, for her in her carriage, then
drove to All Souls', Langham Place, where Edward awaited
them 'gaily attired in bridal array' as far as a white waistcoat and
a gardenia in his buttonhole could achieve that effect. Their

fellow-artist Sir David Wilkie gave the bride away, and she went on to lunch with her new sister-in-law. Her parents joined them for dinner and Henrietta went home with them.

This was in March. In August the pair went on their honeymoon to Iver in Buckinghamshire, and there the bride wrote the news to her parents. Her mother never forgave her and some of her friends followed this example. In an improving tale misery would, sooner or later, have ensued, but there is no moral at all in this true and happy story. It was a perfect marriage of true minds as of true hearts; they had love and work and success. Henrietta had every desire fulfilled. Before she was twenty she was complete, as a woman and as an artist. She had children and one of them, her son Leslie, born when she was nineteen, inherited his parents' gifts; he became the famous caricaturist 'Spy'.

Henrietta continued her career; the Wards had all the freedom of Bohemia without the poverty. They lived in St. John's Wood which was then almost rural, though so near the centre of town as to be also urban: a region of pleasant houses each in its garden, and by no means misnamed The Wood. London was still surrounded by villages and country ways: Regent's Park had fields and a farm of its own, and on the other side of the town Brompton was a village with lanes where the nightingale sang, Chelsea 'a lovely little village' by the river, its old Church surrounded by fields. Chester and Belgrave Squares were bordered by strawberry fields, and there was a dairy in Marylebone where the dairy-woman was dressed in muslin like a dairymaid in a pastoral play. At a summer evening party one could eat strawberries gathered only a mile or two away and an hour or so ago, with fresh cream from the dairy round the corner and pink sugar.

Henrietta was an even happier Victorian than Charlotte Yonge; she could hardly have known more freedom and certainly no greater happiness in a later age of feminine emancipation. Her happiness was in herself and in her domestic good fortune. It was not always so easy for a girl, exceptionally gifted, to fulfil herself. Charlotte and Henrietta were alike in this that their setting and circumstances did not repress their true selves.

Other girls, perhaps more intellectual but less creative, found themselves hampered, and with more or less effort won freedom for themselves and for others. Most of the pioneers in the higher education of girls were born in the 1820's and 1830's: Anne Clough in 1820, Frances Buss in 1827, Emily Davies in 1830 and Dorothea Beale in 1831, all on much the same social level. They all spent their girlhood in the early years of the Queen's reign; and Victoria, though completely lacking their thirst for 'large draughts of intellectual day', was, in her maturity and theirs, to give gracious patronage to their schemes of education. Women in politics she thought wicked and unnatural but women at college she accepted.

These girls all came of good stock, with a background of culture and breeding. Anne Clough, the eldest of the group, was the daughter of a cotton merchant in Liverpool. Between her twelfth and sixteenth year she lived in South Carolina where her father had an estate in Charleston. The Southern States had a European background and tradition, in some places French or Spanish rather than English, and with Latin ideas about the seclusion of *la jeune fille*. This was relieved by the new trans-atlantic notions of freedom even for *la jeune fille*, so that Anne's youth was more emancipated than that of her contemporaries at home.

Her brothers were sent home to school in England, one of them, Arthur Hugh, being Dr. Arnold's star pupil. Anne did lessons with her mother, reading a great deal of history, much of it American; Rollin, Prescott, Washington Irving, but she was taught to remember that she was English. She read poetry too, and she was deeply religious, having experienced conversion at the age of twelve; the evangelical influence was strong. In the church at Charleston she remembered black people and white worshipping together though seated apart. These were the days of slavery and of the zenith of Southern wealth, ease and grace of living. Anne found the problem perplexing.

E

The South helped to form her, to give her poise and an earlier maturity than she would have known in England. Girls in Carolina were often married at fifteen, and even before that were being formally courted. There were youthful brides in England —witness Henrietta Ward—but they came straight from the schoolroom; the American girl knew a longer and more delightful lingering at the place where brook and river meet.

The Cloughs returned to England in 1836, and the last years of Anne's girlhood were spent in Liverpool, reading and studying at home under the guidance of her brother Arthur, and teaching girls in the Welsh National School which her father (of Welsh blood) had helped to found. Just after her twentieth birthday a change came in the family fortunes; her father failed in business, and they had to move to a smaller house and accept straitened means. The middle years of Anne's life were almost hidden though not empty or unhappy. They were full of study and of teaching, and in 1871, when Newnham was founded, she was appointed Principal; a new life began and we shall see it through the eyes of the late Victorian girls, her students.

Her future colleague—at Girton—Emily Davies, and two of the great headmistresses who were to prepare 'the new girl' for the new colleges were also living studious days. The one nearest her in age, Frances Mary Buss, was a Londoner. Her father was artistic, her mother had a vocation for teaching which the daughter inherited. Mrs. Buss had a school for girls where Frances began teaching after her fourteenth birthday: 'I was in sole charge for a week at a time when I was sixteen . . . and never since have I spent my days out of a schoolroom.'

Her own education at home was solid, and in 1849 she entered the newly founded Queen's College in Gower Street. Among the lecturers was Dorothea Beale, her junior by four years; also a Londoner by birth, the daughter of a surgeon at Guy's. She too had been educated at home, a brief experience of school having been ended by her delicate health. It was a pity, for her girlhood was too solitary and too serious. School life would have brought some companionship and experience of communal life which would have helped her in later years as a schoolmistress. 'Miss Beale never learned to play' it was said of her at Cheltenham.

The rhyme:

> Miss Buss and Miss Beale
> Cupid's darts do not feel;
> How different from us
> Miss Beale and Miss Buss!

was almost true. There was a faint hint of romance in Miss Beale's youth as might be expected for she had beauty—unlike the plain-headed Miss Buss, but neither of these ladies, as far as is known, had to make any renunciation of love for learning's sake. A prick of the darts would have been good for them, or failing that, at least a little fun and mischief in their grave girl-hoods. They were never shatter-brained, indeed they may be said to have been born schoolmistresses fully developed like Minerva. Miss Buss was redeemed by a tincture of humour, by a certain robustness, but Miss Beale was infinitely refined. A strain of frivolity might have crept in when she was sent to school in Paris to be 'finished'; it was a very grand school but it was closed in the Revolution of 1848 and Dorothea came home, ungallicized, to attend private classes and presently to lecture in Queen's College.

The fourth in this quartet of learned girls, Emily Davies, was the daughter of a clergyman of the Evangelical school; her up-bringing was strict, almost puritanical. Novels, card-playing, the theatre were all forbidden.

In 1839 her father moved from a charge near Chichester to one at Gateshead and there remained for twenty-two years; so, in the austere north of England Emily attained her austere young ladyhood.

'We were not much waited on,' she wrote in an account of her youth, 'and did a great deal for ourselves'—even in those days of cheap domestic labour. Emily ironed her own muslin collars and cuffs; she did lessons at home and at the age of eleven helped her brother William to produce a family magazine, that resource of many clever young Victorians. She inserted in one issue an advertisement for a governess which shows no illusions about herself:

'The lady must be a person of great firmness and determination, for the young lady who is the subject of her care is rather inclined to be self-willed. Phrenologically speaking, she has the organ of self-esteem rather largely developed.' This ideal governess must be 'well-skilled in the languages and sciences as Miss D. is anxious to excel all her contemporaries in these branches of knowledge'. The paragon did not materialize, and perhaps there was no real quest for her. Emily was educated at home by her mother and her elder sister, and, as she grew up, by her friends, Jane Crow, a pioneer in education, Elizabeth Garrett, one of the first woman doctors in England, and Barbara Leigh—later Madame Bodichon—who was said to have been the prototype of George Eliot's Romola.

The history of the higher education of girls belongs to the later decades of the century; we see now the youth of the leaders and teachers, serious young women, with high ideals and deeply devout. The Church of England was far from being reactionary in this matter; many of her devout daughters were learned, and many of her clergy approved the new learning, and helped to found the schools and colleges.

These pioneers carried the tradition of Anglican piety into the new world of female scholarship. This was not, however, the only tradition to be continued or revived. The Roman Catholic residuum in England, that faithful remnant long left in obscurity, was enjoying the second spring, as Newman called it, of social and spiritual life, in the 1940's. They were at last freed from political disabilities, and there was a renewal of faith in action, not least in education. It was now permissible for the Religious Orders to open their houses in England and to teach there children who so far had been sent abroad.

In 1842 the Society of the Sacred Heart came to England; the Foundress and Mistress General was Madeleine Sophie Barat (now canonized) a Burgundian peasant who had founded her great society in 1800. Her convent schools had spread over France and Italy, and already passed to Ireland and to America. Two houses were offered to her in England, at Cannington in Somerset and at Berrymead, both former Benedictine foundations. The first Superior at Berrymead, Mother Merilhon, was chosen for her solid virtues: 'We require someone who is mature, prudent, thoroughly religious and calm,' declared Mother Barat. 'Nothing else will do in England.' She knew her England though she had not yet visited this island. The solidity of the education given by the nuns of the Sacred Heart appealed to the English Catholics, and their courtesy won not only their co-religionists but the neighbourhood in general. When they arrived at Cannington the bells of the parish church were rung, and all the villagers turned out to welcome them.

It proved, however, necessary to close this house, for its poverty was great. When Mother Barat visited England in 1844 she decided, regretfully, to move those nuns to Berrymead and make one house. 'These two foundations were like two birds that had but one wing apiece. Now Berrymead, with two, will be able to fly.'

This hope was fulfilled. Berrymead flourished, as convent and as school, and when some years later it was moved to Roehampton, it was, to use the Mother's metaphor, flying with strong wings.

By mid-century the pattern of education for Catholic girls was set; for others a new way was being traced. The Catholic way restored to England a sense of Europe, especially of France; the new schools opened many doors beyond their own.

*Part Two*

# Mid-Victorian

1850–1870

# VI

## MANNERS AND MEN

RUGBY was creating a new ethos, Eton was entrenched in a conservatism yielding only a little to needful reforms. Even more than either of them Winchester was a kingdom in itself, with its own laws, rites and language. There is public school English just as there is Church Latin, and each is a lingua franca within the community. This is only one of the aspects of school life in which the old religion is reflected. Monasticism was to return to England, in both the Anglican and the Roman Communions during the nineteenth century, but the monastic ideal of a community, at least partially and temporarily enclosed, with its own loyalties, obedience and discipline, had been maintained since the Reformation by the public schools. Their very discomforts were a traditional discipline like that of a seminary or a novice-house. That it was the sons of the richest and noblest families in England who endured these hardships was no more an anomaly than it was for a monk to accept the poverty of his Rule, even if he had been a noble in the world.

One chronicler of Winchester, the Reverend F. C. Wickham (most appropriate name), took 1850 as the turning-point in the school history; within that decade two changes were made: 'the opening of college to competition, and the establishment of the first tutors' houses for Commoners.' The rigours of the medieval regimen were being mellowed 'under the kindly rule of Warden Barter'. The boys had no longer to wash 'at a frozen conduit nor to breakfast at ten on bread and cheese and beer, and dine at six off wooden trenchers. . . . But we still slept in the old wooden beds at Chambers, and sat on "scobs" in school'. Thus the monks might have lived, breaking their fast only after hours of prayer and meditation in chapel. The boys' day also began in chapel.

Anthony Trollope and his elder brother Thomas were both Wykehamists, the latter for eight years, from 1820–8. His boyhood is pre-Victorian but his memories of Winchester are substantially the same as the mid-Victorian account given by Mr. Wickham, and may be used for comparison. Both were elected at an examination (so-called) by the Warden:

'Well, boy, can you sing?'—'Yes, sir.'—'Let us hear you.'—'All people that on earth do dwell,' sang Thomas Trollope and, a generation later, Wickham—'Very well, boy, that will do.'

The statutes required scholars to be instructed in plain-song and to sing in the Cathedral; in practice it was enough if they sang a line of the Old Hundredth and went twice to the Cathedral on Sunday besides attending their own chapel.

'The old wooden beds in Chambers' were of oak, black with age. They were hooded—the end-boards being raised and covered like a cradle, and if they were not soft they were snug. Further protection against draughts was given by a screen at the oak door, and a fire burned all night on the hearth. It was the duty of one of the junior boys or 'inferiors' to tend the fire with faggots, and if fire or night-light went out he was, in modern slang, 'for it'. Each boy had by his bedside an oak chest to hold his clothes and serve as seat; above it was a tall desk with cupboard curiously called 'toys', and holding not playthings but books. Chaucer's Clerk of Oxenfoord may have had some such piece of furniture to hold

'*at his beddes head*
*Some twenty bokes clad in black or red*'.

The surplices for chapel hung round a pillar in the middle of the room.

In Trollope's time the prefects washed luxuriously in Chambers, but inferiors at the pump in the quadrangle. 'In severe or wet weather it was not sybaritic.' Yet Trollope claimed that it would 'have been difficult to find a healthier collection of boys than we were'. By 1850 this austerity was relaxed; everyone washed indoors and in hot water; one of the duties of fags was to tend the boilers.

Trollope's schoolday began at half past five with chapel, then school, and breakfast only after three or four hours of work. Beer was still the only drink permitted. Tea and coffee were regarded as luxuries, effeminate if not actually dissipated. Naturally they were smuggled in, and tea on a tray, now regarded as a mere spinster's delight, had all the savour of the forbidden. If a master caught any boys feasting on tea he would smash the service: 'What are all these things, sir? William of Wykeham knew nothing, I think, of tea.'

Luncheon then was a mere nuncheon or snack of bread and cheese; only on Sunday was there a midday dinner of roast beef; on other days dinner was at a quarter past six, and consisted of 'good Southdown mutton' with potatoes and beer. There was a relic of monastic charity in the office of 'prefect of tub', the tub being the receptacle for the remains of the meal to be given to the poor.

The mid-Victorian Wykehamists still rose early for chapel at six, but they had breakfast at eight, before school, with tea instead of beer. Both tea and coffee were by that time permitted; indeed there was a recognized 'mess' in Chambers in the evening of tea or coffee and bread. The diet was altogether more liberal with a one-o'clock dinner and supper in the evening.

The ritual and language were unchanged. Boys still went 'up to books'—in ordinary English, into class, the prefects to the library where they were taught by the headmaster. They wore the black gown with white bands which gave them an air half clerical, half legal.

They played games between twelve and one; at six o'clock on winter evenings they were locked into Chambers, and from seven to eight was 'toy time' a paradoxical term for 'prep.'. Prayers in chapel ended the day.

Long before Arnold created his praepostors the prefectorial system was part of the Wykehamist tradition. Each prefect was tutor to two or three inferiors, tutor both in the old sense of guardian and the modern one of coach. He defended, or should defend his charges from bullying, saw that they conducted themselves in a manner becoming a Wykehamist, and supervised their work. For each pupil or fag he had a fee of £2. The prefects were judge, jury and court of appeal. 'An appeal to the master would have been as much thought of as an appeal to Jupiter or Mars.' They could order and inflict punishment or 'public tunding', i.e. beating with a stick. This, Trollope said, was 'judiciously ordered for offences deemed unbecoming to the character of a Wykehamist and a gentleman' and was rarely inflicted; it fostered 'a high tone of moral and gentlemanlike feeling'. Even in an age when a small boy's life at school could be purgatory if not hell, the ideal of William of Wykeham was tolerably well realized, and these manners made their men perhaps a little juster and gentler than their contemporaries.

This rule of prefects may be seen as a reflection of the oligarchy which long prevailed in England, a form of primogeniture, of respect for seniority, a sense of hierarchy. Each prefect had his special function; the prefect of chapel called the roll, the prefect of hall kept order at meals, and also arranged the holidays or 'remedies': a pleasant term. In Wykehamist language 'holidays' were 'holy days' in the old sense of red letter or saints' days.

On remedies and on summer evenings this prefect led the school in procession to 'Hills'—that is to St. Catherine's Hill outside the city—the eighteen prefects, the seventy scholars of William of Wykeham's foundation and the hundred and thirty commoners who were pupils of the headmaster, walking in order. On the Hill they were free to roam and play until an inferior was bidden to call *Domum* and summon them home.

'Manners makyth man' was their motto; their scholastic injunction: *Aut Disce aut discede* was carved on the schoolroom wall: the learning illustrated by a book and inkstand, the departing by a sword, the career of soldier being the honourable alternative to that of scholar or clerk in holy orders. A third fate was suggested in the words: *Manet sors tertia caedi*—with a

rod depicted as the lot of those who would neither apply themselves to learning or to the defence of their country.

The learning in the fifties as in the twenties remained severely
classical. Trollope 'left Winchester a fairly good Latin scholar,
well-grounded, I do not think I can say more, in Greek, and very
ignorant indeed of all else. . . . I never had an English grammar
in my hand'; but he contrived to write good English, and to
deplore the 'vast number of solecisms, vulgarisms and grammatical atrocities' of a later generation who professed to have
been trained in English.

Wickham, admitting the limits of this classical education,
pointed out that the scope of reading was very wide. The Latin
and Greek texts were read rapidly, to be appreciated as literature
and remembered for style, not analysed in the Melvinian manner.
History and English literature were taught indirectly by allusion
and frequent quotation. It was taken for granted that the boys,
being sons of gentlemen, had a gentleman's knowledge of literature; they came from homes where books made a background,
were read and discussed. Such culture was, like good manners
and a knowledge of the world, assimilated rather than 'got
up'.

Latin prose was taught most thoroughly; not only were the
boys set passages for translation, they were given a theme for an
essay or 'gathering'. Latin verse was hardly less important, and
every inferior must produce every day a *vulgus* or Latin epigram
on a given theme. The prefects' compositions were called
'varyings'.

Divine learning was not ignored; it was the other side of the
shield of education. A certain amount of theology was as essential as Greek for entrance to the universities. Boys were taught
Scripture and the Prayer Book, and attended chapel daily. In
spite or because of this, the religious atmosphere had sunk to
zero in Trollope's time; it rose under a new headmaster, Dr.
Moberly, a friend of Keble and disciple of the Tractarians. He
gave sound instruction in school and in private prepared boys
very thoroughly for confirmation—'the hinge upon which the

whole life of a boy from the beginning to the end of his school-days turns.' This sacrament 'ought to be the strength of boyhood and so it ought to be given then and there when boyhood wants its strength'. He taught sound Eucharistic doctrine, and he indicated, if he did not urge, the approach to Confession, not as an emotional outlet but as spiritual discipline. Such teaching was an act of courage as well as of faith; the Tractarians were suspect of hidden popery and Moberly came under this suspicion for a time. By modern standards his observance of the Christian year in school was very moderate; his Good Friday Prose was not a meditation on the Passion, but merely a discourse on the events in school during the past year.

With his colleague the Warden (Dr. Barter) he made many reforms. He build a separate boarding-house for the commoners. These pupils had hitherto lived apart from the scholars (who were in Chambers) in the headmaster's house. A new one had been built to hold 'they Mulberries' as an old countrywoman once called the twelve young Moberlys, but even so there was too little room for the boys. The new boarding-house was the first of many and the beginning of the modern system of houses each under a housemaster. Moberly also urged the admission of more commoners and the introduction of a really testing examination.

In education itself he was conservative. Appointed in 1835 he reigned till 1866 and saw little need for change in the curriculum. Giving evidence before the Royal Commission on Public Schools in 1862 he declared: 'In my judgment you cannot bring French in as a co-ordinate subject of instruction with the two chief subjects of education, classics and divinity, or even with the third, mathematics. We can find neither the time in the week nor the teachers.' Mathematics he had himself introduced, appointing a master and arranging classes, but French and history, botany and other subjects while of value and interest, were best studied out of school, at home in the holidays: 'I have found it useful to offer prizes annually for the best collection of wild flowers made in the year in the neighbourhood.'

There must have been many appeals to sisters and their gover-

nesses who went on botanizing walks after a morning of French
and history in the schoolroom.

Winchester of the 1850's is seen through feminine eyes in
Anne Moberly's memoir *Dulce Domum*—named from the school
song. She writes of the magic of that song which made a Wykehamist at all times and in all places 'realize afresh his deep love
and loyalty to the school' which 'could only be demonstrated
by shouting the beloved song at the top of his voice and in company with those of the same mind'.

This he could best do on the last day of the summer term,
which was called *Domum*, when as many old boys as could
returned. Some were at the ends of the earth but they remembered: 'There was one who sang it at intervals all day in the
Australian bush.'

For the Moberlys it 'became identified in our minds with
the loveliness of a summer evening; the sunset lights over the
meadows and St. Catherine's Hill fading in the twilight; until
the deepening darkness compelled the company to adjourn to
Chambers' Court for another and last singing of *Domum* followed by the always touching strains of *Auld Lang Syne*; and
the outline of chapel and tower and school against the evening
sky'.

Charlotte Yonge was often with them and she too recalled
this midsummer magic: 'There is no forgetting the wandering
in the twilight or moonlight; the meeting old friends . . . the
singing louder and louder each time; the hats waved; the losing
of all one's companions, and then all turning up again in the
drawing-room full of fun and anecdote.'

On the next night there was the *Domum* ball, and on one occasion a prefect said to his partner, one of the Moberly girls: 'I
hope you are not heavy, for I am not strong.'

The headmaster's house may have been called by the poetic a
'rosebud garden of girls'. There were eight daughters, the
flower of Victorian femininity like their mother, that lovely and
gracious and almost exotically refined lady. They were completely of this world yet so utterly of their period that to us they

appear to move behind a golden mist of time, to walk as in a tapestry of medieval ladies.

They were all educated at home, the elder reading with their mother and helping her in many ways. Alice, the eldest, was her special companion; Mary was the domestic daughter, an exquisite needlewoman, making her own dresses, gifted in painting and music—the last being a gift shared by all the family; Edith was as active as a girl could be in that period, loving an out-of-doors life, with gardening in summer, skating in winter, walking at all times. She was a special favourite of Charlotte Yonge who sent her the first copy of *The Daisy Chain*. Anne was bookish, and she was to become the head of one of the new colleges for women at the end of the century.

They lived graciously; the family memoir is haunted by the fragrance of flowers, of fresh country air, by music. They sang naturally in part-songs and glees, often in summer evenings sitting on the lawn. They were devout in the renewed tradition of the Tractarians; their country home was in Keble's parish. They read widely and their talk was most often of books.

This household was not unique in its culture, or in its interweaving of masculine and feminine threads. Its particular interest is in its union of domestic and scholastic elements. The school was always in the background; and the amateur of Victoriana cannot think of Winchester College without 'they Mulberries' any more than the lover of Jane Austen can think of the Cathedral without remembering one grave there.

# VII

## OTHER MANNERS, OTHER MEN: SOME SCHOOLS AND SCHOOLMASTERS

### I

'SUPERCILIOUS cart-horses' is a good bit of invective, and so is 'unadulterated moon-calves'. They were hurled with other gems at his boys by one of the greatest of Victorian headmasters, Edward Thring of Uppingham, and they were well received. A Head who roars is better than one who sneers or snarls; Thring's wrath was mighty but so were his justice and under-standing. For his integrity of mind and character he was respected, for his affection and sympathy he was loved.

Himself a reformer and pioneer he came from the old, un-reformed Eton of the 1830's. He could confirm all that Arthur Duke Coleridge had said of the evils endured by the boys: 'Rough and ready was the life they led. Cruel at times the suffering and wrong; wild the profligacy.'

Thring was Captain of the School and Captain of 'Montem', the last but one to hold that office. The 'salt' or tax collected came to £1,249, given to the Captain as was the custom: a comfortable equipment for Cambridge. More than half of it went, however, in his expenses for 'Montem'—in wine, in breakfast- and dinner-parties and other ritual extravagance. He was left with about £550.

The son of a squarson, a product of Eton and Cambridge, Thring would appear a conventional figure, completely of his class and period. He took Holy Orders, and a comfortable charge or a fellowship or headmastership might have been expected to follow. The last of the three was his fortune, but only after an experience which freed him from the conventional mould, and deeply influenced him in his career.

As a curate in Gloucester he taught in one of the new National

69

F

Schools, founded by 'The National Society for Promoting the
Education of the Poor in the Principles of the Established Church'.
It was an awakening for the young cleric: 'Never shall I forget
it. . . . Everything I most value, of teaching thought, teaching
practice and teaching experience came from that.'

It was no easy task for this son of Eton and Cambridge, laden
with learning and steeped in tradition, to enter 'the minds of
those little labourers' sons with their unfurnished heads. . . .
There I learned the secret of St. Augustine's golden key which,
though it be of gold is useless unless it fits the wards of the lock'.

He made himself fit the lock. 'It was glorious work. There
was a wonderful freshness in those schools, a most exhilarating
sense of life touching life, of freedom and reality.'

He was probably the first headmaster of a public school to
have known such training. In 1853 he was appointed to Uppingham, founded in the sixteenth century by Robert Johnson,
Archdeacon of Leicester, as a 'faire, free grammar school'. Thring
found it in bad shape, with only twenty-five boys. His salary
was £150, his schoolhouse dilapidated. For staff he had one
assistant and one writing-master. The governors, chiefly the
local squires and clergy, were apathetic, some of them hostile.
Thring was to bring the numbers of boys up to three hundred.

'With many bitter tears and weary days of pain of body and
heart, almost in my heart's blood were the foundations of this
school laid.' He was in truth its second founder, a rebuilder and
renewer, making reforms boldly in spite of official and parental
opposition.

'I'm sick of parental jaw'—and he usually forgot it, having a
way of keeping parents in their place. Had he practised this on
the labourers in Gloucester? Certainly his experience there had
trained him in patience and in sympathy with the average boy.
Uppingham was no forcing-house; if anything the average boy
was preferred to the brilliant. As the school grew Thring
divided it into small forms and houses so that every boy could
be known and receive possibly more attention than he would
wish.

There was no Long Chamber at Uppingham; the boys had separate cubicles or 'tishes' (from 'partitions') and studies. There were praepostors, but the Tone was not that of Dr. Arnold. *He* assumed that boys were naturally depraved and in need of reformation. Thring, for all his vituperation, liked the creatures and trusted them.

He could, indeed, roar and he could punish: 'I have yet to learn that a society of boys or men gathered from all quarters can be managed without punishment. . . . I think flogging is the very best remedy for some breaches of discipline'; and he was known as 'the most formidable schoolmaster of his age'. One old boy remembers his Mosaic thunders: 'When boys saw the lines of his upper lip stiffen like iron and the sheet-lightnings begin to play in his steel-grey eyes they did not lightly provoke the discharge. . . . If he broke in on a scene of misrule with his characteristic cry of, "Law-breakers" and the query "Will you obey orders?"—why, we decidedly thought we would.'

Mosaic he was, like many of the great Victorian clerics, in his passion for righteousness. 'The Bible is God's great police-court as well as His Temple,' he used to say, and his religious teaching was neither faint nor prim.

'Till life ceases to be coarse, lessons in coarseness will be needed; also much of modern reticence is not purity but lust.' It was a bold statement in an era of primness, though one often wonders how the Victorians, a generation of Bible-readers, could maintain that attitude, Holy Writ being so conspicuously unrefined, so extremely outspoken in regard to carnal passion. Thring maintained that it was the duty of fathers to teach their sons the lesson of chastity, to warn them against impurity. 'Curiosity, ignorance and lies form a very hotbed of impurity. We pay heavily for our civilized habits in false shame and the mystery in which sex is wrapped.'

He might thunder as from Sinai but he could descend from the heights. The grey eyes could gleam with humour or soften in tenderness, and he was utterly just. There is, after all, something endearing in a Head who roars at delinquents more in anger than in sorrow and who knows that a flogging hurts them more, much more than it hurts himself.

There was punishment for crime but there was no spying: 'I demur to the wisdom of perpetual surveillance and do not mean to allow it here. Boys should be trusted, and if they break trust, punished.' He even commended 'a little judicious blindness and deafness' as 'a great virtue in a wise teacher'.

The boys came to him for help, finding in him the strength as well as the hardness of a rock. His 'paternals' or talks to boys in trouble or at some moral or emotional crisis were truly fatherly, probing with tenderness and understanding, drawing out the suppressed grief or guilt or temptation. He was feared for his wrath but never for his moods, and the small boys feared him least. One of his most cherished memories was of two little brothers, newly come to school, who could not read a letter from their father in India. It did not occur to them to ask help from a senior boy or an assistant master. They went confidently to the Head; *he* would read it to them. He was generally known as 'The Man', sometimes, more flippantly as 'Teddy'; but 'The Man' suited him.

The school regimen was conventional; he taught the classics soundly and well and encouraged games as 'an opportunity specially devised by Providence to enable small boys to work off their original sin'. Long walks on half-holidays were approved, and there was a good deal of freedom after school and evening prep. and prayers. His ideal was to make school 'better than home' with domestic security, warmth and kindness as well as the discipline and companionship of a community.

II

Those mid-Victorian years saw a renaissance in school life. Old foundations were reformed, and new were made: Cheltenham, Marlborough, Malvern, Clifton, Glenalmond and Loretto were all begun in the middle decades. The railway made travelling easier, and boys were more readily sent from home.

There might not be a public school in every county but there was one in every region of England, and they were invading Scotland as well. Public school education was more and more accepted as the norm. There was, no doubt, a desire on the part of parents to rid the house, for a time, of some of their young, the Victorian family being so large and ubiquitous, and, even under the sternest father, not always subdued. School took the place of the noble household in which medieval youth had been trained as pages and squires.

Wellington was founded in 1858 as a memorial to the great Duke, to provide a good education at moderate cost, chiefly for the sons of officers. The boys at first wore a uniform of green cloth with brass buttons and plaid trousers, designed by their patron the Prince Consort who disliked any such hint of clerical or monastic dress as a gown or cassock. This wearing of the green did not last long; when the neighbouring railway station was opened, travellers used to give up their tickets to the boys who looked so like ticket-collectors.

Wellington began under a young and vigorous Head, Edward Benson, the future Archbishop. He came from Rugby where he was assistant master under Temple—whom he was to succeed, at one remove, in the Primacy. His own school had been Birmingham Grammar, whence he had gone up to Trinity, Cambridge. He was appointed by the Prince Consort on the recommendation of Dr. Temple, and took something of Rugby to his new school, including the system of praepostors. However much he might approve the rule of boys by boys, in theory, he himself, according to his son Arthur 'dominated the whole place'. He was a born administrator, a great ruler, knowing his boys and never forgetting a face; an inspiring teacher, but 'I doubt if he was an educator of the first rank, because he did not desire that his pupils should develop on their lines but on his own'. In this he was the antithesis of Thring; for all their resemblance in force of character, Benson lacked that humorous and patient sympathy with the ordinary boy: 'His temper was high, he brooked no opposition, and he had little or no sympathy for the weak or erratic.'

Thring had been taught by teaching the poor, Benson had himself been poor, as poor as any Scot, but it had hardened rather than mellowed him. He was one of a large family, early left fatherless; when he went up to Cambridge in 1845 he was well equipped intellectually (it was said that he could recite five or six books of the Aeneid before he left school) but materially too poor to enjoy college life. In later years he used to recall the misery of living in a circle, or on the edge of a circle of wealthy friends. Like many a Scots student he earned his fees by tutoring in the vacation; in that of 1848 he was at Abergeldie and saw the Queen and her family on their first visit to Balmoral. His expenses for his first year came to £90. Much work, little sleep and little exercise made his regime, one highly untypical of the Cambridge of his day.

His greatest friend was Lightfoot, another future Bishop. They were both deeply interested in Church matters, and with some others founded a Holy Club with the motto, *Non nobis, Domine* and the objects of prayer, devout reading and good works. Benson's religious views were singularly unswerving; in a period when liberalism on one hand, Rome on the other, drew many away from the Anglican fold, he did not waver, though he was fascinated by Newman—by that time a convert to Rome—on hearing him preach in the Birmingham Oratory.

'He spoke with a sort of angel eloquence,' Benson wrote to Lightfoot. 'Such a style of preaching I never heard before and never hope again to hear.' Newman's appearance startled him: 'May you never turn Romanist if you are to have a face like that—it was awful: the terrible lines deeply ploughed all over his face, and the craft that sat upon his retreating forehead and sunken eyes.' Benson was further shocked by the Roman devotions: the Litany of Our Lady and by Newman's lifting his biretta and bowing at her name as well as at the Holy Name of Jesus: 'How painful it was to think that he had once been an English Churchman!'

This young man was already setting in a rigid mould, his hard youth having strengthened him in character, in self-discipline and integrity but not in tolerance or sympathy. It helped to make him an autocrat who ruled every detail of school life. But he did care for the boys and tried to make the school atmosphere that of a family. Every Sunday two of the Sixth were bidden to breakfast—'as much a necessary accompaniment of breakfast as my father himself' in his son's memory.

His public appearances were magnificent, especially in chapel, and chapels were frequent: twice daily and thrice on Sunday. Once Charles Kingsley, whose sons were at the school, came to preach, and by a curious process of unreasoning on the part of the governors, Benson was reproved for thus encouraging a Ritualist and Romanist—after Kingsley's literary duel with Newman! The boys were interested but not awed: 'We knew he had written *Westward Ho* and *The Water Babies* and knew the books by heart. But that did not astonish us; we supposed that any of the Wellington masters might have written just as good books if they had chosen to do so.'

Autocrat as Benson was, remote as he might appear he was loved as well as feared. When he left Wellington for Lincoln the boys showed this in an ovation. Benson was overcome: 'My dear, dear boys,' he said, his face wet with tears.

### III

To return, briefly, to the older foundations. Rugby under Temple, the third Head in succession from Arnold, knew some innovations. Temple introduced science, a gymnasium and a Rifle Corps. His personal influence was immense, with all the sternness of Arnold, perhaps even more, for Temple was a man of rock, rough-hewn, rough-spoken, but he was of fire too, and the fire had warmth. His religious teaching was deeper than any that had been received, and his Saturday classes of preparation for Holy Communion were well attended and much valued by the boys. Flippancy was not encouraged. Overhearing a boy say: 'I have entered for the Confirmation Stakes,' Temple crushed him forthwith: 'Well, you're scratched now.'

Rugby was by this time influencing other schools as old boys and assistant masters were appointed to headmasterships. Kennedy took the Rugby ethos and the system of praepostors to Shrewsbury where he reigned from 1836-66. He began the moral reformation of the school with religious teaching on the lines of Arnold's, and introduced a hint of modern subjects. French was taught, though not in the Sixth, the boys at that stage having presumably put aside such childish things; there was a whiff of history and geography, and a very faint one of mathematics, Kennedy himself, it was alleged, being unable to do a sum.

His Latinity was excellent and creative. He wrote a Grammar, and composed a mnemonic for the use of the ablative for which many generations of struggling Latinists have blessed him unaware:

> *A ab absque coram de,*
> *Palam clam cum ex* and *e,*
> *Sine tenus pro* and *prae,*
> And unto these if 'rest at' be intended,
> Let in *sub super subter* be appended.

He may further be remembered, outside his school, by the epigram he published on the Restoration of the Roman Catholic Hierarchy in England by Pius IX and Cardinal Wiseman:

> *Cum Sapiente Pius nostras iuravit in aras.*
> *Impius O Sapiens! Insipiensque Pius!*

Rugby touched Harrow through Dr. Vaughan, a pupil of Arnold, one of the first Rugby set, a friend of Arthur Clough and married to a sister of Arthur Stanley, altogether in an atmosphere of incredible earnestness. An old Harrovian described him as 'bred in the school of Arnold, with the velvet glove hiding the iron hand'.

Such a hand was needed; like most of the early and mid-

Victorian headmasters he had to put down drunkenness and
other evils. The velvet glove could be adroitly applied, as
when a young Highlander arrived wearing the kilt. Vaughan,
foreseeing the attitude of his Sassenach schoolfellows kept him
in his own study until a tailor had made him a pair of Saxon
trousers.

For Vaughan, as for Moberly, the classics and divinity were
'the be-all and the end-all' of education. French, History,
English and other kickshaws were of little account: 'He taught
scholarship and nothing but scholarship of the straitest kind, but
this he taught admirably.'

Recognizing, however, other needs and demands in education, he helped to found a new school, in Harrow though not of
'The Hill': a modern and middle-class establishment 'to meet
the wants of a class of residents in Harrow who may not desire
for their sons a high classical education and who yet are reasonably unwilling to confound the natural division of ranks by
sending them to the National School'. The fees were to be
'easy to the class in question' but 'above the reach of those who
are properly contemplated by the National Schools'.

Latin was to be compulsory and free, other subjects such as
English, History and Geography were extras and paid by fees.
Wednesday and Saturday were half-holidays. The boys attended
on Sunday morning for a Scripture lesson but went to church
with their parents. Most important was the condition that 'the
boys will regard themselves as entirely separate in all respects
from those of the Public School, and will on no account mix
themselves with the games, etc., of the Higher School'. This
rule was made in the interests of the new boys—'to secure
them from any interference or annoyance from the Public
School.'

Towards the end of his reign Vaughan received on his staff
one of Harrow's most loved and famous masters, Edward Bowen,
who said, incidentally, that Vaughan 'invented discipline'.
Bowen came in 1859 and was made a housemaster in 1863, not
entirely to his delight: 'The only form in which boys are a

nuisance is in the house,' he complained. 'One is so tied up to hours and the parents will keep writing letters, and there is always the chance that the boys will set the house on fire.'

Of these three evils the worst was the irruption of parents whom most schoolmasters would wish to abolish at least during the school-life of their young.

Bowen's work for the school was, apart from the imponderable of his personal influence, twofold: the first part being his shaping of the Modern Side. This was begun in 1869, with Latin retained, but Greek dropped in favour of History, Modern Languages, English, Mathematics and Book-keeping. Bowen had the flexibility of mind to accept new ways, and the wisdom to insist on a high standard for the boys. The Modern Side was not to be 'a refuge for the destitute' of intellect.

His own teaching was lively and he taught the boys to teach themselves. In history a battle was not merely mentioned but described in detail; his classes usually began with an account of the news of the day.

His other gift to Harrow was in song. He gave the school its own treasury of verse: *Willow the King, Byron Lay, Giants of Old, The Voice of the Ball*, above all, *Forty Years On*:

> *Forty years on when far asunder*
> *Parted are those who are singing today,*
> *When you look back and regretfully wonder*
> *What you were like in your work and your play;*
> *Glimpses of notes like the catch of a song,*
> *Visions of boyhood shall float then before you,*
> *Echoes of dreamland shall bear them along.*
> *Follow up! Follow up!*

He had that talent for inspired fooling which is one of the most endearing qualities of the Victorian intellectuals; at its height in Lewis Carroll but divertingly present in a host of songs and rhymes. In another song Bowen wrote of an ideal, Platonic and fishy Harrow:

*Underneath the briny sea*
*Where be fishes and mermaids three,*
*There lies Harrow as it ought to be.*

Fantasy could invade the schoolroom and nonsense tweak the
tail of the solemnly couchant lion of the public school spirit,
though not, perhaps, at Rugby.

# VIII

# TWO SCOTTISH SCHOOLS

I

*GLENALMOND*

IN mid-century the public school came to Scotland where the tradition of high schools, grammar schools and merchant foundations was old and strong; but there was place for a new way. Glenalmond was a Church school founded by a group of Episcopalians of Tractarian views, of whom the most notable were Dean Ramsay, Mr. Gladstone, and James Hope the husband of Sir Walter Scott's granddaughter and heiress Charlotte Lockhart, who later assumed the surname of Scott.

The Episcopal Church in Scotland, no longer persecuted and no longer a mere 'shadow of a shade' was growing in numbers and vitality, and had never suffered from lethargy. Many of the gentry and the army, and some of the professional classes were Episcopalian, but they were a minority, and there was no school in Scotland where their sons could be bred in their hereditary faith and where ordinands could be prepared for the Church. The theological faculty in each of the four universities was Presbyterian. The new foundation was planned as school and seminary together.

A site in Perthshire was offered by its laird, George Patton, and duly inspected by Mr. Gladstone and James Hope. Years afterwards, Gladstone wrote to Hope's daughter that their decision to buy this land had been—'I do not say assisted . . . but cheered up . . . by a luncheon of grouse newly killed and roasted by an apparatus for the purpose at the moment, and bedewed by what I think is called partridge-eye champagne': surely the most genial foundation ever laid.

The school was opened in 1847, the theological college a year later. The first Warden was the Reverend Charles Wordsworth,

FASHIONS FOR THE YOUNG, 1866
From a coloured lithograph

GLENALMOND: THE BUILDINGS
From the architect's lithograph

GLENALMOND: THE CRICKET TEAM

who came from an assistant mastership at Winchester, though not himself a Wykehamist. He was a nephew of the poet, and a son of Christopher Wordsworth, Master of Trinity, and had all the family seriousness unmarred by any humour. His sub-Warden Moberly was a nephew of the famous headmaster of Winchester, a Wykehamist and New College man; so, much of the tradition and idiom of the ancient English foundation were carried north. The boys' desks were like the 'toys' at Winchester and called by that name.

Glenalmond opened with fourteen pupils, the first to arrive, a day too soon as it happened, being Lord Henry Kerr, afterwards Lord Lothian, who was pressed into service by the Warden engaged upon arranging his library. The boys had to bring each a Bible, Prayer Book and Greek Testament. They wore black gowns or cassocks. 'Though ugly and clumsy,' as the school historian has pointed out, 'these gowns were found to make useful receptacles for birds' eggs and other forbidden things.' In like manner the top-hats worn on Sunday often concealed towels for surreptitious bathing.

Not only the theological college but the secular school had the discipline of a seminary. The full offices of Matins and Evensong were recited in chapel every day, and on Sunday the Litany was said. Every Sunday, too, there was a celebration of the Eucharist, an observance rare, as yet, even in the devout little Scots Episcopal church. The senior boys had to learn the epistle for the day in Greek. Mercifully the sermon was, as a rule, brief, and the music was good. The boys loved singing. Surplices were worn in chapel to the scandal of Presbyterian neighbours who regarded those vestments as rags of Popery. The rumour that they were worn for cricket was, however, false.

Cricket, football and fives were part of the public school ritual which the Warden tried to teach 'those stubborn highlanders'. They had no objection to games as such, but were slow in accepting them as a rite or a *mystique*. They had been accustomed to play games for fun, and they still preferred the freedom, which was granted them of country walks, of plant-collecting and of fishing.

Their small numbers at first made possible a good deal of liberty, physical and intellectual, outside school hours and possibly within them as well. A rule may imply its own occasional infraction and one of the rules was: 'The hours of study are to be strictly devoted to the school business. All other reading at such times is forbidden.' The boys did read, widely and independently.

At first the standard of scholarship was not high, for there was little tutoring by the staff and the small numbers did not make for competition. As for discipline, the Warden though benevolent was strict, his severity proceeding from lack of humour rather than from harshness of temper. He punished some boys for indulging in an illicit feast of fried eggs and herring by making them translate a chapter of Ecclesiasticus into Latin. The offence was magnified by having been committed on a fast, the Vigil of St. Simon and St. Jude—though at least the law of abstinence had been kept.

Life at Glenalmond was austere. The building itself was cold and was lit only by oil-lamps. In winter, the boys rising at half past six had to dress each by the light of his own small lamp which he carried about with him. They did not breakfast until eight o'clock when they had bread and butter with tea or coffee. The fees were low; at first only £70, with a reduction for the sons of the Episcopal clergy.

The rules were manifold, covering the weekly allowance of clean underwear (three shirts and cravats, three pairs of stockings, one flannel waistcoat, one nightshirt and cap) and prohibiting bird-nesting and the keeping of pets, bows and arrows and gunpowder. This indicates a venturous type of boy. Other commandments forbade such amusements as name-carving on desks and tables, snowballing or playing hockey in the Quad, and walking on stilts on the grass.

The life of the young theologians at Glenalmond was a brief and not altogether happy one. These poor sheep would seem to have been mocked and tormented by the lay goats in the school. This was only to be expected but it would not have occurred to the pure mind of Mr. Gladstone.

The curriculum was wide, including modern languages. The Royal Commissioners who reported on the school in 1868 were impressed by the amount of time given to these and to mathematics, and also by the number of chapels: 392 in the school year. Saints' Days were kept both as holy and as holidays.

This report stated that: 'The boys for the most part, indeed almost exclusively, belong to the higher classes in Scotland. There is less mixture among them than at any school we have visited.'

Such exclusiveness was rare in Scotland. The Episcopal Church was not entirely 'the lairds' kirk' as has often been asserted; there were many poor Episcopalians, especially in the north-east, who, like their forebears, had never swerved from their ancient faith. They, however, could not afford even the modest fees asked by Glenalmond, so their sons must attend the parish school and endure the cry:

> Pisky, Pisky, amen!
> Doun on yer knees and up again!

to which they could retort with spirit and justice:

> Presby, Presby, dinna bend!
> But say yer prayers on man's chief end!

Glenalmond grew steadily in numbers and in the 1860's had a hundred boys. The Warden then was Dr. Hannah, nicknamed The Gru (or Grue): 'The origin of the title is lost in the obscurity of the ages which have clothed it with reverence,' but it is supposed to derive from the Scots word for greyhound, and to have been bestowed on the Warden for his alertness of look, mind and movement. The staff always included some notable scholars and churchmen, among them Dr. Bright who wrote the great Eucharistic hymn:

> And now, O Father, mindful of that Love
> Which bought us, once for all, on Calvary's Tree.

The Modern Side was developed in the seventies, and a Rifle Corps was started. In 1875, doubtless to their relief, the ordinands moved to the Theological College in Edinburgh; and through the latter decades of the century the little school, founded upon a luncheon, grew and prospered.

II

*LORETTO*

Meanwhile a near contemporary was growing to maturity. Loretto, at Musselburgh near Edinburgh, began as a preparatory school that sent boys to one of the English public schools or to the Scots universities where students went up at a schoolboyish age. In Catholic Scotland the 'Chapel of Loreet' or Loretto had been a shrine of Our Lady and a place of pilgrimage, hallowed by an image of her brought from the Holy House in Italy. In 1862 the school came up for sale and was bought by the man who was to make it new, as Thring did Uppingham.

This man was Hely Hutchinson Almond, the son of a 'povre persoun of a toun', an Episcopalian clergyman in Glasgow. He went to Glasgow University and from there to Balliol with a Snell Exhibition. At first he was not over-happy at Oxford: 'There was an absence of, a dislike of enthusiasm and originality which always rubbed me up the wrong way.' The Scots student, manifold though his faults may be, is rarely a half-warmed fish.

'Jowett told me I had no chance of a Second in Classical Moderations, so I got a First to spite him'—and a First in Mathematics as well, and did not fail to point this out to the Master. This lad like Benson and many another was too poor fully to enjoy what Oxford could give; but he discovered the river:

'To the pale-faced student who had spent his afternoons in aimless wanderings about the streets of Glasgow, the river was a revelation. . . . It opened his mind to a new set of virtues. His love of the open air, his passion for health, his appreciation of manly endurance, his reverence for loyalty and public spirit were to him the gifts of the river.' Isis made a devotee of this plain-living, high-thinking Scot and he declared: 'The Balliol Eight did me more good than all the prizes and classes I ever won.' We hear, far off from Elysian Fields, the applause of George Hughes and of Old Brooke.

There was brain in him, however, as well as brawn, and force of character even more than either. He came to Loretto as mathematics master when he was noted for 'the bewildering rapidity' with which he taught his subject, and for his keenness in games, the latter a new spirit in Scottish schools. After a year at Loretto he went to Merchiston where he introduced rugby and cricket, and where the headmaster, Dr. Harvey, introduced boxing, having once subdued a rebellious pupil by fisticuffs, not flogging. Then came his purchase of Loretto which he made in every way his own.

It was very small with only fourteen boys and a few private pupils known as 'pewters'. One of these was Andrew Lang who spent the summer before going up to Oxford at Loretto, reading Greek and playing cricket—two of his many loves. His memory of Almond was of his brilliant, casual way of teaching, his widely ranging talk that touched all things in heaven and on earth, and his playing games 'with the zest of a boy'.

The numbers increased rapidly, and the school developed its own atmosphere. The regimen was bracing rather than severe. Discipline was maintained, if necessary by flogging or by 'skytes', or slaps, but much more by games which subdued the devil in the boys while toughening their bodies. There was a cult, very new in those days, of hardihood. Loretto boys played golf in all weathers: 'If I was a gentleman,' one caddie vowed, 'ye'd no' find me playin' gowff on sic a day. I'd be sittin' a' the aifternoon at the fireside, drinkin' sherry and blawin' clouds.'

Loretto had its own games beside the orthodox rugby and cricket. 'Goosie' was played between two goal lines each defended by a player who tried to capture the others as they ran. 'Dex' was 'a little cricket' played with a spurtle for bat and any kind of ball. Twice a year the boys were taken to Gullane to play on one of its classic golf-courses. In winter they skated and

G

watched the curling on Duddingston Loch. The apple-wives came with their fruit, men set up stalls for hot coffee; it was bliss and magic.

School might be Spartan with open windows and cold tubs even when the water froze, but the food was ample and excellent: no frugal breakfast of tea and bread and butter, but a hearty Scots meal of porridge and milk, followed by herring or a Finnan haddock or bacon, with baps, those large, soft floury rolls, fresh from the bakery. There were 'elevenses' of home-baked bread made by the steward who was known as 'The Skipper'—'What appetites we had in those days,' one old boy recalled, 'and what lovely complexions!'

The latter were due to fresh air, cold water and a general observance of the laws of health that would now be taken for granted. In those days Almond's ideas were startling. When everyone else wore layers of clothing his boys went blissfully free in tweeds and open-necked shirts, discarding waistcoats and top-coats unless in the coldest weather, and going bareheaded except on Sunday. They wore flannels for games, and their boots and shoes were foot-shaped. 'Mothers were distracted, sisters were horrified' by 'that man Almond's freaks' but the boys abounded in health.

The cult of games spread slowly; it did not touch the universities till the seventies, and it was long opposed by some parents who thought it a waste of time, by ministers who thought it a carnal vanity and curiously by some doctors. Loretto might claim to lead the movement. Almond's pattern of education gave 'character, physique, intelligence, manners and information' in that order. Intellectually he believed in the classics as the foundation of all learning, and taught them well. Morally and spiritually he taught the way of service and loving-kindness: 'Don't bother yourselves about your states of mind. Just do your duty always and think more about other people than about yourself. Don't be introspective.'

Loretto was officially Episcopalian and the boys used to attend St. Peter's Church, Musselburgh, in the morning, and in the afternoon often walked to St. Mary's, Dalkeith, for Even-song. This was the private chapel of the Duke of Buccleuch and was famous for its choir; the Duke maintained a choir school. It has been claimed that this was the first Episcopal church in Scotland to restore the regular Sunday celebration of the Eucharist. The boys liked going to church, and loved the music. Sunday was a happy day with a good deal of freedom.

In school the Head gave weekly Bible lessons and religious instruction in the old Scottish Episcopal tradition; he taught the Real Presence in the Blessed Sacrament. Holy Week was strictly kept and on Good Friday the boys wore black ties and heard a sermon on the Passion. When Almond married, in 1876, the Old Boys gave him a school chapel as wedding gift, one of iron which was replaced in 1893 by a stone building. The boys then had their own choir and wore surplices, without however caus-ing a riot in Edinburgh.

Almond, as might be expected, liked and admired Thring. 'Very strong and eminently lovable' he found him, adding: 'It's a treat to read the way he sat upon selfish, narrow and ignor-ant parents.'

These two great headmasters resembled each other not only in being allergic to parents; they both liked the ordinary boy. Loretto, like Uppingham, was no forcing-house. Almond could punish, but he never snubbed a boy and in difficult cases he would appeal rather than threaten or denounce. 'If you soften him you win,' was one of his maxims. His influence was strong and when, in the seventies, his boys began going up to Oxford, they made a good impression by their character and manners and were dubbed 'the blameless Hyperboreans of Loretto'.

Something of the nature of Rugby had found its way to Uppingham and Loretto, but in both it was reformed, charged with a warmer and gentler spirit.

# IX

## FEMININE WORLD: *THE MONTHLY PACKET* AND THE SCHOOLROOM NOVEL

IN the world of school there was the cult of games and manliness. The feminine world knew the cult of girlhood. The charm and importance of the years between childhood and womanhood were more fully realized in mid-century than ever before.

> *Standing with reluctant feet*
> *Where the brook and river meet,*
> *Womanhood and childhood fleet*

—girls were cherished, though not without some discipline. The meadow where brook and river met could be a very pleasant place.

Female education was still largely domestic and convention was strict, but the needs of girls were being more and more recognized, and one of the first to fulfil them was Charlotte Yonge, grown now out of her own early Victorian youth. If the primary dedication of her work were *Pro Deo et Ecclesia* the secondary was to English girlhood.

In January, 1851, she produced the first number of *The Monthly Packet*. She was twenty-eight, by our standards a young woman, by those of her generation approaching middle age and certainly of the age of discretion, solidly educated, highly cultivated, a devout gentlewoman. Already she was known as an author in both the *genres* she was so brilliantly to develop: in *Abbeychurch*, *The Two Guardians, Henrietta's Wish* and *Scenes and Characters* she had written the first of those family chronicles which were to enthral generations of readers, and in *Kenneth, or The Rearguard of the Grand Army* the prelude to many historical tales. A series of sketches *Langley School* had appeared in 1847 in *Mozley's Magazine For the Young*. So it was as an accomplished woman of letters that Charlotte Yonge began her venture. The first number of *The Monthly Packet* was introduced by her editorial: 'If the pretty terms "maidens" and "damsels" had not gone out of fashion I should address this letter by that name to the readers for whom this little book is in the first place intended—young girls or maidens or young ladies, whichever you like to be called, who are above the age of childhood, and who are either looking back at schooldays or else pursuing the most important part of education, namely self-education. It has been said that everyone forms their character between the ages of fifteen and twenty-five, and this magazine is meant to be in some degree a help to those who are thus forming it: not as a guide, since that is the part of deeper and graver books, but as a companion in times of recreation which may help you to perceive how to bring your religious principles to bear upon your daily life, and may show you the examples of both good and evil of historical persons, and may tell you of the working of God's Providence both here and in other lands.'

It was a large purpose but it was amply fulfilled in a manner more entertaining than might have been expected. Charlotte was a born story-teller, one might almost say a born entertainer. Her creative zest enlivened all her work, and her *Monthly Packet* was, from the first, full of good and varied contents. She herself contributed the cameos from history which were to become a schoolroom classic; a series of historical novels, beginning with *The Little Duke* and another of family chronicles, beginning with the brief but delightful *Castle Builders*. Religious instruction was given in her Conversations on the Catechism in which a Miss Ormesden (alias Miss Yonge) explained Church doctrine and practice to a little group of girls. Other contributors wrote 'accounts of foreign lands', translations, usually from the French, articles on social and literary topics and brief reviews of new books.

It must be emphasized that there were still very few books

for girls, and that new books were not easily procured. A lending library might hold a good deal of rubbish, and a girl, spending her pocket-money upon new books, wanted guidance. There was a real need for the *Packet* or miscellany that would contain a little of everything good, and indicate where more was to be found. It was taken for granted that readers of *The Monthly Packet* were young gentlewomen, living in an atmosphere of leisure, comfort and culture, the daughters of the country gentry, the clergy, the professional classes. If it found its way into a farmhouse or the home of a superior tradesman, so much the better, but it assumed the standards and point of view of the upper middle class, and it was essentially Anglican.

'It is the special desire and prayer of those who address you through the pages of this magazine that what you find there may tend to make you more steadfast, dutiful daughters of our own beloved Catholic Church of England, and may go alongside in all respects with the teaching, both doctrinal and practical of the Prayer-book. For we live in a time of more than ordinary trial and the middle path seems to have grown narrower than ever.'

This path had been forsaken by Newman and many others, and there were recurrent attacks, from Rome on one side, ultra-Protestantism on the other, against Anglican pedestrians. Charlotte all her life walked that middle path unswervingly. She did not attack or disapprove of Roman Catholicism in its place, which was on the Continent; it was a very good religion for foreigners. But in this country Catholicism was represented by the Church of England, and by the Episcopal Church in Scotland for which she had a warm admiration.

Her readers must be strengthened in their loyalty. One article on *The Choice of Books of Amusement* gave a warning not only against immoral books but against 'anything that can at all unsettle your faith'. There were three perils: infidelity, sectarianism and Romanism. To the first a girl was not likely to be exposed; the second, as a well-taught Churchwoman, she was bound to ignore as beneath her; the third was insidious, attractive and dangerous and its spell could easily be conveyed in fiction.

Charlotte's energy in these years was tremendous; even while *The Monthly Packet* was being introduced she was creating a masterpiece in *The Heir of Redclyffe*. The *roman jeune fille* had come into its glory, for this was a best-seller, captivating not only the schoolroom but the drawing-room and library, the college and the camp. Officers in the Crimea found an escape from the splendours and miseries of war in that romance of true love and spiritual conflict. It was a domestic picture of Pre-Raphaelite fidelity, and it possessed, as Alice Meynell has pointed out, the quality of holiness that had not hitherto been found in fiction.

Sir Guy Morville was the most loved hero of that decade, as Amy was the ideal heroine. She was almost faultless, but was too humble and too lively to be a prig. Philip, the villain of the piece was neither rake nor ruffian but, what Charlotte detested more, a Pharisee. Guy was her own favourite, and 'the author of *The Heir of Redclyffe*' as she was henceforth known by the public was 'Guy's mother' to her friends.

In Amy and Laura Edmonstone we have the first full-length portraits of Victorian girls. The family in *Scenes and Characters* are vivid sketches, but these new heroines are painted in detail. The background is delightful, and the house so familiar that one seems to have entered it in the body.

The chief rival to *The Heir of Redclyffe* among Charlotte's books was *The Daisy Chain* which appeared as a serial in *The Monthly Packet*. In this she introduced one of her most famous families, the Mays, who were to live as long as their author, and a heroine, Ethel, who was the essence and likeness of every eager and awkward young girl as Amy was of the gentle. The Mays were to grow old naturally, to marry—and to marry into a family of later creation, the Underwoods of *Pillars of the House*. Charlotte was by this time creating a world as real as that of Trollope's Barsetshire.

*The Monthly Packet* reviewed many books, some now forgotten, others among the classics. *Cranford* was commended as 'the best of all the sketches we have seen of an uneventful country-town life, and an excellent lesson in the respect that may be united with a full sense of the ridiculous'.

Any book recommended must be of impeccable morality, but morality was not enough. Charlotte herself was a sound crafts-woman and demanded professional quality in others. An anony-mous novel, *Blanche Mortimer,* or *Unconscious Influence,* was dismissed with a gentle finality; the author was obviously very young, very serious, very artless: 'We think so well of her that we predict that in a few years she will wish her story still in MS. . . . As friends of the later years of girlhood we are anxious to impress on young ladies that it is a pity to rush into print, and they will be sorry for it by and by. . . . Write, but be content with showing your stories to your own friends.'

# X

## INCARNATION OF A HEROINE

CHARLOTTE YONGE created the ideal Victorian heroine
and helped to form the Victorian girl, but even before her
portraits had been painted, a girl was growing into their pattern
of young ladyhood. If Charlotte is the perfect Victorian, Lucy
Lyttelton is her heroine incarnate.

She was born in 1841, the second daughter of the Fourth Lord
Lyttelton and his wife Mary, who was a sister of Mrs. Gladstone.
Her station in life was a little more exalted than that of Char-
lotte's heroines who were, as a rule, of gentle but not lordly
birth. The Lytteltons belonged to the great world of Court and
Society but they were not worldly. They were serious, devout
and cultivated; they spent much of their time on their estate of
Hagley in Worcestershire. Lucy's 'Uncle Billy', the Reverend
the Honourable William Lyttelton, was Rector, and Manor and
Rectory ruled the village with benevolence.

The family were as numerous as any of Charlotte's creation:
twelve of them, ranging from young ladies to babies. Lucy
began her diary when she was thirteen. One of her first entries
announced the engagement of Uncle Billy to Miss Emily Pepys,
a daughter of the Bishop of Worcester, 'a very worthy person'
in the opinion of her future niece, 'charitable, young, amiable,
humble, good-looking'. Lucy acquired a much-loved aunt, and
was drawn into parish work which she enjoyed. At a school feast
she was impressed by the appetite of the youthful guests: 'Six
rice and six plum-puddings, two legs of mutton, besides lots of
beef, bread and beer.' No pallid bun-and-milk affair!

Life for Lucy and her elder sister Meriel went on tranquilly,
with lessons in the schoolroom, visits to the village, riding with
Papa, and reading aloud in the evening. Their grandmother the
Dowager Lady Lyttelton used to read to them. When they were

in town they and their cousin Agnes Gladstone were bidden to a Children's Ball at Buckingham Palace where they had a private and domestic interest: their grandmother the Dowager had been governess to the royal children of whom the eldest, the Princess Royal and the Prince of Wales aged with Meriel and Lucy.

'We were rigged, figged and launched into two carriages in tolerable time, and our dresses were simply magnificent. A beautiful muslin frock trimmed with ruches and daisies,' their gloves also trimmed with daisies and 'a wreath of two rows of daisies on our polls'. It was almost too thrilling and Lucy had 'the bathing feel' which in Glynnese, the family language, meant butterflies in the stomach, the chilled and sinking feel one has before an ordeal like going in to bathe. All went well, the Queen being particularly gracious: 'Oh ecstasy, she shook hands with me . . . I kept hold of her dear hand as long as I could.' Lucy danced a good deal, chiefly with her cousin Willie Gladstone and the ball ended at ten o'clock with the National Anthem: 'Oh, didn't it thrill me!'

That was in May, 1855; the next great day was on 22nd July when their mother's birthday coincided with Meriel's confirmation. Next day another baby was born, the eleventh in this long family.

Parties, whether a school feast or the Queen's Ball, occurred but seldom. Lessons were the rule and there was now a French governess. Mademoiselle had none of the elegance expected of her countrywomen, being 'more hugely fat than imagination can picture or tongue describe' and looking 'as if an immense pillow had been laid on her chest. . . . Mamma looked like a poplar beside her'—in spite of eleven babies. Mademoiselle was, however, cheerful if not shapely, and 'chattered away while she was still further enlarging herself with some mutton and tea' which sounds a horrifying meal for a Frenchwoman.

The family spent Easter of 1856 at St. Leonards, in an 'enchanting house into which we all packed delightfully tight'—Meriel, Lucy and their younger sister Lavinia sharing a room, and somehow contriving to pack themselves into the schoolroom with

Mademoiselle's 'more than portly form'. There was hardly any
place 'wherein and whereon to put anything' and the Victorian
girl had so many many things to put on shelves or into drawers
and cupboards: workboxes, desks, albums, diaries, trinkets and
treasures.

Life went on as at home with lessons in the morning, a good
deal of reading, music and dancing classes, and in the afternoon,
driving with their mother. After Easter they went up to London
where Meriel and Lucy attended another ball at the palace,
wearing white tarlatan dresses trimmed with pink, having ruched
skirts and wreaths of pink roses on their 'polls'. Again Lucy
had the bathing feel, and again unalloyed pleasure to follow. She
was presented to the Queen by 'Aunt Pussy' (Mrs. Gladstone),
danced nearly every dance and had wine at supper and ices 'which
were delicious'. The ball ended so late that she stayed in bed
next morning 'till I don't know what o'clock' and felt delightfully dissipated.

Back at Hagley they had a new governess: 'a nice, real, comfortable English one, ladylike and pleasant-looking.' The word
'ladylike' is coming into use as favourable comment upon those
in whom breeding is desirable though not to be taken for granted.
A governess would be 'ladylike', the village schoolmistress
'almost ladylike'.

The new governess set a time-table of Italian on Monday and
Thursday, French on Tuesday and Friday, English on Wednesday
and Saturday. In French they read Racine, Lamartine and
Bossuet's *Histoire Universelle* which they translated into English
then back into French, comparing the result with the original.
In Italian they read a Goldoni comedy and *Le Notti Romani* by
Metastasio. For history they had Dr. Arnold's *Rome* and Reid's
*English History*. Altogether they read widely and thoroughly,
being trained to read with a purpose. This schoolroom was, no
doubt, one of the best in England but it was not unique. Girls
with a good governess were trained in memory. Lucy and her
sisters had quantities of poetry by heart; literature was part of
their daily life and background.

*The Monthly Packet* came to Hagley and was not only read with delight but used for lessons. One of Charlotte's serials, *Pigeon Pie*, was set for translating into French.

There were many visitors to the house, Matthew Arnold among them. 'I don't like Mr. Arnold,' Lucy wrote in her diary, adding the rhyme about Dr. Fell. 'But I can tell partly; he seems light and vain and does not talk sense.' This, from a lady of fifteen is pungent. 'Vain' is not surprising. Mr. Arnold was, as J. S. Phillimore said about Marcus Aurelius, 'a great and good man and he knew it'. But to call this apostle of high seriousness 'light' is rather like describing Queen Victoria as a social butterfly.

The clue was given in the next sentence: Mr. Arnold did not kneel in church because there was no hassock, a poor excuse and 'rather a horrid one for a strong man' when delicate women knelt devoutly. He also advised going to the dissenting chapel to hear good preaching. The root of the matter was not in him, he was a trifler with doctrine and no better than a dissenter himself. Mr. Arnold reciprocated the dislike; he found the high seriousness of Rugby lacking in this Etonian family.

Croquet-parties were newly fashionable and usually included the schoolroom. Far more exciting, however, than any game or party was the dedication of the parish church after it had been restored, enlarged and adorned with new windows. It was a tremendous event for Lucy and her sisters, as it was for the girls in *Abbeychurch* where the climax is the dedication of a church; and so life proves the truth of art and heroines are incarnate.

The church was decorated for Christmas by the party from Hagley which at New Year (1857) was full to the roof with Lytteltons and Gladstones, eighteen of them being under seventeen years of age.

'The dear old house is choked, overflowing, echoing with children. The meals are the fun.' Upstairs there were two tables for breakfast, the nursery and the schoolroom; at one, Miss Smith the governess presided, 'dispensing drinkables' while Lucy dealt with the eatables; at the other, Meriel.

'The noise pervading the room, as much from scolders as from scolded, from bellowers as from bellowed at, from children, boys, women and girls may be imagined, mingled with clatter of crockery, pouring of tea, hewing of bread and scrumping of jaws.' These Glynnes or half-Glynnes had a genius for words: 'scrumping' is precisely right for the eating of toast, 'hewing' for the cutting of bread-and-butter 'door-steps'.

The young folk acted a play for their elders. 'Rehearsals are ceaseless, lessons droop, disorder prevails.' Lucy found it bliss; Miss Smith's opinion has not been recorded.

Another baby was on the way, and Lucy knew about it, and was anxious for her mother. The Victorian girl was not so ignorant as is commonly believed; it would hardly have been possible for any senior in a large and increasing family to believe any fairy-tale about the coming of babies. In due course, the child arrived and was christened Alfred. 'Papa dares to think of Frederick, my abomination.' (But she married a Frederick.) Mamma appeared to make a good recovery but she was very fragile.

That summer, Lucy was taken to Oxford for 'one of the happiest days I have ever spent'. She was chaperoned by Mrs. Talbot, and had breakfast with John Talbot in his rooms: 'an elegant spread' and a substantial one, with 'a beautiful sort of hashed fish . . . obtained after some little difficulty caused by some regulation against the importation of fish for breakfast'. (One recalls the breakfasts of the wealthy set in *Tom Brown at Oxford*.) Everything delighted Lucy; the sitting-room grate 'of the most scholastic and collegiate appearance' and the toast 'cut in a collegiate way also, triangles of an impressive appearance'. The ample breakfast did not spoil her appetite for luncheon: 'One of my notes of Oxford was the vast quantity everybody eats, myself included.' Luncheon, offered by one of the guests at breakfast, was 'an excellent spread, in fact a very ample dinner'. Lucy was no niminy-piminy miss trifling with her food in affected delicacy.

There was a visit to Eton, too, with Papa and Aunt Pussy, Meriel and Cousin Agnes, to see brother Charles play fives. They attended chapel where 'the flood of boys looked impressive enough, especially when they all stood up with a sort of rushing noise', but there were no clear responses, 'only a mutter and whisper'.

Lucy was being prepared for confirmation, for her as for Charlotte Yonge and her heroines the beginning of a new life. She was confirmed on 4th July, by the Archbishop of Canterbury (Sumner): 'I shall never forget the touch of the hand on my head: "Defend, O Lord, this Thy servant with Thy heavenly grace" . . . and the glorious rush of trembling calm that followed.'

The strength thus given was to be sorely needed, for in the following August Lady Lyttelton died. She had never fully recovered from the birth of her last baby. 'It is all over, all left behind. The everlasting morning has dawned on that weary night.'

Lucy and Meriel must be companions to their father and mothers to the younger children, and when Meriel married, Lucy became mistress of the house. While still in the schoolroom she was preparing for life in the world. One of her tasks was to bring an old copy of the *Peerage* up to date by copying in the births, marriages and deaths from *The Times,* 'in the sanguine hope of improving my knowledge of people's families, titles, relations and circumstances'.

Her first dinner-party was at the Bishop of Worcester's, where, as chief lady guest she was taken in to dinner by the Bishop, and bowed to, after dessert by her hostess, as a signal to leave the gentlemen to their wine. 'I didn't know if I was on my head or my heels' but it was glory. Soon after, with Meriel away, she 'ordered dinner for the very first time in my life. Oh dear'.

She enjoyed social life, even when the bathing feel occurred or when she found herself 'exhausted with behaving properly' and realized, to her own surprise, that she had 'kept clear of all scrapes'. Lucky in cards, she won ten shillings at one game and spent four shillings of that on a new pack, 'gold-backed with green ivy pattern, for whist in the evenings at home. I trust they are not intensely vulgar'.

In 1859 she had her first London season as a débutante. The family travelled 'in the open britschka'—their own carriage placed in a railway coach, Papa on the box where he collected all the smuts and arrived with 'the complexion of a stoker'. It was a dazzling season, and Lucy had a delightful capacity for enjoyment. The Queen was still her adored lady: at a ball in the Palace dancing quadrilles 'with majesty and grace in every movement of her little form. I thought my heart would crack with excitement'; at the opening of Parliament reading her speech from the throne 'in her clear, musical voice'. At the ball the Prince of Wales and Princess Alice waltzed together very gracefully 'so unlike the fluttering whirls in a tight embrace that one sees elsewhere', and at another ball, the Duchess of Teck 'in spite of her imposing size danced and valsed beautifully'. Lucy's admiration for royalty was not extended to the peerage; at the opening of Parliament she found very few beauties among 'the fat, wizzy peeresses' (wizzy being probably a Glynnese portmanteau word holding a mixture of wizened and fuzzy).

The exiled French royalties were in London and Lucy danced opposite the Comte de Paris who captivated her with his 'look and manner and the beautiful old French courtesy.... And there he is, descendant of that ancient, glorious race, banished from his country with that upstart Napoleon on his throne. . . . What with awe, respect, compassion and gratitude I was nearly out of my mind'.

Breakfast-parties were still much in vogue, although the hour was what we should call cocktail-time, and the party was usually an informal dance: Lady Marian Alford's at seven in the evening, with eight hundred guests at one time or other. There was a cold dinner, and afterwards the guests danced to music by the band of the Grenadier Guards, and Lucy had the Comte de Paris for partner in the Lancers. At half-past ten thirteen of them packed themselves into a 'break' and drove to Tring station, and so back to London by train arriving at seven o'clock on Sunday morning 'feeling wicked'.

It is unlikely that Lucy missed church for all that. She was not only devout but a connoisseur of ritual and sermons. Westminster Abbey was disappointing: 'Everything was got through in the most disgraceful, slovenly manner.' One Sunday Meriel, now married, and she drove in a hansom to All Saints, Margaret Street, and 'who should we get out in the very eye of but Lord Cowper who was probably shocked at the sight' of young ladies unescorted and in a hansom. It was still rather daring, and Lucy could not have gone by herself, in London. Once in Brighton she did go alone to church, but coming back 'pretended to belong to two elderly ladies in succession, who, I don't think found out that they were escorting me'. On another occasion she shocked herself by walking alone on the pier, 'which, it suddenly struck me, was scampish'.

For all her circumspect ways and sheltered life she was no prude, nor was she unaware of what might befall the unguarded. At Hagley she had long serious talks with Aunt Emmie at the Vicarage about the 'people to be prayed for'—the old and sick and poor, babies and women in childbirth, and one girl who had been 'led into evil'. As mistress of the house she had trouble with servants: 'It's a most lamentable thing, the want of common Christianity in servants'—and she had to settle their quarrels. One maid was prosecuted for stealing and sentenced to fourteen days in prison. Lucy visited her, finding her 'in strapping health and unchanged in manner', but before she left, the girl was in tears.

Life at Hagley had many duties, some of them heavy for a girl in her teens. She learned something about life outside her own secure world. During one bad winter, a tradesman who had been ruined, stole some meat for his children. They were found tearing it to pieces, like animals. Lucy was discovering things she never forgot.

Still, the parties and pleasures continued, especially in town. At one very grand ball she danced again with the Comte de

Paris and felt a 'stomach-ache of thrill' beside which the ordinary bathing feel must have seemed like tiddly-winks. She saw picture exhibitions, including one of 'glaring, absurd Pre-Raphaelites with every face bright pink, and every sky of lilac, tin leaves and grass like coarse stuffs, and lunatic attempts to render every atom as it is instead of as it looks'.

There was a Christmas house-party at Hawarden where they skated by day and danced by night; an expedition to Cambridge to see Gladstone receive a doctorate 'amid mingled cheers and hisses'. After the graduation came lunch in the new hall of Caius, a concert, a service in King's Chapel, a party.

Balls were delightful, but devout joys ranked even higher, and there was a tremendous one at Hagley, at Easter 1862, when the vestry 'consented unanimously and joyfully to the Choir Surplices!!! We went wild with excitement' and the procession of the surpliced choristers looked 'wonderfully pretty', all of them behaving 'with the utmost gravity and discretion tho' it must have been very shy the first time'.

For all the grief of her mother's death, this was a golden girl-hood, filled with love and laughter. Lucy's marriage, at twenty-three, to Lord Frederick Cavendish was one of complete happiness until the end of earthly joy came for her in the assassination of that dearly loved husband in Phoenix Park. This sorrow only deepened the grace given her in girlhood; till the end of her long life she kept the sweetness, the charity, even something of the gaiety of her youth.

# XI

## SOME LEARNED GIRLS

IN this decade of *The Monthly Packet* and *The Heir of Redclyffe* the second generation of scholar girls was growing up, preparing unconsciously for the headship of the new schools and colleges. One of them was Elizabeth Wordsworth, grand-niece of the poet and born, in 1840, into a family even more exaltedly clerical than Charlotte Yonge could create. Her father was, at the time of her birth, headmaster of Harrow; later he was appointed Canon of Westminster, and finally became Bishop of Lincoln. Her brother became Bishop of Salisbury, her uncle, whom we have met at Glenalmond, Bishop of St. Andrews. Elizabeth grew up in the setting of vicarage, cloisters and Cathedral Close, in an atmosphere of learning and piety. She was ten years old when her famous great-uncle died, and she remembered spending the summer of 1850 at Rydal Mount where 'Aunt Wordsworth' was 'kind and quiet', Aunt Dorothy a little odd—the result of meningitis.

From 1851 till 1869 Canon Wordsworth held a country charge in Berkshire, and Elizabeth knew the rural England that lives for us in Hardy's novels. In church they held to the old ways, there was no organ, the precentor gave the tune with a pitch pipe and the people sang the metrical psalms of Tate and Brady, *Hymns Ancient and Modern* being still unknown and unwanted. At Christmas the mummers and the carol singers came round, in summer the Benefit Club marched in procession with a band and banners, and bunches of flowers on poles. The men danced on the Vicarage lawn, dressed in their Sunday black: 'To see them hopping about, dodging the flower-beds on the lawn and looking indeed like the proverbial Englishman who takes his pleasure sadly, was a sight not easily to be forgotten.' After their dance they had dinner in the school. There was the annual tithe dinner, too, for the farmers, a jolly affair with the punch bowl in circulation. In dress, the village clung to the old fashions of smocks for the men, sun-bonnets for the women, while old Nanny Grundy who kept a dame's school, wore a red cloak and a black, coal-scuttle bonnet with a white frill under the brim.

Elizabeth was educated at home, with a good deal of theology and Church history as well as the usual subjects. Her mother was extremely musical, as was a governess who introduced her girl to modern music as well as to Handel and Mozart. The vicarage gave parish concerts of unusual quality. She was confirmed at fifteen after intensive preparation, some of it from Prideaux' *Connection of the Old and New Testament*—a book so learned and so long that 'I don't think we ever got to the end . . . but I have not forgotten the delight I felt when the dear old historian got to a particular date and added the words: "It was about this date that the prophetess Anna was born." It seemed like the first snowdrops of Spring.'

She was of the age and class of girls for whom *The Heir of Redclyffe* was written, and she gave it full admiration:

'It was as regards fiction what, to the Tractarian Movement, *The Christian Year* and some of Newman's poems had been as regards poetry. It represented the love of beauty both natural and spiritual which characterized that large section of English society which was recruited from our cultured home life, our universities, our cathedral towns and our country parsonages. We felt in it the influence of Shakespeare, Sir Thomas Malory, Dante, Scott, Wordsworth, Southey, Manzoni and even Keble's *Praelections*.'

In 1857 she went to school in Brighton, more happily and profitably than Frances Cobbe some twenty years earlier. She learned a good deal of French and a little German, continued her music and had drawing lessons: 'But how South Kensington would have anathematized the methods which were then prevalent. We copied black-lead drawings on Bristol board, we did sketches with ready-made sunset and moonlight "effects" of pink and grey respectively which looked really imposing when touched up with Chinese White by the master's steady hand; we did, I think, a little perspective . . . and we filled pages on pages with "touches" as they were called, that is copies of the master's drawing of foliage and the like.'

On Sunday the girls learned passages of Scripture by heart and read *James on the Collects* between breakfast and lunch, and 'some good little S.P.C.K. story-books in the afternoon'. The education may have been, for the most part, superficial, but it gave the future principal a knowledge of girls and their ways which she would not have acquired in the domestic schoolroom. It also made her realize the need for games. There was no exercise for these girls but in dancing-class, in long 'crocodile' walks and, for a few, in riding, and with so much repression of energy there was a good deal of silliness, overmuch interest in dress, a tendency to flirt or to imagine flirting with the Italian singing master: 'If some of this enthusiasm could have been expended on a tennis or a hockey match it would have been better for both mind and body.'

At seventeen she left school which 'technically speaking closed my education', but music and drawing lessons continued at home along with the real culture absorbed from her parents' talk, from the background of books and scholarship, the very air of home. Much was still lacking; she knew nothing of science or mathematics and, like Charles Lamb, would not have been surprised to find the sun rising in the west: 'We did just know that the earth went round the sun.' She and her sisters 'never learned more than the very rudiments of English grammar and to this day if I want to know what part of speech an English word is, I have to turn it into Latin'. Perhaps it did not greatly matter: 'When you have once taught a boy or girl to read, you have put the key of knowledge into their hands.' These girls were given the freedom of a large house of literature. They were trained in handiwork as well: in drawing, even if superficially, in needlework, and 'to use our wits and our fingers to write legible hands'; and they were taught to read aloud, that almost lost domestic art.

In 1861 when she passed from girlhood into womanhood, Elizabeth was sent abroad, to Dresden and to Italy, to learn wider ways of learning and of the world.

Her exact contemporary, a future headmistress of a great new school, was Louisa Lumsden, born in Aberdeenshire, the daughter of an advocate, with a good inheritance of brains and a love of books. Scott was dearly loved as were *Gulliver's Travels, Don Quixote, The Pilgrim's Progress*—the great romances which have been adopted as their own by children of every generation. The Lumsdens were Episcopalian in a region of Scotland where Episcopacy is traditional, but the children were not, for all that, spared the Shorter Catechism. They had to learn it as a week-day lesson, as well as the Church Catechism on Sunday.

After a period at a private school in Cheltenham, Louisa and her sister Katherine were sent to a *pensionnat* in Brussels, the Château de Koehelberg. They were happy in a freedom unknown to their English school. The château had a large garden, the girls were taken for walks but not in 'crocodile', and for picnics, and the feasts of the church were celebrated: St. Nicholas by the interchange of presents, Holy Innocents by the rule of the girls over their school world, following the medieval tradition of children's authority on that day. Then came carnival with all the gaiety of Continental Catholicism, a fancy-dress ball and *tableaux vivants*. On Sunday they all went to their own church; there were no lessons and there was no grimness. Louisa's memories make a singularly happy contrast with Charlotte Brontë's *Villette*.

From Brussels she and her sister returned to another English school, near London, which was kind but dull and superficial: 'Accomplishments made the whole curriculum' and 'obedience was the supreme virtue'. They missed the cosmopolitan atmosphere of the château. At seventeen Louisa came home to a free and happy country life. There were still lessons, Latin with a tutor, and, 'like Mary Bennet' she made extracts, but unlike that dim damsel she made interesting extracts, collecting much country lore in old tales and traditions, proverbs and weather-lore. It was a gay girlhood; the sisters used to go to dances in

Aberdeen, seven miles away, dance all night, drive home and be up early again to walk the dogs. Their activity was hampered but not prevented by the fashionable dress: the many starched petticoats, the full skirts, the new crinoline.

These two learned girls were to carry the best of the old ways of learning into the world of education. A third scholar, ten years their junior, was equally to know both worlds. Jane Ellen Harrison, born in Yorkshire in 1850, wrote of the governesses who had educated her (more or less) till she was seventeen that they were all 'grossly ignorant, but they were good women, steadily kind to me' and they taught her 'how to come into a room, how to get into a carriage, also that little girls should be seen and not heard and that I was there in the schoolroom to learn, not to ask questions'. Her father held a simple creed: 'All foreigners were Papists, all Papists liars, and he "wouldn't have one in his house!"' Consequently, his daughter longed above all things to see a Papist, and in further consequence realized in maturity that 'never in this world shall I be able to speak French'.

What she did learn were lists of dates, lists of the Kings of Israel and Judah, signs of the zodiac, and the table of weights and measures, and every day three verses of the Bible and a quantity of poetry, most of it learned while lying on a back-board. This gave her a well-stored memory and a perfectly flat back. 'When nowadays I see the round backs of my young friends and watch them slinking round doors as though they were criminals and not English gentlewomen, and especially when they fail to get up when addressed by their elders and betters, I sometimes sigh for a little "deportment".'

The mental discipline had value, but she deplored much waste of time: 'Victorian education was ingeniously useless. Every day I spent an hour indoors doing exquisite hems and seams' but 'I cannot to this day make the simplest garment'.

She learned a little Greek helped by the curate whose interest in her proved to be more than scholarly. Partly in banishment, partly for the usual 'finishing' she was sent to Cheltenham where she fell into deep disgrace with Miss Beale. A boy friend at home who had helped her with her Latin sent her a postcard of good wishes on the eve of the London matriculation examination. It ended 'Give my love to the examiners' and was signed 'Peveril'. The subsequent interview with Miss Beale was shattering: 'You are too young and, I hope, too innocent to realize the gross vulgarity of such a letter, or the terrible results to which it might lead.' In spite of this indiscretion she was well placed in school. She already knew three or four languages by book though she could not understand spoken French; now she learned arithmetic and elementary mathematics, both well taught, and chemistry which she found exciting. On the other hand—'I carried away from Cheltenham College a dislike for history which has lasted all my life', and this although it was Miss Beale's own favourite subject. Lessons consisted mainly of 'moralizing on the doings and mis-doings of kings and nobles' and with a bias. Miss Beale was Cromwellian, Jane, like all right-thinking youth, a Royalist.

A picture of a Scottish girlhood in Edinburgh is given in the memoirs of the novelist, once popular and still readable: Mrs. Walford, born Lucy Bethia Colquhoun. She and her sisters had German governesses, approved by serious families as being solid, respectable and above all, Protestant. The Colquhouns' governesses were treated as members of the family and used to play and sing at Mrs. Colquhoun's parties.

Edinburgh in the fifties and sixties was an intimate society ruled, in a particular sense, by the Law. The Season was from February to Easter when the Court of Sessions rose for vacation. This brief gaiety, however, was unbroken by any Lenten abstinence; Lent, being a Popish invention, was not regarded by good Presbyterians. Holy Week or no Holy Week, parties continued. Theatres were forbidden in some families but there were concerts, and the parties were many and delightful. Balls were balls, not mere informal dances with the carpet rolled back. The best of all were the regimental balls where hardly a black coat was to be seen, all the men being in uniform or the gallant kilt. The ballroom was massed with flowers, and on one occasion fountains of eau-de-Cologne played into silver-gilt basins. At another peacock pie was served for supper, the peacock being the regimental badge. It was all very high, wide and handsome.

Amid all this grandeur there were graver and higher pleasures: lectures were popular, especially a course arranged by Miss Catherine Sinclair, aunt of the young Colquhouns, and author of the immortal *Holiday House*. These were known as The Ulbster Hall Lectures from the name of the Sinclair place in Caithness and were high social events, followed by supper with negus and hot jelly.

Sermons were taken as intellectual treats and Lucy Bethia heard some of the best preachers of the day. And at the very peak of godly amusement there was the bazaar, at which girls in their prettiest frocks and bonnets helped their mothers to sell unlimited quantities of incredible forms of fancy-work in aid of the poor, of orphans, of foreign missions. How far the bazaar stimulated this fancy-work and how far the latter evolved the bazaar is a fine problem.

Lucy began writing at thirteen but wisely put her manuscript away until she was eighteen. Then she wrote a tale of Edinburgh life—*The Moderator's Breakfast*. Her first novel, *Mr. Smith*, was a story from real life and proved delightfully successful; and at nineteen, already a woman of letters, she married.

# XII

## DAUGHTERS OF GREAT MEN

ANOTHER novelist of talent was Anne Thackeray, born in 1837. Her girlhood was rich in experience. She and her sister Minnie were much in their father's company and met many famous folk. When Annie was sixteen and Minnie thirteen Thackeray took them to Rome for the winter. They had an apartment in a palace in the Via della Croce near where the Brownings lived. The ground floor was rented by a pastry cook from whom they bought delicious cream tarts, and Anne was impressed by hearing, from Lord Leighton, that her liking for these delicacies was shared by that eminent and formidable man of letters, John Gibson Lockhart.

He was spending that winter in Rome, ill, aged beyond his sixty years by sorrow and overwork. Before the new year was out he would lie at Scott's feet in Dryburgh. Anne saw him driving to the Campagna with Mrs. Sartoris-Adelaide Kemble, the singer, one of the most gracious of his friends: 'He gazed straight before him like some solemn, brooding eagle, silent and mysterious . . . wrapped in cloaks and wore a soft travelling cap not unlike that hood in which Erasmus is commonly depicted. . . . The pale, beautiful face was still before me as if it belonged not to the present but to some medieval figure out of one of the galleries. . . . The incident, such as it was, impressed me—the sick man, the strenuous life behind him, the feeling of the great campagna outside the walls, the friend's good company, the glorious warmth of land and sky.' Lockhart was as dark as a Spaniard and she remembered his 'eyes of jet set in a face of ivory'.

Mrs. Sartoris and her sister Fanny Kemble were both kind to the girls who used to visit the former in her 'big Roman drawing-room with a great window to the west, and the colours of the room were not unlike sunset colours', with quantities of flowers and, against all that beauty the beautiful figure of the hostess in grey satin, with her golden-haired little son in white.

These girls were being educated in the most delectable way: they were taken to galleries and studios, met the cosmopolitan society of Rome: 'charming Scotch people, gracious English ladies, enterprising young Americans', and absorbed the atmosphere of a city hardly changed since the Middle Ages. They lived in antique splendour in 'great vaulted rooms with marble tables and gilt arm-chairs and swinging lamps'. In that setting their father wrote *The Newcomes* and drew the pictures for *The Rose and the Ring*.

The galleries were full of treasures, the streets of life: 'monks in their flapping robes and sandals', cardinals with their attendants, Pio Nono himself on foot, blessing the people as he went, his coach following, peasants and artists' models, Romans and foreigners, every type of humanity.

From Rome they went to Paris where they saw Mrs. Sartoris again in the Rue Royale: 'Her houses seemed like succeeding Paradises upon earth' to those girlish eyes. They dined at a round table with pink candles and had ices for dessert, then were taken to the theatre where they had a glimpse of George Sand.

Mrs. Sartoris read Anne's first efforts at writing and was encouraging and helpful: 'Read your MSS. aloud to yourself' was her advice. Fanny Kemble gave her a moment of enchantment. They were sitting in her room, bright with flowers and with some American mocking-birds, as gay as the flowers, in a cage. A chance question from Anne brought a re-creation of a scene from *As You Like It*: 'Suddenly . . . the little room seemed transformed. . . . There stood Rosalind and Celia themselves, there stood Jaques, there was Orlando—and there was Mrs. Kemble again in her chair.'

And Mrs. Kemble herself, in girlhood, had heard her great kinswoman, Sarah Siddons, speak, unforgettably, the witch scene from *Macbeth*.

To be the daughter of a genius was for Anne a most pleasant

experience. Another girl would have agreed with her that an eminent papa added to the richness of life and was not in himself formidable.

Gladstone's daughters grew up happily if somewhat haphazardly. One of them, Mary, born in 1847, might, like her cousin Lucy Lyttelton, have walked out of a Charlotte Yonge novel.

She wrote, in later life: 'My governesses from ten to seventeen treated me as half-witted, so I grew up a nonentity. I have never outgrown it.' On the contrary she was never a nonentity and she grew into a girl of quick mind and sympathy, but her formal education was erratic. She was fluent in French and Italian with some knowledge of German, but in other subjects was half-taught. She read 'furiously but inconsequently' and her mind was 'kept like a kind of domestic pet to be fed upon literary titbits'. In one study she did achieve concentration—in music. She practised singing and pianoforte thoroughly, and her musical taste and knowledge were developed by Hubert Parry.

'Anything that is appealing in my pianoforte playing, anything that is tender or wistful or passionate is entirely owing to Hubert; it was he who first revealed to me how to express in music the emotion of a human heart.' Hubert Parry had recently married Lady Maud Herbert, daughter of Lord Pembroke. Mary met him at Wilton 'in all the glow and glory of a first love' and heard him play a Schubert Rêverie and a Chopin Prelude: 'Never in this life can I forget the effect on me of his rendering of these two pieces. Shall I not remember them in another?'

Like Lucy she had happy memories of a Children's Ball at Buckingham Palace. She was dancing with George Herbert, the future Lord Pembroke. Neither of them was sure of the steps and the Queen came down from her dais, joined their hands and showed them how to pirouette. But there were only occasional splendours until she 'came out' at seventeen. Her allowance was increased to £8 a year (her sister Helen in the schoolroom had £7), she was given a watch and a waterproof cape and was so entranced by these possessions that she carried the watch in her

hand and wore the cape on a bright June day in St. James's Park. As a grown-up young lady she also wore her first bonnet.

Like Lucy and indeed like all the Lytteltons and Gladstones she was deeply religious. When Lucy became engaged Mary gave her a copy of *Holy Living and Holy Dying*, and when Helen was confirmed, noted with pleasure that she had been given a number of religious books: 'amongst them *Sacra Privata*; she is going to have St. Thomas à Kempis's *Imitation of Christ*'. One of her first visits by herself was to the Bishop of London and Mrs. Tait when she took flowers to the old women in a work-house: 'a happy day though away from all my relations'.

She was bridesmaid at Lucy's wedding and helped her with her shopping; one day they bought eight silk dresses, two muslins and a shawl.

In the year of her coming-out her father was returned as Prime Minister. On 9th June, 1864: 'At 3 a.m. Mama woke us up to say that the Government was triumphant. . . . It is mostly owing to Papa's beautiful speech on Monday.'

When this loyal daughter went to the Ladies' Gallery to hear Papa and his rival Disraeli, she found the latter 'simply full of stuff and nonsense' and 'very ungentleman-like' while Papa was 'nobly grand'.

Now, in her first season, there were parties and pleasures in abundance; an occasional breakfast-party at the comfortable hour of ten, and many balls, the most brilliant being at Chiswick, given by the Duke of Sutherland. The Prince and Princess of Wales were present and 'in the country dancing I had to take the Prince's hand'. Afterwards she danced 'a romping tempête' with Lord Cavendish: 'immense fun, only my bridesmaid's frock all torn to pieces'. She might enjoy 'a romping tempête' but she was not allowed to waltz.

At one house-party the guests sat in the dark while two of them, Lord Halifax and the Bishop of Oxford told ghost stories and discussed Roman Catholicism, both favourite topics with the Victorians.

In 1865 she was taken on a round of visits to Scotland,

beginning at Drumlanrig, the Duke of Buccleuch's; an exalted party that included the Duke of Teck. He was not alarming in royal dignity, he even acted as cook on one of their picnics. From Drumlanrig they went to Inveraray where Mary drove to an otter hunt with the Duke of Argyll's heir Lord Lorne. He was two years her senior, and a charming host to 'a raw, seventeen-year-old girl' who was more than a little in love with him. This kind and serious young man would, no doubt, have delighted Gladstone as a son-in-law but a loftier destiny awaited him. He married the Princess Louise, the first Princess in many decades to marry a subject. It was held an honour for him by the world but not by an old clansman in Argyll: 'Och, the Queen will be the proud woman the day, her daughter married on the son of MacCaileain Mor.'

At Inveraray there was plenty of sport by day, and in the evening more serious occupation. It was a true Scottish home of the period, with a spiritual atmosphere not greatly different from that of a manse or some grave professional household.

'We had a great discussion of the Scottish Established and the Scottish Episcopal Churches.' The Campbell tradition was Presbyterian, Gladstone was a passionate High Churchman. Dean Milman was among the guests and he used to read aloud his translation of the *Agamemnon*. The famous Free Kirk minister and philanthropist, Dr. Guthrie, was also staying at the castle. The atmosphere was not wildly dissipated, but Sabbath discipline was so far relaxed as to permit the young people to go for a long walk over the hills on Sunday afternoon: 'Our talk was of the deepest interest ranging over endless subjects.'

In November the Gladstones were in Glasgow for political meetings and some of 'Papa's fine speeches'; thence to Newbattle Abbey and Edinburgh for his speech as Lord Rector of Edinburgh University. There was another house-party for which Mary had a new ball gown of white tarlatan and 'a black silk gown with a morning and evening body'—an anticipation of the modern 'separates'.

In 1866 the family spent the winter in Rome, staying in the

Piazza di Spagna. Rome was dirty and the Tibor muddy, but nothing could mar the impressiveness of the Eternal City or of St. Peter's. Papa led Mary with her eyes closed until she stood under the dome, 'so that its full beauty and grandeur could burst upon me at once'.

They had an audience with the Pope: 'He began to talk and trolled on very good-naturedly and laughing a good deal', about Rome and Italy, poetry, Milton, the Atlantic Cable, the Queen, Scotland, so that 'altogether we were much pleased with his tenderness and simplicity'. All the same 'there was something excessively ludicrous in all this'.

They went to Vespers in the Church of the Sacred Heart, Trinità dei Monti, where the singing of the nuns was very sweet; and made a party to the Catacombs with Dean Stanley and Lady Augusta, under the guidance of Mgr. Nardi of the Pope's Household and of his archaeologist Monisgnor di Rossi: 'Such an extraordinary party, especially as Monsignores are not allowed to drive with females' though Deans may do so. Mgr. Nardi 'later said some very extraordinary things' which remain, unfortunately, unrecorded.

There was a round of visits to galleries, studios and villas; to the theatre and opera, all interspersed with Italian studies and reading Dante with Papa. In November Mary celebrated her nineteenth birthday and was given lapis-lazuli earrings by Mama, a ring by Papa, a turquoise cross and a photograph of Rome by Uncle Stephen Glynne, and a cast of the head of Michelangelo by her sister Agnes.

At Christmas the young Gladstones sang carols outside their parents' bedroom, and they all attended Mass at St. Peter's where Mary sat by 'a pious female who did her utmost to convert us' with no effect. In the evening they sang hymns together at home. On Holy Innocents' Day they saw some of the ceremonies of the children's feast and heard a boy preach in Ara Coeli; and on New Year's Day Mary heard Liszt play and had to play to him, 'which brought on a slight attack of palsy. He was more exciting than anything I ever heard'.

Nearly sixty years later, in 1924, Mary, grown old, wrote to her daughter about that winter: 'Rome was extraordinarily romantic and lingers in my mind as a vivid personal experience. The three men we chiefly consorted with—Sir William Richmond (in love with Agnes and she with him) Lord Odo [Russell] in love with me (so he pretended), then Lord Lorne, the most exciting, and I was what would now be called in love with him.' Romantic memories were manifold: 'The love duets with Lord Odo, the wonderful rides on the Campagna with Lorne, playing to Liszt and he playing to me'—and always the high seriousness in the background: 'Lord Acton's and Dean Stanley's talks with Papa and an exciting reading of Dante with the latter every morning.'

It was still the Rome Anne Thackeray had seen: the capital of the Papal States before the unification of Italy, the seclusion of the Pope in the Vatican and the compensatory Decree of Infallibility.

Home once more, Mary had the 'tremendous treat' of being received by the Princess of Wales at Marlborough House, the Princess 'very sweet' but the honour inducing something of the bathing feel until 'the Baby came in which took away all awkwardness' (the Baby being the Princess Louise Alexandra, future Duchess of Fife and Princess Royal). 'I can't tell you what a treat it was and how it seems almost a dream,' Mary wrote to Lavinia Lyttelton. 'I hope you won't be bored with such a troll.' Troll in Glynnese meant a long ecstatic account, a rave, or in plain Scots, a haver.

Mary was to be for many years yet the daughter at home. She did not marry until she was nearly forty when she married the Reverend Harry Drew and was profoundly happy.

Like Lucy Lyttelton and like Anne Thackeray she carried the zest of youth into maturity and old age. They might, these daughters of eminent fathers, have been either freaks or nonentities, crushed under the weight of paternal fame or self-assertive in eccentricity. That they were so natural and so delightful is a tribute both to themselves and to those famous fathers.

# XIII

## OXFORD IN THE FIFTIES

I

IN 1853 two young men, Edward Burne-Jones and William Morris came up to Oxford to begin a lifelong friendship. The latter came from Marlborough, then a new school begun ten years before. He had entered in 1848 in his fourteenth year. The school was growing but was still unformed, which was perhaps all to the good as far as this pupil was concerned. He would not have taken kindly to a strict code.

Games were played only by a few, most of the boys preferring long country walks. Morris walked with a purpose, investigating Roman remains and the ancient stones at Avebury and Silbury. He read omnivorously, chiefly archaeology and romances; he was religious with a leaning towards Anglo-Catholicism, influenced both by his reading and by the tone of the school which, being new, had escaped the usual heritage of eighteenth-century lethargy.

Morris was remembered afterwards for his strength and vitality and, like the young Walter Scott at the High School of Edinburgh, for his story-telling. He used to entertain his dormitory with nightly sagas. He was not unhappy at school but it was a bad phase in Marlborough's history, and he was taken away at Christmas, 1851, and put under a tutor. Home life was extremely comfortable. His father had been a wealthy business man, a good specimen of the new class which was so to develop, and even his early death did not leave his family in reduced circumstances. They lived in The Water House, Walthamstow, a square Georgian building not lacking in dignity outside and inside handsome and spacious, with some features likely to appeal to romantic eyes, such as the great hall and staircase and the gallery with window-seats. Here Morris used to sit and read.

Behind the house was a lawn, and a moat encircling an islet planted with aspens—'a sort of fairyland for all the children who almost lived on it' and a setting for imagined tales and adventures. It was to appear in more than one of Morris's romances. All his life he loved this type of landscape, low-lying, watered by streams, as he loved old churches and houses made gentle by generations of habitation. A letter he wrote, while still at school, to his sister Emma might belong to any period of his life, holding as it does so much of himself—his love of church art, the beauty of the Easter anthem; of antiquities in a Roman entrenchment, and an old Norman church discovered in his wanderings; of this blending of land and water in landscape. He had floundered into a water meadow but was undeterred. The letter ended boyishly with a request for a cake and some biscuits, stamps and writing-paper, a pen box and his silkworm eggs.

Emma married a High Church cleric and largely because of her influence and their mutual sympathy Morris thought of taking Holy Orders. His tutor, who was also in the High Church tradition and a good scholar and teacher, strengthened this resolve. Morris matriculated in 1852 but had to postpone going up until 1853 as Exeter, his chosen college, was full. The same delay befell Burne-Jones. The two met at the examination, and when in the following year they began the new life together, they began also one of the immortal friendships of artistic history.

Burne-Jones was, like Morris, of the middle class though much less wealthy. His father was an art dealer and frame-maker, perhaps an artist *manqué*. His son described him as 'a very poetical little fellow, tender hearted and touching, quite unfit for the world into which he was pitched. . . . He believed all good things that were ever said of anyone, and was altogether unworldly and pious' and the gentlest of parents. Edward's mother died young and he was an only child, which developed his inherited dreaminess and remoteness. He was by no means a recluse, however, and made good friends at King Edward's Grammar School, Birmingham. Two at least of them, Cormell Price and Richard (later Canon) Dixon, were to be lifelong.

I

His home life was quiet but happy in the tenderness of his father and an aunt who helped to bring him up. There was money enough for comfort, for many books, even for a little elegance and luxury. To the other boys Edward was enviable 'as he was evidently lord, and did as he liked, asking whom he would to visit him' and as he always had 'money and nice things about him'. His money was spent chiefly on books—poetry and history and romance—and he and Price used to spend their half-holidays reading in the old cemetery, not from any touch of necrophilism but because it was 'the only public space within easy distance which was quiet and planted with trees'.

He was a day boy at the grammar school, as were most of the pupils, and was first put into the English or modern or commercial side by his optimistic father who, believing all things, intended him for a business career. Soon he was transferred to the classical, for though never a brilliant or exact scholar he had an obvious leaning towards the humaner letters. He was tolerably happy, though conditions were austere. The school was richly endowed and charged no fees, but like the public schools, saw no reason for pampering the boys with creature comforts. There were only two classrooms for some four hundred and fifty boys.

'The Babel was awful,' one of them told Lady Burne-Jones in later years, 'but it taught us to shout and was probably good for the lungs.' The leg muscles were also exercised as they did not sit for lessons. 'The younger boys would be half dead with fatigue, and quite incapable of attention before the hour was up.' The teaching was forceful rather than evocative: 'A boy never dreamt of asking explanations of his difficulties; the free use of the cane alone could drive us forward.' To this Edward added: 'We were plunged into Caesar without a word of explanation'— not even of the fact that these Commentaries were 'the Diary of the man we had learned about in History. . . . For a dullish boy it was hopeless'.

For boys of eager mind it was good if harsh training and the school produced some fine scholars and great Churchmen—

Lightfoot, Westcott and Benson among them. With the sternness, too, there was a good deal of freedom that would not have
been possible in a public school. There was no cult of games,
no ethos; again as well for this particular pupil.

Cormell Price said that he always recognized Edward by his
laugh. 'There he would be, ready for any fun.' The laugh
remained with him, though the melancholy that dwells in every
Celt was in later life to find more expression in his art. In his
schooldays he had a tremendous capacity for jokes, both verbal
and practical, and a talent for caricatures and comic drawings,
too much suppressed by the mature artist. The official report on
his drawing was that 'he might be better if he exhibited more
industry'. None the less his sketches in letters, one of some little
black devils playing cricket, are pleasing to the frivolous. The
melancholy was apparent too: 'He did not leave on me the
impression that he was happy,' Dixon told Lady Burne-Jones.
'He was high-spirited, boisterous, humorous, but with melancholy underneath.'

Like Morris he was an ardent Anglo-Catholic. Two of his
letters, to a cousin, are packed with exposition of doctrine. They
are too sincere and too objective to be priggish, but they are
pathetically serious for a boy of fifteen. He seemed destined for
Holy Orders. Meanwhile there was Oxford, the city of dreams
and spires, and there, to Exeter College, he came in January,
1853.

At first both he and Morris were disillusioned. Enchantment
was to come and to last, but the first chill was bitter. Edward
had dreamed of a holy place lit and warmed by the piety of
Keble and Newman and Pusey even though they had departed;
he found it cold and barren. The two young men, lonely but
for each other, went for long walks together, talking out their
disappointment. Then insensibly the vision of the sweet city of
dreams was recaptured.

'A glorious place, godlike,' Edward wrote to his father. 'At
night I have walked round her colleges under the pale moon
and thought it would be heaven to live and die here.' The dons

were majestic, the men generous and good-natured, he made friends. There were some from his old school, Dixon among them, at Pembroke, and at the heart of everything was Morris. The two had everything in common with a contrast in temperament and character which dovetailed them into unity. They worked and they read and they played.

'Tell me all you know of home affairs,' Edward wrote, to his father; 'don't give me advice above all things. . . . In return for all these I may graciously inform you of my health and estate, the former is increasing rapidly, the latter decreasing alarmingly'. His wine bill was for 12 dozen Madeira at £2. 2s. a dozen, three dozen claret at £3 a dozen, and two dozen champagne at £3 10s. There was also a bill for the hire of horses, one item being for 'tandem an pair to Woodstock an back, with leader's knee broken an trappins likeways—£5. 10 6', and another: 'Dogcart to Abbingdon with sharves all broke reglarly to sharters—£2. 19.' Discount for cash was allowed, and came to twopence.

Writing to Cormell Price he passed from a eulogium of Tennyson to a lighter note: '10 o'clock evening. I have just been amusing myself pouring basons of water on the crowd below from Dixon's garret, such fun, by Jove.'

Oxford in those days was truly a sweet city, compact as a walled town of the Middle Ages, with meadows bordering the streets and old grey colleges. 'Children gathered violets in the Iffley Road within sight of Magdalen.' There were no suburbs, no industrialism. 'The Oxford of 1853 breathed from its towers the last enchantments of the Middle Ages'—so J. W. Mackail has written in his life of Morris. Changes and reforms were in sight and the currents and cross-currents of thought kept the river of life from being stagnant. There was the reactionary stream, cold and heavy, but there was also the torrent of the Anglo-Catholic revival with the equally torrential flow of liberalism. Had Morris only turned his creative energy in later years to writing a tale of contemporary Oxford, he would have captured the aspect and spirit of the place as no other could do. He and Burne-Jones and their friends read, with delicious sadness and delight, *The Heir of Redclyffe*. Miss Yonge had told something of the effect of Oxford on Guy her hero, but like her greater predecessor Jane Austen, she was too wise to attempt description of any way of life she did not know. Morris might have written the masculine complement and counterpart of her masterpiece. Indeed these two friends might almost be incarnations of her ideal young men, living a life beyond the scope of her narrative.

Tom Brown's verdict, 'It's an awfully idle place' might have been repeated by them though they did not themselves choose to be idle. One of their contemporaries has left a pungent account of a typical lecture at which the men read in turns a translation from a crib of the set book, and answered questions put by the lecturer in a form that clearly expected the answer 'Yes'.

A reading man could, of course, read, a rowing man could row. Most of them probably did a little of the first with a good deal of the second. Some lapsed into idleness and vice, others, like our friends, went their own way in friendship, purity of heart, ardour of mind.

They both read enormously. Morris in particular had that faculty essential and akin to genius, of selecting precisely what he wanted:

'He never seemed to be particularly busy,' Burne-Jones said of him and always had 'plenty of leisure for fishing, for amusement if it amused him' but he would not play by rule. 'He had a great instinct at all times for knowing what would amuse him and what not to read.' His tutor admitted that 'Mr. Morris had no difficulty in mastering the usual subjects of examination' but found him 'rather rough and unpolished' with 'no special literary tastes or capacity'.

They read the new and exciting poetry of Tennyson, the prose of Ruskin, with the old romances, the *Morte d'Arthur* and Chaucer. Both drew a great deal, Morris architectural details, Burne-Jones flowers and foliage relieved by devils. Their discovery of

their true vocation as artists rather than priests was being made
and in this enchanted, enchanting Oxford they came to their
decision, and passed from preparation to their fruition. |There
are few men of great talent and achievement in whose maturity
we can see so clearly and enduringly the young men of nineteen who met in Oxford and began life and friendship together.

## II

Oxford in those golden days for youth may be seen through
feminine eyes long before 'the sweet girl graduates' became more
than a poet's fantasy. Mrs. Jeune, the wife of the new Master of
Pembroke, came there in 1844 with her husband and children.
'The society here strikes me as ponderous and wanting in
ease. . . . There seems no lack of young ladies in Oxford, but if
they always sit so unnoticed as they did, in an innocent row last
night, the young men are in little danger from their charms.'
She enlivened that society by her own pleasant personality,
and in due course by the charms of her eldest daughter Margaret.
After being educated at home by their parents, Margaret and her
younger sister Lydia were sent to a French boarding school
'in a beautiful part of Paris, fine air, nice garden, twenty-five
girls, the most part French, the mistress a nice, sensible person'.
It was well recommended by some friends, Mr. and Mrs. Buck-
land: 'The latter certainly gives but a bad account of the morals
of French schools but the education given in them is, she says,
wonderful' and in this particular one the morals also were sound.
Margaret and Lydia were accordingly dispatched to Paris.
'The house is so desolate without them,' but they wrote cheerful
letters home, their only complaint being the lack of fresh air and
exercise. Papa on a visit to Paris found them happy and well,
making excellent progress in their studies and popular with the
other girls. It was a cheerful school even on Sunday when the
only obligation was to go to church once. Some of the girls
even played dominoes!
In 1855 they returned home and Margaret 'came out' at parties

at which we may be sure she was not permitted to sit in an innocent row and be bored and boring. A Hogmanay party in Mr. Hozier's rooms in Balliol was delightful, with dancing, a magic lantern and a Christmas tree. The Master made sure that no guests would outstay the Old Year, by advancing the clock one hour. At midnight (Master's time) the host served a grace-cup and the company, led somewhat surprisingly by Mrs. Liddell, mother of Alice, sang *God Save the Queen* and *He's a Jolly Good Fellow*.

Margaret received many compliments: 'She is certainly very superior to most of the other girls here, and has a fine bearing which distinguishes her,' and which was probably due to Paris. In May, 1856, she had her seventeenth birthday: 'an age of peculiar interest to a young girl in which she enters first on life as a young woman'. Her gifts were a pleasing mixture of the edifying and the gay: a Bible and a trinket, a book on geology and a bouquet. There were many other parties, there were holidays at Boulogne and at Brighton and a course of baths at Malvern. At home she read and studied a little, and embroidered a flag for the Pembroke boat. Her grandest ball was in the term 1859–60 when the Prince of Wales was in residence. He danced with Margaret, was a delightful partner and brought her decorously back to Mamma. Altogether he made an excellent impression by his charm and dignity and his observance of college rules.

Most people, indeed, liked this exalted young man, with the notable exception of his mother. The harshness with which she treated him had deep roots in her nature, perhaps in that of her race. Enmity between monarch and heir was an old and tragic story in the Hanoverian succession. Besides disliking him, the Queen distrusted her son and this feeling was shared by his father. They looked on him as more than ordinarily prone to evil and thought to pluck him from the depths by harsh rules and restrictions. There was much good and much sense in some of the rules but the attitude of repression and surveillance was wrong and the marvel is that the boy was not embittered and distorted for life.

The memorandum sent him on his seventeenth birthday began:
'Life is composed of duties, and in the due, punctual and cheerful
performance of them the true Christian, true soldier and true
gentleman is recognized.

'You will in future have rooms allotted to your sole use'—
not to enhance his dignity and freedom but 'to give you an opportunity of learning how to exercise yourself unaided by others
and to utilize your time in the best manner.'

It meant indeed a new loneliness separated even from the
companionship of brothers and sisters. He must not leave the
house without reporting to his governor, Colonel Bruce. The
Prince Consort addressed a further memorandum to the gentle-
men-in-waiting who were to form 'a good set' for the heir who
could not mix with other young men. A certain amount of
relaxation was permitted but not overmuch; conversation, literature and the arts were much to be preferred to cards and billiards,
and it was desirable to hear poetry, 'amusing books or good
plays read aloud'. Colonel Bruce and the other gentlemen
doubtless did what they could with the result that to the end of
his life the Prince and King detested books and cared little for
the arts and for intellectual conversation.

The admirable part of the instruction was on his attitude to
others, especially to servants: 'They have not surrendered their
dignity that belongs to them as brother men and brother Chris-
tians. You will try to emancipate yourself as much as possible
from the thraldom of abject dependence for the daily wants of
life upon your servants.'

The young Prince needed no exhortation to be 'courteous
and kind'. He may have needed the warning—no laughing at
people and no practical jokes 'which should never be permitted'
and which were to be extremely popular in Marlborough House.
His own good taste might have made him 'borrow nothing
from the fashions of the groom or the gamekeeper' in dress.
Where the system went almost tragically wrong was in being
excessively intellectual and in keeping him apart from his contemporaries. He was no more a lover of learning than was his

mother, but his father imposed his own German pedantry. The young Prince would never have made a scholar but his intelligence was good; he observed and understood men and life.

The worst lack was of companions. Before going to Oxford he had spent some time in Edinburgh, living at Holyrood and attending lectures at the university. Playfair's lectures on chemistry interested him; he liked finding things out. But the company provided for him in the ancient palace that had seen Mary Stuart and Prince Charles Edward in their brilliant youth, was 'distinguished but unjoyous'—to quote from an article in *The Quarterly Review* in 1910.

His guests were such men as the Lord Advocate, Lord Melville, the Provost, the Sheriff, and Professor Playfair. It is extremely unlikely to anyone knowing the traditions of Edinburgh that these reverend seniors were unjoyous in private; but the Prince could not be allowed to savour the true joviality of the Scot.

At Oxford he did not live in college but in his own establishment with Colonel Bruce in charge. 'The only use of Oxford is that it is a place for study, a refuge from the world and its claims.' Colonel Bruce might arrange some 'convivial meetings at dinner' for the Prince to meet the dons and a discreet choice of undergraduates 'who otherwise have no means of meeting familiarly those from whom they expect to derive the benefits of education'. Which of the two groups were less happy and convivial is left to the imagination.

One tutor reported the Prince as lacking generosity, enthusiasm and tolerance; the second want might be true but the other qualities were never absent from the mature man.

Every desire, even the most laudable, was opposed. He wished to attend the early Celebration of Holy Communion, but this, in the Prince Consort's view should occur only twice a year, at Christmas and Easter and then in private. He might go oftener if he felt 'a real yearning of the heart' but such a yearning was hardly understood. There was perhaps a fear that an emotional, impressionable and lonely youth might turn to Rome with her guidance and suavity and worldly wisdom. When he called upon the Pope during his visit to Rome in 1859 the Queen wrote: 'Bertie's interview with the Pope went off extremely well. He was extremely kind and gracious and Colonel Bruce was present. It would never have done to let Bertie go alone, as they might have hereafter pretended God knows what Bertie had said.'

In all the story of Victorian harshness no chapter is more pitiful than that dealing with the most exalted youth of all. The tyranny which hedged him was more severe than any which flogged the boys at Eton or Winchester.

# XIV

## TWO ECCENTRICS

PUBLIC or grammar school education was the norm for boys of the middle and upper classes, but among them were irregulars, even eccentrics, and one of the most startling was Augustus Hare. Adopted by a widowed aunt from a father who regarded his offspring merely as a litter to be got rid of, he was reared in that religiosity which holds all pleasantness as sin. In her perverted way his aunt-mother, as he called her, loved him, but he knew no comfort or fun, no companionship with other children. From this purgatorial childhood he passed into another purgatory of boyhood, which might have been called hell had it not, in time, come to an end.

In 1847 he was sent to Harrow, a delicate boy of thirteen, utterly unprepared for the new discipline. He was bullied at first, and ragged, which he survived comparatively unscathed. Fagging was hard labour with punishment for every lapse such as letting his fag-master's fire go out: 'He makes me his fag to go errands and do all he bids me, and if I don't do it he beats me. But I don't mind much. . . . I am rather lonely still, with none to speak to or care about me. . . . Yet I like Harrow very much.'

The sincerity of that statement might be doubted, were it not that even the hectoring he received was better than the desolation of home. The school was a stern place under Dr. Vaughan, and an assistant master, Oxenham, who had 'the power of flogging and does flog, even for the least fault, for he really enjoys it'. He was 'very old, very stern, very indolent and very preachy' —a deplorable catalogue.

Augustus went for part of the Christmas holidays to the palace at Norwich where his uncle Edward Stanley was Bishop, and began a happy friendship with his cousin Arthur Stanley, the

future Dean. Christmas at home was utter misery, and return
to school a relief.

'That I got on tolerably well at Harrow is a proof that I was
never very ill-treated there.' It would have taken a deal of ill-
treatment to impress the victim of that aunt. Other boys suffered,
and not only in body. The small boys were sent to buy beer for
their seniors. If caught, they were flogged by the Head, if they
refused to go they were flogged by the bullies: 'What with
fagging and bullying, servility was as much inculcated as if it
were likely to be a desirable acquirement in after life.'

The teaching was bad and he learned nothing. His health
declined and he had to wear an iron plate on his spine. After a
year of school he was taken to Torquay for a summer of unrelieved pain and weakness. There was no attempt at cure, for
his aunt-mother believed in the moral validity of pain; the boy
*ought* to suffer. Pain was sent by God 'as a tract to draw its victims
to heaven'. It is a miracle that this victim did not die or go mad.
Physically he was starved, mentally fed upon tracts and sermons.
A tutor was engaged for his piety with no pretence of learning.
Augustus grew steadily worse and reached the verge of suicide.
Then came a change though not much for the better. He was
sent to an establishment near Bath where there was no effort at
teaching, the only alleviation being a certain amount of freedom
and of country air. He gained a little strength but intellectually
this was a period of sterile misery.

Through the intervention of Arthur Stanley some relief came
in occasional visits to London and more frequent visits to Bath,
to that rich and splendid eccentric, scholar and near genius, Walter
Savage Landor. In his house the boy was fed, physically and
mentally. Landor was a gourmet and used to do his own mar-
keting, when Augustus went with him, and afterwards dined
delectably on turbot and veal with fresh vegetables and a currant
tart. The house was full of pictures but with few books, for
Landor used to give them away. Thanks to a prodigious memory
he had no need to re-read or consult what he had once absorbed.
His talk enriched his visitor.

Even with such interludes these schooldays were 'two and a half years of misery ... I still feel, in passing Bath by railway, sick at the recollection'.

He was again next sent to the Reverend Charles Bradley at Southgate, again by the intervention of Arthur Stanley. Conditions there were reasonably comfortable. The food was wholesome and plentiful enough and each boy had a fire in his study bedroom. But the greatest change was intellectual: 'Mentally I owe everything to Mr. Bradley' who had 'a wonderfully pleasant way of teaching.'

The boys had to work hard but they worked with understanding and zest. The master was stern, but if he barked at them he expected them to bark back: 'He continually asks me if I do not think him to be the most annoying, tiresome man I ever met, and I always say: "Yes, I do think so." In return he says that I am sapping his vitals and wearing him out by my ingratitude and exaggerations, but he does not think so at all.'

There were excursions to London and to places of interest, Hatfield among them, and once a visit to Lady Louisa Stuart, daughter of the Marquis of Bute, granddaughter of Lady Mary Wortley Montagu, and friend of Sir Walter Scott. Augustus saw the opening of the Crystal Palace in 1851 by the Queen, gorgeous in cloth of silver and wearing her crown.

'I never was happier anywhere in my life than I have been here, and I have done more, learned more and thought more in the few months at Southgate than in all the rest of my life put together.'

In summer he was taken on foreign tours. His first visit to France meant an enlargement of mind. He saw the old Paris before Napoleon III and Hausmann rebuilt it, visited Rouen, Amiens, Bayeux, Lisieux and Caen and in the last town was left with a French family to learn the language. His host was the Protestant *pasteur*, Monsieur Melun. There were races on Sunday afternoon and in the morning Monsieur preached against them, so in the afternoon he had no congregation because they had all gone to the races or, as he put it, to perdition. The boy enjoyed Caen but would have enjoyed it more had he had any money.

His allowance was £10 a year out of which he had to buy his boots, gloves and hats. His aunt was wealthy but miserly in a complicated way: if the boy had more money he would spend it in riotous living.

He was approaching manhood now and Oxford lay ahead with the further destiny, not to be argued, of Holy Orders. In 1853, aged nineteen, he went up to University College, furnished by his kind Aunt Kitty Stanley with an introduction to Jowett.

'At nineteen I was just beginning to feel something of the self-confidence which boys usually experience at thirteen.'

Jowett proved a good friend to this raw young freshman, giving him not only the coaching he needed, but a still more necessary knowledge of the world. Thanks to his help Augustus passed his examinations, but there could be no thought of Honours: 'My mother would only have wondered what I wanted them for, and had I gained them would have lamented them as terribly ensnaring,' for to her secular learning was as pernicious as worldly pleasures.

He found Jowett Christian in action if not always in teaching, and his steadfast kindness brought a little warmth into the bleak young life. There were a few friendships and some amusing and amazing encounters. One was with a certain Mr. R., a prototype surely of the so-called Oxford Group of the 1930's. Mr. R. believed in truth in all its horrid nudity and having replied to a greeting: 'How are you?' with 'Quite well, thank you', wrote to the inquirer: 'Dear Sir, When I told you yesterday that I was quite well I really had a headache. This has been upon my conscience ever since.' The recipient showed the letter to a friend who forthwith reproached Mr. R. with another untruth in addressing as 'Dear Sir' a man whom he was known to dislike. At once the truthful one wrote: 'By calling you Dear Sir I may have led you to suppose I liked you which I never did and never can do.'

Augustus met the almost legendary Dr. Routh, President of Magdalen, who had been born in 1755, had seen Dr. Johnson, and whose mother had known a lady who remembered seeing Charles II at Oxford exercising his dogs. Dr. Routh lived mentally in eighteenth-century Oxford: 'I have seen two under-graduates hanged on Gownsman's Gallows in Holywell—hanged, sir, for highway robbery.'

If he did not find in Oxford the enchantment discovered by his unknown contemporaries Burne-Jones and Morris, Augustus Hare yet gathered some treasure and found the beginning of the way of freedom.

About this time another irregular, though a happy one, went up to Cambridge: that ripe eccentric, scholar, novelist, Church-man and hymn-writer Sabine Baring-Gould. He was born in 1834, of an old Devon family, his father a retired cavalry officer. The family estate was at Lew Trenchard in Devon, but much of his boyhood was spent abroad. First came two periods of more or less orthodox schooling, the first at King's College in Somerset House, London. It was a dismal place, the classes held in a basement. Sabine boarded with one of the masters whose house-keeping would have been commended by Mr. and Mrs. Squeers. Supper consisted of bread and scrape with sky-blue diluted milk. One evening there was an argument about whether the bread would stick to the ceiling. Sabine threw his slice aloft and it did, and had to be dislodged by a footman with a broom. When reprimanded Sabine made the diplomatic defence: 'Please sir, I proved to the other boys that we were not skimped in butter, and they will all write home on Sunday and praise the way in which the butter is laid on.'

His next experience was at Warwick Grammar School as a day boy, his parents having moved to that town. In spite of delicacy he enjoyed those schooldays; because of the delicacy he was taken to dancing class in a sedan, 'probably the last or almost the last in England to ride in that conveyance'. After a bad attack of whoop-ing-cough he was ordered to the South of France, and the family spent the winter in Pau, the beginning of a long sojourn abroad.

Mr. Baring-Gould had a tutor for his sons, but had his own theories of education. One was that Sabine would make a mathe-matician, a view contradicted by facts, another that memory should not be cultivated at the expense or reason and understanding.

This was unusual in a period when everything was learned by heart: irregular verbs, dates and reigns, Kings of Israel and Judah, major and minor prophets, tables, collects, psalms, pages of poetry and prose. Sabine regretted later the lack of this element in his education:

'No man of mind but must rejoice in knowing things by heart. . . . No one ever had a well-trained memory without afterwards having good reason to entertain profound gratitude towards those who secured him the boon.' He read widely, but fairy-tales were withheld, and the German legends he discovered for himself had the sweetness of forbidden things. The books approved for the young Baring-Goulds were *Sandford and Merton* and Dr. Aiken's *Evenings at Home*.

The future author of *Onward Christian Soldiers* was not trained in militant Christianity. His father disapproved of dogmatic religion and the family heard long, dull sermons of merely ethical content, while Sabine realized instinctively that dogma is, in the strict sense, edifying. Having begun geometry he found that 'what the first principles of Euclid have been to geometry, astronomy, etc., the dogmatic statements in the Nicene Creed have been to Christian theology'. Incidentally and flippantly, his father gave as one reason for belief in an overruling Providence the fact that 'it had furnished boys with a portion of their anatomy not covering any important nervous ganglions, nor harbouring arteries, but overspread with a dainty tissue of nerves rendering sensitive to pain, and to which chastisement might be applied without danger'. He was not, for all that, a harsh parent by contemporary standards.

The Church atmosphere in Pau was decidedly Protestant, the chaplain 'of the Colonial and Church Society type. That suffices as a description'. Sabine was searching for the Catholic tradition in the Church of England. English society was full of eccentrics, the most distinguished being Mrs. Trollope, mother of Thomas and Anthony: 'a good-natured, somewhat vulgar old lady.' English boys were known as '*les petits Godams*'.

It was an irregular life compared with that of school but it was disciplined intellectually, and rich in experience. Apart from a brief return to England in 1849 the years from 1848 to 1850 were spent in France, travelling in the great family coach, settling for a while in some such place as Pau. It was a happy boyhood, the antithesis of that of Augustus Hare. There were many 'moments unforgettable'. One was the first glimpse of the Pyrenees: 'turquoise blue, tipped with silver . . . beyond the sombre sea of pines'. The children clapped their hands with joy, their mother rose to look, their father took off his hat. The tutor 'put his ignited cigar inconsiderately into his pocket where it promptly burnt a hole in his coat' no doubt to the further joy of the children, and the groom, a good Devonian, admitted: 'God bless my soul! Them's bigger than Dartmoor!'

Another picture was of an hotel in Brittany, build round a courtyard, with the bedrooms opening on a gallery, and meals served at a real table d'hôte with the host presiding. The women still wore their costume with exquisite coifs. One day Mr. Baring-Gould met a girl going to drown herself for unrequited love. He listened with sympathy, advised her first to go home and leave her coif, and slipped a five-franc piece into her hand. The girl went home—but there was no more talk of drowning.

The boy was living in history and mature enough to be aware of it. He saw France on the eve of revolution, and the downfall of Louis Philippe: 'Never, probably, did any king fall so lump- ishly and was so little regretted.' The family visited some aristo- crats of Irish descent who had come to France with James VII and II, and taken French nationality—the Count and Countess Walsh. They were royalist and legitimist, regarding the Comte de Chambord as the *de jure* King of France, Henry V.

Sabine made archaeological discoveries. In digging up flower roots he came upon some cubes of mosaic. The farmer who owned the fields told him there were 'whole pictures' under- ground. The local English helped him to excavate some pave- ments of lovely mosaic, and a whole villa might have emerged had not French jealousy intervened: the field must be handed over to the town of Pau, and was henceforth neglected.

K

Intellectually and in worldly experience the boy was ahead of most of his contemporaries. For academic coaching he was sent, in 1851, to Cambridge, to the Reverend Hervey Godwin. There he was treated with much kindness and so much confidence that he was begged to help Mrs. Goodwin choose her clothes; apparently her taste was deplorable and Sabine's excellent.

About this time he was confirmed, without any preparation, by the Bishop of Ely. His recollections of church life in Cambridgeshire were not edifying. The church he attended had a monthly Celebration of the Holy Communion when the altar was spread with a tablecloth and had a bottle of wine, covered with a napkin placed in the centre. Others were served by College Fellows who rode out to take Morning Prayer, retired to the vestry for a luncheon of sandwiches, came back into church to gabble through Evensong, then rode back to dinner in Hall and wine and gossip in the Common Room.

When Baring-Gould entered Clare in 1853 he found enough like-minded companions to form a Holy Club, the Society of the Holy Cross. The members made rules for themselves of prayer, study and almsgiving. They attended the only church in Cambridge, St. Giles, which had a weekly Eucharist, and during Lent attended Evensong, every Wednesday and Friday, in King's College Chapel instead of dining in Hall.

Among them was a young Scot, Maclagan, a future Archbishop of York. Already he carried mitre and crosier in his baggage, and knew the danger, for a would-be prelate, of too much zeal on the Catholic side. Finding that the Club kept minutes and a list of members, he resigned: 'He was a canny Scot, and a Scot like a fox sweeps his tail over his traces.'

Catholic scruples were generally deprecated. One youth went to the Dean of his college with some trouble of conscience and received counsel: 'Take a glass of good old tawny port. If it continues, take another. Should it not then subside, my dear fellow, then take a third.'

# XV

## MID-VICTORIAN SCOT:
## YOUNG VELVET COAT

ROBERT LOUIS STEVENSON, precisely mid-Victorian
by birth, hardly fulfils the accepted idea of a Victorian Scot.
Yet neither the Queen's reign nor the city of Edinburgh were
lacking in wild laddies. The society that deplored the poor
Stevenson parents' having so much trouble with their son had
little cause to be startled; it had seen worse.

The fragile child who had listened through the long, white
nights for the rumble of carts that meant the coming of day,
grew into a comparatively healthy and active boy. His schooling
was varied: a year and a half at Edinburgh Academy, a short time
at a boarding school in England, then back to Edinburgh to a
small private school kept by Robert Thompson who had been
tutor to two other men of letters in embryo, William and Henry
James. Louis read widely, always with 'a fixed idea that literature
was his calling'. He was well informed and not unconventional
in his learning. To the accepted subjects of Latin and mathematics he added French, thanks to frequent holidays abroad with
his mother. These holidays would not seem to have left any deep
impression on his mind, but he gained an ease of speech and manner unusual in a schoolboy, and was so fluent in French that it
became his second language and a quickening influence on his
own style.

He was described at this time as 'long, lean and spidery'
with an expressive face and 'soft brown eyes that seemed already
to have drunk the sunshine from southern vines', while 'about the
mouth and in the mirthful, mocking light of the eyes there
lingered ever a ready Autolycus roguery'.

The Puck and Ariel were stronger in him than the Shorter
Catechist although that being also lurked within him; and under

the mocking and travelled youth there still lingered the child who had played at pirates, explorers and shipwrecked mariners in the Manse garden at Colinton. He still preferred games mixed with make-believe to orthodox sport, even to golf which in a young Scot is eccentricity bordering upon heresy. What he would have made of Rugby and Rugby of him is a matter too deep for present pondering.

'At the age of fourteen I bought a certain cudgel, got a friend to load it, and thenceforth walked the tame ways of the earth my own ideal, radiating pure romance, still but a puppet in the hands of Skelt.'

He learned to dance, though never well, and to ride which he loved. On horse or pony he could be cavalier or highwayman, fugitive or solitary horseman against the evening sky. There was a holiday at Peebles where he made friends with a brother and sister about his own age, and long afterwards the girl recalled a wild dash through Tweed, herself on a white pony called Heaven, Louis on a brown Purgatory, her brother on a black Hell.

'That part of the earth was made heaven for me by boats and bathing,' Louis himself wrote, 'and the fascination of streams and the delights of companionship and those (surely the prettiest and the simplest) of a boy and girl romance.'

Other holidays were spent at North Berwick, already a favourite resort of Edinburgh citizens, with the pleasures of fishing, bathing, and 'crusoing', a word he defined as meaning 'all extempore eating in the open air, digging perhaps a house under the margin of the links, kindling a fire of the sea-ware and cooking apples there'. It was the period of 'The Lantern Bearers'.

Even with foreign travel it was an intensely Scottish boyhood, nurtured on Scottish history and tradition, on the ballads and Border legends, on tales of the Covenanters—'My style is from the Covenanters'—and on Scott, with the particular Stevenson inheritance, from his engineering father of tales of 'shipwrecks, out-lying skerries, pitiless breakers and great sea-lights'.

In his father's library Sir Walter Scott dwelt genially among Calvinist divines and commentators on Scripture, and Louis was captivated by *Rob Roy*, until he encountered Di Vernon. He had still the schoolboy's contempt for this love-business, but in young manhood that gallant girl was to bewitch him and he was to read the novel with increased delight.

He was already trying his prentice hand on writing, starting many school magazines full of horror tales, and attempting a play about that versatile citizen of Edinburgh, Deacon Brodie. The Deacon was a respectable carpenter by day, a housebreaker by night, and prospered in both activities until found out and, in the word of his judge Lord Braxfield, 'hangit'. The play came to nought, but it was the germ of *Dr. Jekyll and Mr. Hyde*. At the age of sixteen the Shorter Catechist in him took command for a time, and he wrote a *History of the Pentland Rising*. His proud father had it printed and bought most of the copies.

So it was as a fledgeling if unacknowledged author that Louis went up to Edinburgh University at the age of seventeen, to study for the degree of B.Sc. in engineering and so equip himself to follow his father and grandfather in their profession. Latin was still essential and he attended 'on occasion' the lectures of Professor Sellars and still more occasionally those of Blackie in Greek. The latter, no stickler for exact scholarship or profuse attendance, was dimly aware of this abstinence:

'I don't seem to remember your face,' he expostulated mildly when asked for a class ticket.

'Probably not, sir, but I hope that will not prevent you from giving me a certificate.'

Already 'dear Louis of the blooming cheek' was justifying Andrew Lang's description of him. He was given the certificate, but another professor, Fleeming Jenkyn, in his own subject of engineering, was less *complaisant*:

'It is quite useless for you to come to me. There may be doubtful cases; there is no doubt about you. You simply have not attended my class'—but in the end he too conceded the certificate.

By his own confession Louis 'acted upon an extensive and highly rationalized system of truancy 'which probably cost him as much mental agility and concentration as would have taken him virtuously through his classes. Had he gone to Oxford or Cambridge he would have found such truancy prevented by proctors and tutors, but he might have been less tempted to roam, the southern ways of learning being so much ampler than the Scottish, so much closer to the primrose paths of idleness: 'The English lad goes to Oxford or Cambridge, there in an ideal world of gardens to lead a semi-monastic life, costumed, disciplined, drilled by proctors'—so he wrote of the difference between the Scots and the English university. For the Scots student there was the experience 'of crowded classrooms, of a gaunt quadrangle, of a bell hourly booming over the traffic of city streets. . . . His college life has little of restraint and nothing of necessary gentility'. In both these omissions it suited this vagrant, though he missed the genial culture of the south. In Scotland, 'all classes rub shoulders on the greasy benches. . . . The first muster of a college class is a scene of curious and painful interest; so many lads fresh from the heather hang round the stove in cloddish embarrassment, ruffled by the presence of their smarter comrades'. He recalled the kindness of Professor Blackie in 'putting these uncouth, umbrageous students at their ease with ready human geniality'.

In favour of the Scots way there was this democratic atmosphere with almost complete freedom: 'Our tasks ended, we of the North go forth as freemen. . . . Till the bell rings again we are masters of the world; and some portion of our lives is always Saturday, *la trève de Dieu*'.

The danger lay in misuse of freedom with or without money. Thomas Stevenson distrusted his son's prudence, and on the principle that hard-earned money should not be lightly squandered kept him on an allowance of 2s. 6d. a week, increased in time to £1 a month. Even in those days it was hardly enough for *menus plaisirs* and the lad began to haunt low pubs and corresponding company. He chose to wear shabby clothes, and in particular a velvet jacket which seemed to him daringly Bohemian and artistic.

'The queerest looking object you could conceive,' a fellow-student remembered him, 'a slithering, loose flail of a fellow, so like a scarecrow that one almost expected him to creak in the wind.' Under the velvet coat he wore a black shirt with a tie 'that might have been torn from a castaway carpet'.

The shabbiness of poverty has never been despised in Scotland, but the shabbiness of youthful eccentricity is another matter. Stevenson was considered, not unjustly, a *poseur*.

'We simply thought him a fool and expressed that opinion with all the freedom of our kind'—to which Louis replied in kind. He had a way of sneering.

When vagrancy deepened into dissipation he was avoided and these years of first manhood were misery to his parents and to himself:

'Days of green-sickness and they were often miserable,' his cousin and first biographer, Graham Balfour wrote afterwards, and Louis himself confessed: 'My acquaintance was of what would be called a very low order. . . . I was the companion of seamen, chimney-sweeps, thieves; my circle was being continually changed by the action of the police magistrate.'

For the son of solid, respected and kirk-going parents and the grandson of a minister it was almost unspeakable: almost, but not quite, for Edinburgh spoke about it at length and with a horror not untinged with enjoyment.

They were not, however, altogether wasted or unhappy these years of difficult youth. He had many good and reputable friends and his parents were hospitable. In his former nursery, now his own domain, in Heriot Row, he might entertain his own guests; his cousin and comrade since boyhood, R. A. M. Stevenson the artist; Charles Baxter, wise and kind and witty; Walter Simpson, son of the great surgeon, with whom Louis made his *Inland Voyage*, and James Walter Ferrier, 'the most complete and gentle gentleman I have ever known'.

'It was the period of Jink. Jink was a word of our own,'

which meant 'doing the most absurd acts for the sake of their absurdity'.

Perhaps the best friend of all was one, half a generation older than himself, mature in wisdom but youthful in spirit, Fleeming Jenkyn, the professor over whose eyes he had so signally failed to pull wool. Mrs. Jenkyn, a young woman of great charm and intelligence, called on Mrs. Stevenson. In the midst of their polite conversation a voice spoke from a shadowy corner of the drawing-room: 'My son,' Mrs. Stevenson told her guest who sat entranced by the youth, 'who talked as Charles Lamb wrote', and who, when he escorted her to the door was seen as 'a slender, brown, long-haired lad with great dark eyes and a brilliant smile and a gentle, deprecating bend of the head'.

'Who was he,' she wondered, 'this young Heine with a Scottish accent?' Invited to visit her he replied like an eager child: 'Shall I come tomorrow' and was told 'Yes'. At dinner Mrs. Jenkyn told her husband: 'I have made the acquaintance of a poet.'

Like all young things, especially the brilliant and eccentric, he needed mothering, and he never escaped or tried to escape from semi-maternal affection and domination: his mother and, in childhood his aunt and his 'second mother' Cummie, and now Mrs. Jenkyn who though young herself was senior enough to be motherly. A little later there was Mrs. Sitwell, and finally he married a woman nearer his mother's age than his own, who ruled him as a loving matriarch.

His *Apologia pro Iuventate Sua* is offered in various essays: 'If you look back on your own education I am sure it will not be the full, vivid instructive hours of truancy that you regret,' he wrote in *An Apology for Idlers*, but rather 'some lack-lustre period between sleep and waking in the class'. He acquired some scraps and remnants of knowledge in an occasional wakeful attendance, but valued more all that he had learned in 'that mighty school of education'—the streets: the school of Dickens and of Balzac. A confessed and impenitent idler he yet was 'always busy on my own end which was to learn to write . . . I lived with words'.

He kept two notebooks in his pockets, 'one to read, the other to write in'.

At college he learned the use of the spoken word, at the famous Speculative Society—of which Scott, Jeffrey, Brougham and many other men of letters or of law had been members. Like his hero Archie Weir, he chose to speak against capital punishment, but made no great impression on his audience. The Speculative was the nearest approach to a Common Room a Scottish student could know. It owned handsome rooms where members might read, gossip and even smoke without leave from authority. Here, in the library, was conceived one December day, a University Magazine, with four editors, including Stevenson and James Ferrier: 'I went home that morning walking upon air.'

The magazine lived for four months 'in undisturbed obscurity and died without a gasp' and without any shock to the hopes of its editors. The first number was edited by all four editors, the second by Louis and Ferrier, the third by Louis alone, 'and it has long been a solemn question who it was that edited the fourth'.

Looking back on his student days he deplored the lack of any 'University feeling' in Edinburgh: 'There is such an entire want of broad college sympathies and ordinary college friendships that we fancy no other University in the kingdom is in so poor a plight.' There should be more than 'a building of classrooms, a Senatus, and a lottery of somewhat shabby prizes' to fuse the students into an organic unity and so blend their diversity as to help each of them to lose his own worst crudity: 'As you send a man to an English University that he may have his prejudices rubbed off, you might send him to Edinburgh that he may have them ingrained. . . . A common weakness is the best master of ceremonies in our quadrangle. . . . The studious associate with the studious alone, the dandies with the dandies. . . . We are apostles of our own caste and our own subject of study instead of . . . true men and loving students.'

Louis must learn the practical side of his profession of engineer, and so went in the vacations to various seaports. One year he went to Anstruther: 'I am the only person in Anstruther who dines in the afternoon,' he told his mother. He asked for wine but none was to be had, so he must be content with green ginger. For diversion he went to see some strolling players in the town hall, and on the way home was lured, by one glorious voice, into the schoolhouse where they were practising the psalms for Sunday.

From Wick, another year, he wrote of a storm: 'A cold, black, southerly wind with occasional rising showers of rain. It was a fine sight to see the boats beat out a-teeth of it.' In another, more violent, he watched the battling of a schooner with some alarm until he remembered 'the verse I am so fond of' from one of the psalms:

> But yet the Lord that is on high
> Is more of might by far
> Than noise of many waters is
> Or great sea billows are.

The Shorter Catechist was not muffled by Velvet Coat and he enjoyed the company of the Free Kirk minister, and discovered such edifying books as Aikman's *Annals of the Persecution in Scotland*, enthralled by which 'I almost forgot to drink my tea and eat mine egg'. He also read George Herbert, 'a devout cove but awfully twaddly!'

In 1870 he went to Earraid in the Sound of Mull, the island on which David Balfour was to be marooned. There he met the artist Sam Bough, to their mutual pleasure. They had read the same books, the old poets: Chaucer, Shakespeare, the Elizabethans.

'Where the devil did you read all these books?' Sam Bough asked. 'And in my heart I echoed the question,' added Louis. They sat together in the stern of the lugger that took them to the island, 'our feet upon the baggage in a beautiful, clear northern eve'.

These were days neither of green-sickness nor of misery, giving an education better than that of the streets, wider than that of the classroom. He was growing into manhood, and he liked this work and valued the family tradition: but his vocation as writer was compelling. A year later he told his father that he did not want to be an engineer. To profess himself an author would be absurd; by way of compromise it was decided that he would read for the Scottish Bar like his great predecessor, Walter Scott.

That calling too he was to forsake, but his training in law as in engineering strengthened his mind and enriched his art. His many youthful selves—the child absorbed in make-believe, the lantern bearer, the foolish Velvet Coat, the apprentice engineer and lawyer all lived in the teller of tales, as did his own father, at once so stern and so tender, who could comfort a frightened child with his stories.

# XVI

## A SAINT, A JOURNALIST AND A PLAY-BOY: SONS OF THE NORTH-EAST

STEVENSON'S poverty at college was imposed as discipline. There were others for whom it was necessity, bravely endured. A boy was born in Kirriemuir in 1836, the only child of a poor mother whose husband had deserted her. The boy was Alexander Whyte, in later years to be famed and loved as a preacher and a mystic, a minister of the Free Kirk yet devoted to St. Teresa, uniting in his unique and saintly personality Catholic devotion with Calvinist theology. He went to the Free Kirk School in Kirriemuir and then to Webster's Academy, but he was so poor that he must leave school at thirteen and begin to earn his living. He was apprenticed to a shoemaker. Cobbling, like weaving, can be a contemplative occupation and the boy used to read at his work. 'A gey puir shoemaker he was,' declared a candid friend, the father of another famous son of Kirriemuir, Sir James Barrie. It was said without rancour, merely as a statement of fact. Reading was a necessity to him as well as a pleasure; his only other recreation was fishing—also of the contemplative sort.

After five years' apprenticeship to a trade he would never master he was appointed teacher in a little country school four miles from the town. He walked there and back, and in the evenings studied to keep ahead of his pupils. His salary was 7s. a week. After a time he was promoted to the Free Kirk School at Airlie, with a salary of £10 a year with his scholars' fees in addition. A kind minister helped him in his studies, and he continued to read everything he could lay hands on, being remembered long afterwards as 'the mannie that could never speak to you for reading'.

He had entered his twenties before he could go up to King's College, Aberdeen, and so his student days lie beyond our scope.

His victory over circumstances was noble but not uncommon; he was one of a great multitude of poor lads, some of whom fell by the way from frailty of body and the dire blows of poverty.

A few years later, in 1866, a boy of fifteen came to Aberdeen with little more material wealth and with equal zest for learning. William Robertson Nicoll was the son of a Free Kirk minister in Lumsden, who was passing rich on two hundred pounds a year, and on that income contrived to rear a family and to acquire a library of 17,000 volumes. Young William read omnivorously. At the age of eight he began Latin in the parish school where one master, assisted by a pupil teacher, taught some hundred and thirty pupils in a single classroom. In winter the children were joined by farm servants who filled their inactive days with learning. The dominie was a scholar with a love as well as a knowledge of the classics. 'He was one of those who awaken the soul,' this particular pupil said of him.

At fifteen young William was sent to Aberdeen Grammar for intensive coaching for the Bursary Competition, and in the same year went up to the university.

'We went too young to college . . . too young to have a fair chance. The first two years I hardly understood what was going on. . . . In spite of our happiness, and it was very real I think now that we were too young and too poor.'

It was an austere life with four classes a day and intense study. The curriculum was chiefly classical but in his third year the boy attended the Logic and the English Literature classes, both under the same professor, Bain. As a teacher of logic he was excellent, but in literature 'as dry as the sands of Arabia'. He had no feeling for poetry, especially love poetry of which he sometimes declared that it 'exceeds the bounds of propriety', as indeed it often does, like love itself.

Other professors were more inspiring, notably Geddes in Greek, and there was always the resource of reading in the University Library. This was not altogether approved: browsing was frivolous, leading a man astray from the paths of prescribed learning. Magazine reading was almost as deplorable as drink or gambling. Still less was there any encouragement of games or any social life. For these lads there was little of the culture that lies beyond books; it was not easily accessible and they were too straitened to seek it.

William's bursary of £11 a year paid his fees with a little over. The rent of his attic was 4s. a week, and he spent 4s. on food, 2s. on other expenses. 'To live on £1 a week was uncommon and was considered luxurious and extravagant.' He did not, however, starve, for boxes of good country fare came regularly from home and were shared with others. Sometimes, when the bursary had just been paid and they were in funds, he and a friend would treat themselves to a penny tart between classes. There were good friendships, and the lads were young and full of the joy of youth and love of learning; this particular boy had good health from his country rearing; but others were less fortunate—to them he may have seemed rich—and many of them died from overwork and undernourishment. Tuberculosis took many victims.

William graduated at nineteen, and by that time he had appeared in print, with a poem in the popular new weekly *The People's Friend* and an article in the same paper on Fielding— not precisely the author to be expected in a Free Kirk library.

After graduation he proceeded to the Theological College of his Church and there spent four years in the study of divinity, Church History and kindred subjects. He was now keeping himself—by tutoring, by writing—and altogether earned about £100 a year. His days were packed with work: tutoring in the morning, classes in the afternoon, and in the evening, writing and study, and sometimes more tutoring. At twenty-one he was licensed to preach.

A third North-Easter born to fame was James Matthew Barrie, born in 1860, the son of a master-weaver, in the Kirriemuir he was to re-create as Thrums. The Barries were not poor, and already the eldest son, Alexander, was at Aberdeen University preparing himself for a distinguished career as school-

master and inspector of schools. He and his eldest sister Mary
were to prove second parents to young Jamie (whom we may
name thus familiarly in his boyhood). For him the way was made
plain and comparatively easy by this elder brother. He went to
school first in Kirriemuir, then to Glasgow Academy where
Alexander was classics master, then back to Kirriemuir, and
finally, at thirteen, to Dumfries Academy in the opposite corner
of Scotland from his birthplace. Alexander had been appointed
H.M. Inspector of Schools in that area, and Jamie lived with
him and Mary.

It was a happy school life. Surprising as it may be to those who
know only the legend of Barrie as a leprechaun of genius, he was
a normal and orthodox schoolboy. He worked reasonably well,
and played a good deal: football and cricket, skating, and pro-
digiously long walks. One Saturday he and a friend walked to
Carlisle, thirty-three miles from Dumfries, in nine and a half
hours; another time they did a twenty-four-mile walk in the
morning and in the afternoon Jamie played football, 'after which
I was missed from school for a month'.

In the holidays he went fishing, like Alexander Whyte, and
like him he read copiously though at a less exalted level: chiefly
adventure stories, Ballantyne, Fenimore Cooper, Mayne Reed
and others beloved of boyhood, and these he used to dramatize
and act with his companions. He used to devise ploys like
Stevenson's, discovering a smuggler's cave on the Nith, leading
expeditions and explorations, lighting camp fires; but he was
never a solitary dreamer.

He was not ready, as his brother had been, to go up to the
university at sixteen; and thanks to that brother, spent two more
years at school, years of gradual maturing, in which he made his
first great friend and hero, James Macmillan, a brilliant boy
whose career ended sadly soon. Macmillan died at thirty. 'I
never admired any boy so much,' Barrie said, long afterwards.

They went walking together, one of their walks being in the
hope of meeting Carlyle who was living at his old home of Eccle-
fechan: 'Macmillan and I used to walk up and down, lifting our

hats every time he looked our way . . . but all the notice he took of his slaves was to brandish his staff at us once, threateningly, which filled us with a boastful joy.' They went canoeing, and they read their chosen books together at a ruined keep near the town, 'a spot heavy with romance. . . . There we talked poetry'. The pair began a story which was never finished, and Jamie contributed to the school magazine. He was secretary of the dramatic club but 'never called any committee meeting' so 'we got on nicely' until he was deposed, when his successor called so many that 'there was dissension twice a week'. After seeing Toole in a travelling company of players the club produced some of the plays in which he had appeared. Jamie in one 'came out strong as a young lady with my hair tied to my hat'. They sent the newspaper report of their production to Mr. Toole who replied hoping benevolently that 'one of us would write a play for him some day. That amused us very much'. Jamie did indeed write a play, 'a melodrama in six scenes and fifteen minutes in which I played all my favourite characters in fiction, artfully rolled into one. The name of this staggerer was *Bandalero the Bandit*'. He wrote also a novel in some hundred thousand words: *A Child of Nature,* which he described as 'a very cynical work'.

At eighteen, a mature age for those days, he went to Edinburgh University, helped by his brother and with good friends to stand by him, chief of them being that elder son of Kirriemuir, now the Reverend Alexander Whyte, minister of the church popularly known as Free St. George's. To him, recalling his own poor boyhood, Jamie must have appeared a prosperous and sheltered youth, and indeed he never knew penury. He lived frugally but sufficiently well, with even an occasional shilling or two for the theatre.

He made friends, he studied diligently, was neither a recluse nor a vagrant—no velvet coat in him. It was not a grim life but it was still somewhat bleak. When Barrie was installed Chancellor of the University at the height of his fame, he referred wistfully to the establishment of unions, clubs and hostels and the like, since his day: 'The absence of them maimed some of us for life.'

On Sunday he went to church, usually to Free St. George's: 'During the four winters another and I were in Edinburgh we never entered any but Free Churches—less on account of our scorn for other denominations than because we never thought of them.'

Some of his 'memories and portraits' are given in *An Edinburgh Eleven*. There could be no more impressive figure in those days than a university professor, and he remembered with awe, having seen four of them 'marching down the Bridges abreast— an inspiriting sight'. He had Masson in English and perceived his authority: 'He masters his subject by letting it master him; for though his critical reputation is built on honesty it is his enthusiasm that makes his work warm with life.' Masson sometimes began his lecture on the way to his platform.

Blackie, who professed Greek officially and countless other subjects unofficially, had one habit, well intentioned but capable of embarrassment: he used to invite students to his house who had any marked physical defect. These breakfasts 'were lively meals, with eggs served in tureens', but there was always the risk that the guests, surveying each other, might realize why they had been bidden.

Sellars, in Humanity, was very properly 'a Roman senator' of infinite dignity and courtesy, but remote: 'Few got near him; all respected him.'

Some of the professors were recognized eccentrics and produced comic legends. Calderwood, the Professor of Moral Philosophy, was once so misguided as to say, in praise of Handel's *Dead March in Saul,* that he would forgive any student who stayed away from class in order to hear that noble music. Next day, naturally, he received a batch of apologies for absence from *soi-disant* musicians who had stayed at home to practise the March, or who, hearing it in the street, had been too much affected to proceed.

The Scots student was not inhibited. There was fun at times,

L

rising to almost Dionysiac exuberance at Rectorials; there were private and academic jests. Barrie knew a share of 'laughter and the love of friends' in his college days, but the gates into the world were only ajar when he graduated at twenty-one. Then they opened, still narrowly and a little creakingly, and he walked out into a world that was to be large and splendid beyond any schoolboys' dream. Among those who helped to open the doors for him was his fellow-countryman already established in journalism, William Robertson Nicoll.

# XVII

## CATHOLIC YOUTH

BY mid-century convent education had again taken root in England. The Society of the Sacred Heart flowered in a mingling of French and English culture. Two English converts, Mabel Digby and Janet Erskine Stuart, both of whom in turn became Mother-General, brought their individual gifts of personality into the Society, and grafted the tradition they shared—that of English country and county life—on to that of the old Catholic régime of France.

Mother Digby, as she became, was received as a postulant by the foundress herself, Mother Barat; and Mother Digby received and trained Janet Stuart so that the living chain was unbroken. The latter was a great teacher as well as a great religious, holy to the point of sanctity. Her book on *The Education of Catholic Girls*, though published in the present century, so clearly reflects the late Victorian years in which she, as a young nun, was preparing her girls for life in the world, that it may be taken as an exposition of conventual ideals in that as well as in a later period. The essentials do not change.

For Mother Stuart, as for Charlotte Yonge in the other Church, the years of girlhood were of the utmost importance in the forming of character and its edification by religious teaching. A girl must not only be taught her faith but be prepared for 'the warfare of faith in the adult world' her mind 'inured to the duty of defending as well as adorning the faith'.

In this matter she went ahead of Charlotte Yonge who took for granted a spiritual security enfolding her girls; the difference being between a Victorian writing in her own period and a Victorian writing on the threshold of a new age. The similarity is, however, greater than any difference. Both emphasize the virtue of obedience, the value of discipline, the grace of humility and its expression in modesty.

That elder sister of the Society of the Sacred Heart, the Ursuline Order, inculcated the same discipline with a stronger infusion of the Victorian spirit. A Directory for Novices enjoined upon the young religious a steady self-discipline with an impartial kindness towards their pupils: 'You should remember that you are the guardian, as it were the visible angel of the children with whom you are charged. . . . Children are instructed better by example than by precept, and are far more inclined to imitate what they see than to practise what they hear.' The nuns must be very patient, very tactful, adept in the delicate art of appearing to be interested in the frequently tedious affairs of their young.

Surveillance was enjoined: 'Be particularly careful never to leave the children alone.' The Roman Church, that extremely realistic body, has never had any illusions about youthful virtue: children, left to themselves, naturally did what was wrong. Faults must be corrected gently and punishment deferred until the delinquent had recovered from whatever impulse or passion had misled her, and could admit her sin and her contrition. The gravest sins were 'disrespectful conduct at prayers, lies, dupli city, and exaggeration, murmuring, tale-bearing, a spirit of criticism and remarking the faults of others particularly superiors, want of charity and forbearance with their companions, the shadow of disrespect towards clergymen'. Very few sins would appear to be overlooked.

Any sin of pride, especially pride of family, must be rooted out, and in those schools for the daughters of ancient and aristocratic families this must often have been necessary. Yet in all their humility, these girls must maintain a right sense of the difference between them and their servants, to whom kindness must always be shown, but never familiarity. A reserve of manner was commended, especially towards inferiors: 'never conversing with servants except when duty or business may render it necessary.'

These servants, for their part, must know their place. The nuns who might have to teach in a poor school were advised that 'the poor should be deeply impressed with the obligation of, respect, love and obedience to their parents and superiors' and of a 'strict honesty and fidelity to their masters and employers'. They too must cultivate a certain reserve, avoiding all manner of gossip, story-telling and mischief-making; it gives one a glimpse into a great household with the young ladies gossiping indiscreetly with the maid who helps them to dress and brushes their hair, with the maids listening, and conveying the chatter to the servants' hall and perhaps to the village: so piling up a heap of gossip and scandal, a bonfire of jealousy and feuds.

The sense of separation, the memory of persecution and prohibitions lingered among English Catholics long after the Emancipation Acts had freed them from political bonds. Reserve of speech was still cultivated, even among equals and co-religionists, and those convent pupils were taught to be 'affable towards all, familiar with none'. Catholic servants in Protestant households were given a special warning: they must be apart in religion from their employers, never 'join in their prayers, listen to their sermons, read their prayer-books or Bibles, go to their churches or meeting-houses' or even attend their weddings and christenings. Again one has a glimpse of a great house where the staff, led by housekeeper and butler, file into morning prayers, and are marshalled to church on Sunday, to sit in two rows, one male, one female, behind the family pew. The little Irish maid must be very firm, though very respectful, in refusing to attend, and in obtaining leave to attend Mass somehow and some time every Sunday.

The grace of convent manners, the excellence of the teaching of languages, especially French, and of needlework, sometimes led Anglican parents to send their daughters to a Roman Catholic school. The revived Anglican Orders of nuns had not yet had time to establish their own tradition of teaching. The faults alleged by some Protestants against Catholic teaching—the extreme reserve that seemed a lack of frankness, the constant surveillance, the insistence on decorum and modesty were only a development, not always an exaggeration of the domestic discipline of devout Victorian parents.

Among Catholics the value of convent training was, of course, fully valued; but even so, there were families where education at home was believed to be as good a preparation for life. This opinion was held by Maude Petre, born in 1863, one of a large family. She and her sisters had governesses:

'Our education was amateurish but we did acquire the love of work.' There were strict rules—any task begun must be finished—and among so many girls there was room for competition, for the stimulus of mutual criticism. There was also the stimulus of the outer world brought by their brothers who were at school.

Home was a better microcosm than school; at school the seniors were apart from the juniors, at home there was a constant coming and going between many worlds: that of the parents, that of the nearly grown-up brothers and sisters, that of the schoolroom and that of the nursery. They were all separate, yet all under one roof and one parental sovereignty; within that rule there were two separate authorities, for the nursery and for the schoolroom: nurse in the one, the governess in the other. Each domain had its own laws. 'There was even a different standard of conduct. Nursery children were almost uniformly well-behaved and obedient; schoolroom children began to distinguish between the law of conscience and the law of the governess, to the detriment of the unfortunate governess.'

It was, for example, a sin to disobey parents but only a venial fault to disobey the governess, poor woman.

One of Maude's elder sisters, a girl of almost masculine temperament and a strong sense of public school morality, drew up a schoolroom code enjoining: no tale-bearing; no self-pity or complaints of illness; no indulgence in sentiment, or any sign of fear; no care for dress or appearance or for any feminine amusements. Maude obediently if reluctantly tried to force her own feminine self into this mould.

Altogether this schoolroom was as strictly governed as any convent school. Added to its Victorian discipline there was the particular Catholic training in austerity and self-abnegation:

'We were not taught to enter the world as masters but as citizens. It was a world of law.' Their mother trained the girls in a reserve of manner which did not make it easy for them to enter the adult world, or sufficiently prepare them for emotional complications. They were almost cloistered: 'Flirting was not merely foolish or vulgar, it was a serious fault' which indeed 'seemed to me in my early girlhood a more grievous offence than familiarities would seem to even well-brought-up girls of the present day.'

Convention was almost as binding as the moral law, and was indeed its expression. 'We were to be virginal'—a quality deeper than decorum and one by no means merely negative: 'To be virginal is to exclude sexuality from thought' as well as from speech and conduct. Modesty was interwoven with humility and obedience into a strong girdle of feminine virtue.

To modern eyes it may seem something less than a preparation for life in the world; yet in that atmosphere of reserve, even of repression there was joy. That was the quality that lingered in this girl's memory of her youth: *joie de vivre*, a vitality that made work and prayer alike more of a delight than a duty. Piety, which is a form of spiritual joy, was strong in her and her family: the desire always to go another mile in the service of God.

For Catholic boys also there was a return of the monastic school. At Downside, the Benedictines achieved a blend of religion and the public school ethos. The framework—like that of Anglican Winchester—was medieval, the teaching Catholic, the language and customs as peculiar to the place as those of Eton, Harrow or Winchester to those foundations. The Gregorians, as these boys were called, had as distinct a vocabulary as the Wykehamists.

Bread, for example was called 'tommy'; 'fish-pie' was not Friday's dinner but a wavering in the stomach caused by bad food, or more often by nerves: in Glynnese 'the bathing feel' in common speech 'butterflies in the stomach'. A 'bum-tolley' was, to quote Dom Hubert van Zeller, the historian of the school, 'an instrument of punishment made of leather and having a short wooden handle. Origin uncertain, derivation clear'. 'Popery' was not what Protestants mean by that word, but an omnibus or portmanteau for various kinds and expressions of piety: church-going, spiritual reading, objects of devotion; an English equivalent of *bondieuserie*.

Gregorians in mid-century, like their predecessors in 1820 when the school was founded, rose at half-past five and worked, fasting, until half past eight, when they had breakfast. At nine they heard Mass, then went back into school until dinner at one o'clock. School was resumed at three, supper was at seven, prayers and bed at half past eight. Silence was kept at meals except on Sunday. The meals were ample, and certain feasts were celebrated with 'punch nights' when the boys ate plum duff and drank rum punch, both unstinted, and kept up the celebration till midnight. At one special feast, in honour of the twelve best scholars, they drank a delectable white wine called Calcavella.

In other ways their life was austere. Hot water was unknown, and in the depth of winter the waking call of the prefect (one of the monks, not a senior boy) was often: 'No washing today, boys, everything frozen. *Benedicamus Domino!*'

At Stoneyhurst, the Jesuit rule was even more strict. When Arthur Conan Doyle went there in 1871 the curriculum was still medieval. There were seven classes or grades, making a progress of seven years of which the first two were spent at Hodden, the preparatory school. These grades were: elements, figures, rudiments, grammar, syntax, poetry, rhetoric. Conan Doyle was not unhappy in spite of the dullness of the teaching which, for all the medieval names, was merely 'the usual public school routine of Euclid, algebra and the classics, taught in the usual way which is calculated to leave a lasting abhorrence of those subjects'.

The food was Spartan: dry bread with milk-and-water for breakfast, meat for dinner, with pudding only twice a week, bread and beer (or swipes) at the afternoon break, hot milk, and bread and butter and potatoes for supper. It was not, however, stinted in quantity and it was not unwholesome and the boys throve on it.

Discipline was strict and surveillance unrelieved. 'The Jesuits have no trust in human nature and perhaps they are justified.' The masters taught the boys, superintended their prep., played with them or watched their play at recreation, and kept, in rotation, an unbroken night-watch in the dormitories.

Another pupil, himself a priest, Lord Petre found this supervision excessive; it held, to his mind, an element of espionage. He found at Stoneyhurst nothing of the easy relationship that could and sometimes did exist at other public schools between master and boys. 'Vigilance was Stoneyhurst's predominant characteristic.' He remembered waking in the night to see the gleam of the lantern carried by the prefect in charge of the dormitory.

Until the coming of the railway made travel easy, boys stayed at both Stoneyhurst and Downside for the Christmas holidays. The twelve days of feast were duly celebrated. Plays were acted, and at Downside the boys chose their King who in turn chose his Court. He was expected to provide his own robes, crown and throne and to entertain his subjects with banquets; in this way he might spend anything from a hundred to two hundred pounds. Then the railway train carried away all this medieval splendour: 'In the whistle of the engine was heard the voice of the syrens; the king, laying down his crown, followed in the wake of his departing suite'—thus Dom Hubert van Zeller.

It may be an accident of individual recollection but memories of Downside are mellower than those of Stoneyhurst. Lord Petre criticized not only the constant supervision, the lack of ease, but also the intellectual standards. Scholastic training was subservient to religious teaching. He admitted, however, the difficulty of balancing the two, and the importance of the latter: 'The object of all education, Catholic or non-Catholic . . . is to give the highest degree of training to the will. . . . Catholic education is necessarily engaged in the difficult problem of adjusting the natural and supernatural.' The moral and religious

teaching was more positive than at the great public schools:
'In our schools boys must live by the motive of the love of God
daily and hourly inculcated; in "public schools" they must be
content to adjust their conduct by what is honourable and manly
and gentlemanly.'

In some schools there was a positive development in religious
teaching; Dr. Moberly at Winchester was giving his boys more
than merely ethical guidance. In most of them, however, the
devotional and sacramental elements were lacking. There was a
distaste for clear-cut dogma, for piety which might become
emotional, a preference for the *mystique* of games rather than
any mystical devotion. Cricket was, on the whole, preferred to
Confession.

# XVIII

# THE POOR

## I

### THE DISREPUTABLE POOR

THE miseries of youth were not confined to the poor. The discipline of school could be formidable, but this passed in time and beyond these rigours lay freedom and luxury. For the youthful poor there was seldom any escape and worst of all was the lot of the disreputable whose guilt so often came from their misery. Mercifully there was a growing awareness of this evil. The public conscience was becoming sensitive and its goading produced reforms.

There was a touch of self-righteousness about the reformers with more than a hint of Puritan sternness. Young criminals must be rescued but also punished. It was realized that they might have been driven to crime by the appalling conditions of their life, but it was never believed that sin, public or private, was a disease of the mind, an interesting though regrettable form of self-expression.

Something must be done for 'the perishing and dangerous' class of juvenile offenders. How juvenile and how offending they were may be learned from various reports and pamphlets. One ten-year-old boy had eight convictions for stealing and each time had been sentenced to one month or two months in gaol, sometimes also to a whipping. Dickens's descriptions, after a little documentary evidence, begin to appear restrained.

The Factory Acts checked the exploitation of children, the Ragged Schools began the work of teaching and reformation. The Sisterhoods that sprang up in the Anglican Church after the Oxford Movement gave much of their energy and devotion to work among girls and young women, preventing as well as correcting evil. The redemption of the young criminal was

159

attempted by reformatory schools. These sound grim and they were grim, nor were they intended to be otherwise, though a measure of kindness was often recommended. Many of them were modelled on a famous French institution at Mettray, founded by Monsieur de Metz and others, where boys were put to field-work—'not to ensure them a comfortable condition but to prevent them from becoming more depraved. It was a great mistake to believe in the pleasantness of a life of labour', asserted the realistic Frenchman. The work was both corrective and preventive: 'The handling the spade spoils the fingers for the delicate operation of the pickpocket and the till-stealer.'

Neither at Mettray nor in the English institutions was there much formal teaching: 'For passing through a life of honest toil few of those acquirements which are usually though erroneously called education are absolutely necessary,' declared the Recorder of Birmingham in an open letter to Lord Brougham. Field-labour and handicrafts were more important than book-learning.

This was prevention. There was still the problem of punishment. One reformer, a clergyman, urged the separation from the hardened young criminal from the 'comparatively innocent'. In the former their guilt was 'the same as the man's in *kind*' and 'the place for them, by whatever name it is called, must be one of severe penal discipline'.

'Shew Thy pity upon all prisoners and captives.'

Perhaps with a remembrance of that liturgic pleading the cleric added: 'They are, indeed, to be treated, like every human being, with kindness, but here severity is kindness.' He found the name 'Reformatory School' too pleasant, for apparently even the most vicious youth liked school!

'Reading and writing are rather idolized than dreaded.' They were not half-wits, those young delinquents, and knew the value of reading and writing in forgery and other ways of crime.

Solitary confinement was sometimes urged as punishment, provided that 'the cell is not warmed and fitted up as comfortably as a fashionable boudoir, but gives the inmate just as much cold and privation and discomfort' as his health would stand and the

conscience of authority permit. Whipping was to be given only
for such offences as stealing, lying, desertion, trespassing, throw-
ing stones, indecency and insolence: a fairly inclusive list.

Constant supervision was necessary and the staff should be
large enough to provide a master for each small group of boys.
In some Continental reformatories they lived in separate houses
each under a guardian. The masters should be trained, and one
good psychologist added that they should have no physical
defect or oddity of speech or manner; he knew the tendency
even of the decentest boy to mock. At Mettray there was a
training school, almost a seminary, where young men of good
character and background were prepared for this mission work.

One school in London, under a Mr. Bowyer, had a good
record for reform and reclamation. There were some pitiful
cases: boys in their teens were already adept in 'dipping and
busting', that is, in picking pockets and in stealing bundles of
laundry. One lad of fifteen was head of a gang. He was the
dipper or actual pickpocket, while the others hustled the victim
and conveyed away the booty. When in prison, of which he had
fifteen terms, this gifted youth was greatly missed. His first
experience of the reformatory was a failure: 'The superintendents
never understood him. He generally managed to make them lose
their tempers and put themselves in the wrong'—a gift by no
means peculiar to criminals, and of all boyish talents the most
enraging. A second period was more successful. The boy was
well handled, and taught to turn his undoubted talents to respectable use as a carpenter. His force of character was deflected into
being a good influence on his companions. At the time of writing
the report, he was being prepared for baptism and confirmation.

Another was a 'sneaker', stealing goods exposed for sale outside a shop. Yet another, at sixteen, had been three times in
gaol which he regarded more as refuge than as captivity. He
used to sleep in doorways or under archways, or sometimes on
the door-mat of a room in a lodging-house, this last being a
favour conferred on him by some costermongers as payment
for carrying their baskets. Once he found a 'stunning' place:

the great iron roller in one of the parks. When brought to the reformatory he was so tattered that his rags hardly held together. This boy needed care and compassion more than correction, and before long he was trained as a smith, and in every way 'made good'.

Sometimes the work was entirely preventive, as in the case of a country boy who came to London, hoping to find good work and wages. He was directed to this institution by a decent workman, and lived there contentedly and blamelessly, while being trained in skilled labour.

## II

### THE RESPECTABLE POOR

The young and respectable poor went to the village school. The dame school had almost vanished, the dame being replaced by the schoolmaster, or more often the schoolmistress: the latter a superior young person who had some measure of professional training, usually as pupil teacher.

Until the Education Act of 1872 appointed School Boards of management, this village school was generally under the patronage and supervision of the squire and the vicar and their ladies. Tennyson exhorted Lady Clara Vere de Vere to teach the orphan boy to read and the orphan girl to sew instead of spending her time in breaking the hearts of unfortunate and un-coroneted young men, Charlotte Yonge's heroines performed this duty without bidding and sometimes with over-much enthusiasm.

A little book, *The Schoolmistress's Assistant*, published in 1852, aims at keeping both schoolmistress and pupils in their proper station. The three R's should be taught and thoroughly taught, but further than that secular book-learning was not important. The boys would be apprenticed to a craft or become farm labourers, the girls, most of them, go out to service. They must learn all the domestic duties, and be trained in every way, practical and moral, to be good servants. The one useful literary art for them was the writing of a good letter, correct in grammar and spelling, neat in hand-writing, for this would help them in applying for a post. They should also be trained in economics for they would be paid wages, as much as £6 a year at first, and must be taught how to lay out their money and how to save it. A warning against extravagance in dress was necessary.

'Which is the best? [sic]. A smart bonnet or a pair of good shoes? Is not a smart bonnet a foolish kind of thing for a plain person?' Not only was it foolish; it was unseemly. A maid should not try to follow her mistress or the young ladies in fashion. Cheap smartness in those days was tawdry. A maid's Sunday gown ought to be of good material to wear well, and plain enough to serve, in due course, as a working dress.

The patronage of the manor and vicarage was, on the whole, benevolent, and indeed the good squire and parson with their wives and daughters did more than has been realized to save England from revolution. Sometimes, however, there was a condescension that was hard to bear and which must have provoked comment at the fireside or in the inn. One issue of *The Monthly Packet* published a letter, signed Blanche Montgomery, from a patronizing young lady who seems almost too good to be true. As a satirical portrait, a spiritual granddaughter of Lady Catherine de Bourgh, she would do credit to Jane Austen, but nature can surpass art, and it is unlikely that one so scrupulous as Charlotte Yonge would invent a correspondent.

Mrs. Montgomery was newly married to the vicar of a church on the outskirts of a large town: a setting new to this daughter of the manor: 'My husband wished me to get acquainted with everybody and to use my influence with the young women of the middle class to raise their tone a little.' The young women did not wish to have their tone raised, and the poor of the parish were even less amenable:

'I am very fond of poor people, and whenever we were at home we used to go and see them a great deal; but then it was a nice, quiet little village all belonging to Papa and none but poor people'—but of the nicest kind, in neat cottages with 'such charming kitchens with sanded floors and shining oak dressers and meals tidily set out—a fine rout we made if all were not nicely kept. We called them all by their Christian names and scolded if the children were not at school, and as Mamma dressed them all they could not be smart.'

In her new parish the people could afford such trimmings of life as pleased them. One child in Sunday School refused to take 'a tawdry flower out of her hat' at Mrs. Montgomery's bidding. 'Please, Teacher, Father says it be to bide,' was her answer. It was an attitude new and unwelcome to the young lady.

Pretensions to gentility were further shown in the cult of 'the best room', furnished with 'trumpery ornaments' and 'cut paper in the grate'. And these people never said 'Ma'am'. The children in Sunday School addressed her as 'Teacher', and their parents said 'Mrs. Montgomery' in every sentence, which infuriated her. The prosperous townspeople were no less irritating: 'If I try to be very kind and friendly with the tradespeople's wives and daughters they put themselves quite on an equality with me' and the daughters had no interest in literature or any conversation beyond gossip. The only young woman who showed a proper sense of her place was the schoolmistress, 'a very good, humble young woman with no pretensions, and we are great friends. I believe she says "Ma'am"'.

This letter naturally evoked replies: one of dignified rebuke 'on behalf of the women of the lower middle class' who were hurt and bewildered by 'the undisguised contempt often entertained for us by the wives of our clergymen. . . . We can see that our girls, although sometimes well taught, lack the manners of high breeding. We are, however, willing and eager to be taught', but let the clergy-ladies reflect 'how little opportunity our young women have of learning what the society of high-bred people really is' and let them realize that 'the companionship of a true lady might do more than she herself would dare to dream towards preparing those frivolous girls to become unaffected women possessed of the true refinement of simplicity'.

Other correspondents begged Mrs. Montgomery to try to see

the point of view of those she criticized, and one added, rather cynically: 'There is no doubt something very attractive to a number of young ladies in the life of a clergyman's wife'—assuming ample means, leisure and the opportunity of interfering in other people's lives. They could, if devoid of tact, courtesy and charity do much harm. 'So long as clergymen will marry young ladies who can sing, decorate, and talk ecclesiastical nonsense,' so long would the Blanche Montgomeries continue to be a nuisance.

M

# XIX

## DRESS AND THE DRESSMAKER

FROM the forties to the sixties there was an increasing elaboration of fashion. Skirts spread and widened, were flounced and frilled, trimmed with ruching, puffs and knots of ribbon, and finally draped with overskirts in contrasting colour and material. The crinoline came as a measure of relief rather than of bondage, for its hoops gave the fashionable width more comfortably than the multitude of petticoats hitherto found necessary.

In the forties 'the Englishwoman . . . cultivated her feelings at the expense of her body. Physically she was less active than at any period in the century. . . . Her dress, therefore, was admirably designed for passive poses, and it was constructed to check anything approaching unladylike activity'. It was a romantic and a domestic decade, and the young lady wore muslins in delicate colours, or as the weather grew cold, soft cashmeres, poplins and merinos, with a cloak or mantle and a little bonnet for out-of-doors.

The crinoline came in the fifties, at first only for ladies, young or old, for it hardly seemed practical that mere persons could perform the duties of their station walking in a circumference of four or five yards. Such considerations, however, will never impede the descent of a fashion, and before the end of the decade it was said that 'your lady's maid must now have her crinoline and it has even become essential to factory girls'.

The other invention or discovery of the fifties was the sewing-machine. It came from America, and while it increased the speed of dressmaking it also made it more elaborate. Yards and yards of trimming could be added to a skirt already sufficiently elaborate. No doubt it helped the progress *de haut en bas,* for the 'little dressmaker' whose clients ranged from plain to lower middle class and even to young persons, could produce a copy of My Lady's new gown from one of the great houses. Elaboration was creeping upwards, and bodices were frilled and embroidered, trimmed with lace and ribbon, worn with fichus and collars, and with elaborate sleeves.

In the sixties colours became violent and there was a vogue for contrasts, rarely of the most happy. Skirts were enormously wide at the base, often with an overskirt; the female figure distinctly resembled a pyramid, spreading from a tiny hat, and comparatively plain bodice or jacket to that basic amplitude. The world was changing, especially for girls and women with the opening of new schools and colleges, but still the fashions proclaimed a sheltered leisure and wealthy way of life.

The young lady, of course, did not achieve the magnificence of her mamma either in style or in material; muslin and kindred delicate fabrics, soft silks, the adornment of ribbons and wreaths of fresh or artificial flowers with only a trinket or two, or simple parure of coral, turquoise or filigree, were finery enough for the most exalted girl, making her curtsy to the Queen, dancing at the grandest of balls, visiting a great house; but the very delicacy of her dress, the gossamer fineness, the dawnlike freshness imposed rules of labour on the young persons, who with admiration, envy, pleasure or weariness made those clouds of white and blue and pink into ball gowns and party dresses.

Dressmaking was above all the approved occupation for the superior young person. It ranked high above domestic service unless possibly that of the lady's maid, and it absorbed many whose education was insufficient for even the least exacting demands upon a governess.

It was, with other employments and industries, the subject of Parliamentary Reports, one in the forties, another in the sixties. In the former it was estimated that in London alone some fifteen thousand girls were apprenticed to dressmakers and milliners. As in the case of destitute children these documents both prove and exceed the description of contemporary novels. The picture with which Mrs. Gaskell opens her *Ruth* is accurate: Ruth and her fellow-apprentices sit all night, until four or five o'clock in the morning, to finish the dresses for a ball.

In London this went on through the season from April till July and again from October till Christmas, with an extra rush of work before a 'drawing-room' or a wedding, or family or national mourning. Short of being beaten with rods, fed on bread and water, and kept in a cell the girls in some dressmaking houses could not have suffered worse treatment had they been criminals.

One girl had to work from four o'clock on Thursday till ten o'clock on Sunday morning; another had not been allowed to change her dress for nine days, but had been made to sleep, or at least to lie down on a mattress on the floor of the workroom. At seventeen she was totally blind. In some houses they worked on Sunday; in others, the Sunday 'rest' brought its own evils. The principal might refuse her apprentice boarders a fire and dinner, and if they had no friends to visit they lay abed, too weary to seek the fresh air and exercise they needed, or else walked the streets, which often led to doing so in the most disastrous sense of the term.

Most of these girls were between fourteen and sixteen, a period at which even Victorian prudery admitted 'the most important change in the female constitution takes place', and their health, if not their character was ruined. Some of them died young, very few knew a healthy middle age. One doctor declared that no release and relief in later years could undo the harm of overwork, underfeeding and lack of sleep in youth. Of course they fainted at work, and of course they were tubercular. Some employers were compassionate and would have a girl nursed in illness, and spared the heaviest work when convalescent, but others would dismiss the weak and ailing. The plight of the workers was gradually if slowly recognized and pitied; what does not appear to have occurred even to the doctors was the infection of the the work they did. These exquisite ball-gowns must often have been a form of Nessus shirt to their wearers.

A twelve-hour day was not merely common, it was regarded as an ideal. A house was considered to be well conducted if the employees did not work beyond eleven o'clock. Many of the employers not bad of heart, deplored the long, overnight sittings and would willingly have adopted the twelve-hour day—if only it were made general and compulsory. One good lady professed herself 'most happy if any means could be devised to protect the young persons without interfering with the business'. Another blamed the ladies who demanded gowns at very short notice: 'If I refuse a lady she goes to my neighbour who takes her order, so I cannot refuse her without displeasing her and perhaps losing her custom because she thinks me disobliging.' Others, however, pointed out that it was not always practicable to make up even those orders which were given in good time: such delicate fabrics as tulle or tarlatan were spoiled by being made up and laid aside. These gowns were best sent home just in time to be worn.

The decent employers were shocked by the notion of neglecting their girls on Sunday. They 'thought it a very cruel thing if a dinner and a home were not provided on Sunday'. They escorted their girls to church, they held family prayers, and supervised their comings and goings: 'Unless it is known to what places the young persons are going, they are not allowed to be absent.' One unusually benevolent and outspoken lady, Madam Victoire, never kept her staff at work beyond ten o'clock, and declared that she would not put her own daughter to the business: 'No slavery is worse than that of a dressmaker's assistant in London.'

The doctors agreed. One of them said that 'it would be impossible for any animal to work so continuously with so little rest', and the Queen's own physician, Sir James Clark, said that he had long been anxious 'to see something done to rescue those unfortunate girls from the slavery to which they are subject'.

Something was done, in time, but that time was slow in coming, and it was not until the seventies that any 'considerable amelioration' was made. The second Report—of the sixties—shows little improvement on the conditions of the forties. There were some changes. Thanks to some benevolent great ladies hostels had been established for apprentices, dressmakers and others, and the system of 'living-in' was less common. Whether this was an advantage was debated. If a girl went to one of the hostels she was well cared for by a compassionate warden or matron; if not—she might drift into evil ways. Some employers prided themselves on keeping a respectable house and refused to open the door to anyone who came home at what seemed an unrespectable hour. This sounded virtuous—but what of the unhappy creature left on the pavement? It shocked one matron of a hostel. 'Let them dismiss her next morning if they please, but if they only knew how many falls are due to nothing more than missing a train or an omnibus' and so arriving late, the employers would be more merciful.

The conditions in some houses were appalling: girls slept in a crowded dormitory, and some 'have had to sleep with a woman of bad character and even suffering from a loathsome disease'. One social worker thought that given decent conditions the 'restraint and discipline' of the old way was good. 'Love of dress and dislike of restraint were the causes of most evils among young women.' Left to themselves they spent their evenings in 'those terrible places known as music-halls . . . just the places for young girls to be led away'. Even in the kindlier hostels there were lapses. One matron spoke regretfully of having to send away two girls who were 'receiving notes from gentlemen and making appointments to meet them. It might all be very innocent but for the sake of the others I was obliged to send them away. Those we dismissed were particularly pretty and well-mannered'. They would be; those gentlemen usually have good taste if deplorable morals.

One head of a house in Regent Street, Mr. Isaacs, burst into Hebraic wrath over the lack of morals in his young persons, even those who earned as much as £80 a year which should have kept any girl virtuous. 'Letters come, with coronets' and contained, one might be sure, no honourable proposals. 'Such things have but one meaning and commonly one ending. If they are known to dress beyond their means they had better go. Silk stockings and military boots are out of place here.'

Another male employer was positively virulent: 'They are all excessively foolish and ignorant and stupid, and careless beyond belief. Dressmakers seem to be so even beyond all other women.' As his wife was a dressmaker he should have known.

As for the girls themselves, when questioned, some of them admitted their utter exhaustion. At some jobs, such as pinning and tacking the ruches on a wide skirt, they had to stand all day at a board. Others liked the work: 'Everything is so pretty; it is such a pleasure to put one beautiful thing on after another, till the dress gets complete, that you forget to be tired. I should be quite done up in half the time if I were working on crape.'

Even in the best houses, however, conditions were poor. The rooms were often airless, either chilly or stuffy; meals, even when reasonably good, were eaten too hurriedly. The sedentary work meant loss of appetite; these girls lived on bread and butter and tea.

The background to the pageant of Victorian fashion is one of interwoven faults and follies: thoughtlessness on the part of clients, greed or anxiety on that of employers, and among the girls, a pitiful vanity, an emulation of the rich, which could lead to deadly peril. The temptation to yield to the fate commonly said to be worse than death need not have used such very luxurious baits. Merely to rest, to go into the country, to eat well, to have some pretty clothes, would be lure enough.

It is an old song now but a haunting one. We cannot look at Victorian fashion-prints especially those of girls in foaming skirts of tulle or tarlatan, ruched and garlanded and looped with flowers, without seeing behind that rosebud garden the shadows of others, less happy: creeping, beyond midnight, to bed, too weary to sleep, walking aimlessly through the London streets on a dreary Sunday afternoon, sometimes making an assignment and receiving one of those letters, and so going down an easy slope with none to guard their feet. The Victorian ballroom is haunted; the sad little shadows lurk even about Her Majesty's drawing-room.

*Part Three*

# Late Victorian

1870–1900

WINCHESTER COLLEGE

CHAMBER COURT AND MIDDLE GATE FROM CHAPEL ROOF     A COMMONER IN HIS TOYS

CHELTENHAM LADIES' COLLEGE: SOUTH QUADRANGLE, 1894

MISTRESSES AND GIRLS, IN THE 1890'S

# XX

## GIRLHOOD NEW AND OLD

### I

DURING the fifties and sixties the new day schools and boarding schools grew and flourished, the most famous, perhaps, being the North London and Cheltenham, but there were others in London, in Oxford, in Edinburgh, where a tiny St. Denis grew rapidly into vigorous adolescence.

Life did not change greatly for the daughters of the great families, but for clever girls of the middle class there was infinitely more opportunity. The pupil teachers still taught by day in the village or district school, and studied, afterwards, with the headmaster or mistress, then went for a term or two to one of the new training colleges. It was a hard way and their education was, almost invariably, narrow. That most eminent of school inspectors, Matthew Arnold, deplored the utter disproportion between the great amount of positive information and the low degree of mental culture and intelligence in those young people. The more fortunate might stay at school merely as pupils, until they were seventeen or eighteen, then go up for some professional training.

Still more fortunate and adventurous were the girls who went to college, as their brothers did, to study, at university level, their own chosen subjects. The new schools were, after all, a development rather than a revolution. The colleges were altogether a new world.

In 1869 a College for Women was opened at Hitchin some distance from Cambridge. Mrs. Manning was mistress with Emily Davies as secretary. The first student to apply was another Emily, a Miss Gibson, of whom Emily Davies reported: 'She is nearly eighteen, ladylike and intelligent,' and she proposed to read classics. Sixteen students entered in October, one of them being Louisa Lumsden, then aged twenty-nine.

It was a small place for so large a venture: the students had each a bed-sitting-room and they shared a lecture-hall, common-room and dining-room. The strictest decorum was observed; all the old conventions were respected for there must be no shadow of reproach, no whisper of scandal about those adventurous girls. Chaperons sat with them at lectures, for the lecturers were often masculine, being the more sympathetic scholars of Cambridge. But no conventions could irk those young pioneers delighting in a life so new and so ample. They used to waken with the thought: 'I have another day at college.' It was truly their *Dulce Domum*.

There were no games, but the students went for long walks, botanizing, and sometimes singing college songs as they walked. In the evenings they enjoyed the dissipation of cocoa-parties in their rooms.

Another college, founded in 1871, in a house in Cambridge, became known as Newnham. In Oxford, the first foundation for women was Lady Margaret Hall. Elizabeth Wordsworth was appointed Principal in 1878 and in 1879 went into residence, with a few students, in a house in Norham Gardens. The college buildings were finished that year, and she 'first slept in Lady Margaret Hall on the night of October 11, 1879'.

The Hall was named after that royal lady whose career was aply summed up by the Principal: 'Lady Margaret was a gentle-woman, a scholar and a saint, and after having been three times married she took a vow of celibacy. What more could be expected of any woman?' Lady Frederick Cavendish, visiting the new college in November, approved of what she saw but wished 'it didn't sound like a lady who has made a dowdy marriage.'

In the same year was founded Somerville College named after that most learned and most delightful of Scotswomen, Mary Somerville, mathematician and astronomer. Both foundations prospered, but Lady Margaret from the first had a tone and character of its own, derived from the vivid personality of its Principal.

The students were expected to be scholars and gentlewomen, whatever their views and prospects as to marriage or celibacy. (In one of her Sunday evening talks Miss Wordsworth said: 'My dear girls, there is one thing I hope you will never do, and that is be married in a registry office.') Miss Wordsworth was indubitably a scholar and a gentlewoman, even approaching saintliness in her devotion, and like most saints or near-saints she had a wholesome tincture of worldliness. She was excellent company and became a notable diner-out. With her full share of the Wordsworth brains she had also a sense of humour otherwise lacking in the family. In time she became an Oxford legend, almost rivalling Jowett, and there could be no better Head for a new college, especially a female one, than a 'character' just tinged with eccentricity. She loved good company, taking the adjective in more than the moral sense, and enjoyed not only the converse of the saints of Keble but that of 'the heretics of Balliol'. Her comments could be shattering, as when she told a don that Canon Liddon objected to women students because he was afraid of seeing the story of Ruth and Boaz enacted in Christ Church Quad.

She did not suffer fools gladly, still less bores, and appreciated the eccentric, even what by contemporary standards might seem improper. Of two sisters, one of whom took a First, the other a Third, she pronounced: 'I think B (the Third) is really cleverer than A (the First). Of course A knows all the proper things, but B knows the improper—I mean the unusual.' But she really meant the improper!

Of the Oxford of that first decade she wrote: 'These were the days of green serge gowns and Morris papers. . . . Every lady of true culture had an amber necklace, sleeves tight below the elbow and puffed above; any scrap of yellowed old lace she could lay her hands on to trim her dress' and make her look Pre-Raphaelite.

Among the dons was Walter Pater of Brasenose, living exquisitely with the aid of his adoring sisters; one of them, Clara, was a tutor at Somerville. The Paters were not of this world: 'It is simply impossible to imagine any of the Paters in a crowded

railway station or being jostled about or running to catch a bus.'
One cannot easily burn with a hard gem-like flame while running
after a bus.

Both Lady Margaret and Somerville arose under the aegis of
the Association for the Higher Education of Women, with the
help of such namely scholars as Bishop Stubbs, T. H. Green,
A. C. Bradley, Henry Nettleship, Sir Thomas Acland and Jowett,
and of such distinguished women as Mrs. Humphry Ward, Mrs.
Creighton, and Mrs. Talbot. Lady Margaret Hall was opened
by Bishop Mackarness, and the hymn: *The King of Love my
Shepherd is* was sung and became the Lady Margaret hymn. The
atmosphere was very fervent and inspiring but not very comfortable. The house was cold, the paint on the chairs so fresh
that it came off on the sitters' clothes, and there were only two
books in the library: a *Treatise of Science and Colour* and a copy of
*The Newcomes,* thus representing, if inadequately, science and
literature. Soon, however, books began to arrive: some presented
by the cousin college of Newnham at Cambridge, some by Mr.
Ruskin who sent his own works and a set of Maria Edgeworth's
Novels and Tales.

Lady Margaret Hall was Tractarian, 'a hot-bed of ritualism'
in the eyes of critics. The students not only went to church on
Sunday, they visited the infirmary in the afternoon and sang
hymns to the patients, with what effect it has not been recorded.
Occasionally they held an At Home for Oxford shopgirls, trying
to bridge the gulf between the young lady and the young person,
and before very long they had a settlement in Lambeth: the
beginning of a new form of social service.

Meanwhile Hitchin had moved to Girton with Emily Davies
as mistress and Newnham was also in its own college buildings.
The first Principal there was Anne Clough, with Mrs. Sidgwick
(born Balfour) as Vice-Principal. In 1878 London University
granted degrees to women, which so roused the Senatus of
Cambridge that they proceeded to grant a certificate from the
Vice-Chancellor to women who passed the Tripos.

Miss Clough was much respected and, in time, much loved. At

first she appeared a little remote, perhaps too much of the school-mistress, not realizing that her charges were young women, not schoolgirls. On her side she found 'many complications. The young people were feeling their freedom, and they wanted a little more'.

There was, however, much mutual goodwill, with more toler-ance on the part of the Principal than the girls quite realized. Their new freedom was delightful to those daughters of gentle-folk. The livelier spirits might feel repressed at times, but most of them were very serious: 'We were conscious of our privileges as members, however young and obscure, in a great forward movement'—so one of them, Sara Burstall, wrote in retrospect. 'Two things mattered intensely: first that we should do well in our work and justify the hopes of our founders; second that we should avoid giving offence.' To the *noblesse oblige* of gentle birth was added that of their new privilege and vocation.

One student at Newnham in 1880, Frances Gray, had known every type of Victorian education. She came from Dublin, where, up to the age of twelve, she had attended a day school kept by two ladies in a way already old-fashioned. They used *Mangnall's Questions* and *The Child's Guide to Knowledge,* and taught French from a book which 'claimed to furnish young students with a passport to the best society in France' and so included many card-terms. French literature was not read at all, and English only in elegant extracts chiefly from Thomson's *Seasons* and Dr. Watts' *Divine and Moral Songs.* Questions apart from Miss Mangnall's were not encouraged, being considered disrespectful.

They were, fortunately, encouraged at home where, for the next four years, Frances enjoyed a liberal education—as Frances Cobbe had done forty years earlier. She read widely, encouraged by her parents, and learned a great deal from them; she absorbed, besides, the living traditions of Ireland. Her father remembered the days before the Famine of 1847, and an old servant told her the enchanting tales of Irish legendry.

At sixteen she was sent to the new High School for Girls in

Plymouth which had been started by Dr. Temple, Bishop of Exeter, and formerly headmaster of Rugby. The building was barely finished; the staff wore aesthetic green serge gowns 'with tight bodices and trains which vigorously brushed the floor' where the dust lay thick.

In spite of the gaps in her formal education Frances made a name for herself. Having read *The Waverley Novels* all through, without skipping even a word of the introductions, she was able, from her knowledge of *The Pirate,* to answer a question about old Norse. Thereafter 'my encyclopaedic knowledge was a firmly held article of belief in the form'. Her Irish accent and idiom marked her, and she in turn was puzzled by the intrusive 'r' of Southern English: 'No Irish or Scottish ears can tolerate that intrusion.' For some time she heard one girl's name as 'Maria Rabbit', the real form being 'Maria(r) Abbot'.

This was a happy school, with plenty of hard work and some games: rowing, bathing, cricket in summer, and in winter walking. Hockey had not yet occurred. There was a good deal of freedom.

Frances was the first student to set foot in North (later Sidgwick) Hall, Newnham. She did literally set foot there, because the cement in the vestibule was not dry and held her imprint. Presently she was taken over to South Hall to meet Miss Clough and experience 'the comforting of all care that a tired child receives from its mother'. She was introduced to Mrs. Sidgwick and to Miss Helen Gladstone whose talk gave her some fascinating glimpses into political high life. They were all sitting together hemming dusters.

These great ladies brought their husbands and brothers to dinner at High Table, and Frances recalled A. J. Balfour and Henry Sidgwick, the latter at breakfast, quoting Milton as he stirred milk into his porridge.

In spite of her wide reading at home and intensive study at school she felt ill equipped for college, with small Latin and less Greek, but tuition prepared her to hear and enjoy the lectures of such scholars as Jenkinson and Archer Hind.

In 1881 the conditions of sitting the Tripos were laid down:
'Little Go' must be passed or an Honours Certificate in the Higher
Locals taken in both mathematics and languages. To Frances,
algebra was an 'impenetrable mystery' but somehow she came
through that jungle, and in due course passed the Classical Tripos
so well that she was appointed Classical Lecturer in Westfield
College, under the University of London. This was in 1883.
Eleven years later she followed Miss Lumsden to St. Andrews
where the elder lady was Head of the new school, St. Leonard's.
Frances was appointed to the junior school, St. Katharine's,
carrying the traditions of her youth into this new world, and intro-
ducing new ways of her own. She made the children learn crafts,
carpentry, bookbinding and basketwork—as well as their books.

'The ideal education for girls is that by the parents', that by
a good governess came second, and third and least desirable was
that of school. These views were expressed by Charlotte Yonge
in her essays on *Womenkind* which appeared in *The Monthly
Packet* in 1876. By this time Girton and Newnham were under
way. The North London Collegiate School and Cheltenham
Ladies College were out of their first youth, and Louisa Lumsden
after distinguishing herself in the Classical Tripos has gone to St.
Andrews to found her St. Leonard's on ultra-modern lines with
games and gymnastics as well as scholarly teaching. Charlotte
came to accept, if not with enthusiasm, the new ways for girls,
influenced, perhaps, by Miss Wordsworth, and in her latest
novels, the daughters of earlier heroines go to college.

Meanwhile home education by her standards was no superficial
thing. 'The lowest standard for a lady must include, besides
reading aloud, tolerable composition of a letter and arithmetic
enough for accounts, respectably grammatical language and
correct pronunciation.' On that foundation must be built 'facility
in understanding French, history enough not to confuse the
Romans with the Greeks, and some fuller knowledge of that of
England, with so much geography as to avoid preposterous
blunders, dexterity in needlework, and general information and
literature sufficient to know what people are talking about'.

N

The standard was domestic and social rather than professional but this was the absolute minimum. There must be, as well, the physical signs of breeding 'command of the limbs and figure', no slouching or lounging, a graceful walk and posture, the ability to enter a room or a carriage without awkwardness. (This was certainly taught in the old-fashioned school. At one establishment a carriage was kept in the courtyard for the young ladies' to practise getting in and out gracefully.)

Beyond the minimum, it was desirable for a lady to understand book-keeping, both for her household accounts and for those of the charitable clubs she was bound to assist. Music was to be cultivated not only as an art but as 'the readiest means by which a lady can assist in Divine Service'; the lady should also have a sound knowledge of the history of painting, and as much history and literature as possible.

Charlotte had no use for elegant extracts. Her girls were advised to read the classics of poetry, fiction, biography and travel. The writing of essays, biographical and historical, was much to be commended. All this could be achieved with the guidance of mother or governess, and there was, besides, the atmosphere of a cultured home with the heritage of gentle speech and manners.

All this Charlotte took for granted. She had a great deal of sympathy with the intellectual girl, and very little with the trifler, but she hardly realized the difficulties of those who grew up in homes of adequate comfort but of intellectual bleakness or narrowness. She knew the girls of her own class, she was benevolent towards those in the village; the clever ambitious daughters of the middle class she hardly knew at all.

She did realize the difficulties and frustration of the later years of girlhood when the discipline of the schoolroom ended. Many girls at home went on reading seriously, some of them acted governess to younger sisters and brothers, but some put away all but the most trivial books. The girl's period of mental stimulus might end just as her brother's began with his going to college. Until then, she might well have been ahead of him in learning; 'but he makes up on her when he has to be in earnest about study and she has not'. (Charlotte's young men were not among the idle set at college.)

The best strength for a girl was given by religion: 'The religious are those who order their lives by the rule of God's Law, and live as in His Sight.' Religion was no mere affair of the emotions or of aesthetic fancy; it meant obedience, submission, self-oblation and discipline.

While a little distrustful of schools, Charlotte thought the new Cambridge Local Examinations permissible, even useful for a scheme of work: 'As these are conducted in writing and are not competitive, they do not seem to involve anything unfeminine.'

Her fellow-novelist Miss Sewell contributed to *The Monthly Packet* an austere article on the modern girl: 'We shall never find ourselves surrounded by really sensible girls so long as mere glitter is accepted for real talent.' Miss Sewell was doubtful of the value of college education; she was even more sceptical about the possibility of a career in literature. Many girls had ambitions and a flow of words, but it was extremely doubtful if 'these young people have anything to say; and if, when they have said it, they can find anyone to publish it, and when they have published it, they can find anyone to read it'.

She proposed, as a better alternative, the reading and analysis of some profound book like Bacon's *Essays* or Whateley's *Evidences of Christianity* or the Duke of Argyll's *Reign of Law or Unity of Nature*. Précis-writing was an excellent training in clarity of expression.

'Very dry some will say . . . but I am not speaking of what is pleasant and exciting, but of what is desirable in the work of self-education'—so 'put the little tales or the pretty poetry aside. Write if you like, but do not rush into print'.

It was damping but sound advice. The girl at home was only too ready so to rush. Less damping and more effective would have been the encouragement to go up to Newnham or to Lady Margaret Hall.

The girl at home was, in the end, literally to be crowned. The only daughter of the Duchess of Teck who had been Princess Mary of Cambridge, was born at White Lodge in 1867. The girlhood of Princess 'May', the future Queen Mary of loved memory, was like that of any daughter of the manor: simple, devout, practical with a good deal of out-of-doors activity. From 1883 till 1885 the Tecks lived in Florence, and the young Princess made a profound study of art. In these years, and long past her twentieth birthday she read solidly and widely: the English, French, German and Italian classics, and much history. Games and sport made no appeal to her, though she loved walking. Her mother trained her in works of charity and she cared for people, for servants and tenants, for the poor or near-poor in the village, for all sorts and conditions beyond the royal circle.

The influence for good of the Victorian girl upon our throne and country has still to be fully valued, but what one majestic girl began, with such goodwill on her accession, was continued and perfected by another of much greater intellect and wider sympathy.

## II

Learning (in due measure) piety and charity were all part of ladyhood, and around these must lie the fragrance of refinement which was the feminine equivalent of chivalry. This meant a 'shrinking from all that is coarse, gross, sensual or connected with any form of vice or meanness', and it was a moral grace, not an affectation.

'Finery is the exaggeration of this quality. . . . As soon as self comes in, refinement becomes finery. . . . It is simply delicacy towards others and oneself . . . in fact, the outcome of purity of heart.'

As a moral grace it could, of course, be found in girls of the lower class, but in that sphere it was difficult to maintain. Lack of privacy, roughness of circumstance tended to foster 'an obtuseness to the requirements of decorum. A competence is almost needful for the fostering of true refinement'. This ideal imposed a strict rule: 'a sensitive reticence that will take any trouble rather than endure a soil; that will abstain from a book or a newspaper rather than learn details of impurity, and will bear fatigue rather than lounge publicly'.

Charlotte Yonge's regimen for girls was almost conventual, and her obedient readers would not have disgraced themselves in any *pensionnat* of the Ursulines or of The Sacred Heart.

Everything must be done under obedience, and not least, the works of charity. The parish clergyman was the supreme authority and director. Good works were now being more and more directed, and guilds and societies were bringing together those who could give and those who seemed to need help. The new colleges had their settlements or missions and the learned girls as well as the domestic were trained in a sense of sisterhood. The place of youth in the Church was recognized when, in 1874, Mrs. Tait, wife of the Archbishop of Canterbury, and some other ladies founded The Girls' Friendly Society: 'There are few who want friends more than the girls of our working classes. At the age when *our* girls are mostly safe in the shelter of happy homes, these others are sent out to earn their bread among strangers . . . carrying with them only the echoes of a scanty teaching, echoes that fade away into the distance as time goes on, leaving them sometimes at eighteen more ignorant than they were at eight.' The gulf still existed between the young lady and the young person, but friendliness, even when mixed with condescension, was building a bridge.

The Society consisted of Associates, ladies who must be members of the Church, and members who need not have been confirmed, though it was hoped that in due time they would be. 'No girl who has not borne a virtuous character' was to be admitted.

The G.F.S. acted as a benevolent and social club and as an employment agency. There were Homes where girls might stay between jobs, or when on holiday, and a Savings Bank provided for them when out of work. How wide the field was for this beneficence may be guessed from the number of domestic servants in London alone: altogether some 150,000 maids of whom 10,000 were aged between ten and fifteen.

The greatest work of all was done by the revived Religious Sisterhoods in the Church of England. The first to take vows and to found Communities were Lydia Sellon and Marian Hughes, and by 1860 there were at least five such Communities.

The Sisters of the Holy Cross went out nursing the poor in London: Miss Sellon's Society of the Most Holy Trinity sent eight Sisters to the Crimea with Florence Nightingale. The Community of St. Mary the Virgin at Wantage was a teaching Order with a school, and a training college for teachers. Miss Hughes' Community in Oxford, The Society of the Holy and Undivided Trinity, was active in both nursing and teaching, its object being 'to instruct and protect young girls, to visit the poor and ignorant, to nurse in hospitals or otherwise, and to pray for the preservation and increase of the true Faith and by acts of mercy and charity to testify to their love and obedience to Our Lord and Saviour Jesus Christ.'

The Sisters opened a day school 'for the object of affording a good and sound education to the daughters of college servants and small tradesmen'. They also kept an orphanage, and, at the other end of the scale, St. Michael's School for Young Ladies —who used to go to church wearing silk dresses and elegant bonnets and shawls, and who had the benefit of lectures from some of the most distinguished Oxford theologians. The convent kept four cows, and the orphans used to be seen, wearing pink frocks and Norman caps in summer and scarlet cloaks in winter, driving the cows to and from pasture in the meadows by the Cherwell.

There were other Communities—that of Saint John the Baptist at Clewer, that of Saint Margaret at East Grinstead. Some of them had penitentiaries and Homes of Mercy, most of them worked among the poor and tried to guard unprotected girls from evil. In the last quarter of the century religious vocation was a thing to be considered by devout girls.

Charlotte Yonge drew a lovely portrait of a Religious in

'Sister Constance' who appears in *Pillars of the House* and else-where; she herself was strongly attracted towards the life and became an Associate of the Community of Saint Mary the Virgin. She did not describe growth and fulfilment of vocation in any of her heroines—unless, imperfectly, in the wayward Angela Under-wood—but it was from such girls as her heroines, and the readers of *The Monthly Packet* that the first Anglican nuns were formed.

Most of them were ladies, delicately reared, who came from homes of comfort, refinement and ease to live the life of poverty, toil and obedience. How stern the novitiate must be was made clear in a series of articles in *The Monthly Packet*, in 1875, by Canon Littledale. These laid much stress on the virtues of obedience, adaptability and good sense, and none at all on senti-mental piety. The good nun must develop her intelligence, reading the classics of spirituality; she should be practical and above all have character.

'The ordinary young woman who is simply neutral and colour-less, who had neither general sensibility nor any special turn for any particular sort of work, is a snare to any community which admits her.'

No postulant should be admitted just after a bereavement or any emotional crisis. Good sense and good breeding were of great value. 'The first members of the new Society should all be ladies' for they were likely to be more tactful, more adaptable than the uncultivated. Good breeding was itself a form of dis-cipline, a sound preparation for holiness.

# XXI

# GALAXY OF GIRLS

## I

### *PIANO AND PEN*

'OUR governesses never stayed long and they pass before my mind's eye in dreary procession: some English, some German, some with dyspepsia, others with unfortunate natures, perhaps the same thing under different names; nearly always ugly and quite invariably without the faintest notion of making lessons pleasant or profitable.' These were the schoolroom memories of that most spirited of late Victorians, Dame Ethel Smyth. It cannot have been easy for the dyspeptic and dreary ladies. There were six Miss Smyths, all clever, all lively, all critical: 'I think the whole governess system monstrous and unworkable; even as a child I understood how impossible is the position of these poor, unwilling intruders in the family circle. . . . On the other hand, our governesses were specimens of humanity such as few families, however kind-hearted, could assimilate.'

None the less this girl learned to read, and learned all the history she knew from Mrs. Markham, 'till the day dawned for loving Shakespeare'. These two could 'defy the universe as quickeners of the historical sense in the young'. Mrs. Smyth had been educated in France and her daughters had French story-books, but when Ethel and her sister Mary went to school they found they had only a smattering of French and of other subjects. Their chief mental resources were Shakespeare and the Bible. School life was happy and Ethel's talent for music was developed; she sang in the choir, helped to drill the other girls, and was taken to hear Patti sing: a peak of experience. Another peak was reached at her confirmation in an awareness of grace received like 'the insweeping sea . . . that lifts and does not drown', an ecstasy that was to recur like the tides. 'We learned a good deal,'

she said of her school life, 'but I still think among the most
important things was being taught to darn stockings and how to
put clean linen back in drawers, that is at the bottom of the pile.'

Life at home, at Frimley near Farnborough, was a mixture of
country freedom and the discipline imposed by a military father,
Colonel Smyth. In retrospect the delights of freedom predomin-
ated. At the village shop 'kept by a true descendant of Mrs.
Poyser', Ethel bought penny whistles on which she played *Sir
Roger de Coverley* for her sisters', brothers' and her own dancing
on ice. They skated in winter, drove to picnics in a donkey-cart
in summer, went to parties and to parish concerts and penny
readings. The family contributed most of the programme: Papa
recited *The Raven* and *We Are Seven,* Ethel sang duets with Mary.
After a concert at Aldershot they had a very good Press: 'The
applause with which they were greeted was indescribable.' They
followed their coachman's advice to hold their heads up: 'It's
the hattitude as does it.'

Ethel was highly emotional, given to 'passions' and to poetry,
but already music was dominating every other interest, 'like
a *basso sostenuto*' through all the airs and variations of emotion
and aspirations 'such as marriage, travel, becoming a Roman
Catholic or even a nun'. The religious element never failed:
'After my confirmation I held, as I still do, that only one thing
matters, one's relation to God.'

More frivolous notes were sounded often and agreeably. She
loved parties and grandeurs and one ambition was 'to be made a
peeress in my own right because of music'. High-spirited, even
rebellious as she was, she had a profound sense of the grace of
courtesy, of ceremonial, even of convention as hieratic, a 'sur-
vival of respect for office'. When taken to a very grand party
at Wentworth she was impressed by her hostess's curtsying to
Lady Fitzwilliam as lady of the house.

Her girlhood at home did not lack variety: the marriage of
two elder sisters extended the field of country-house visiting, and
there was a very rich friendship with the Ewings: Mrs. Ewing,
the author of so many much-loved stories for children, and her

husband the major, who gave Ethel a much-valued stimulus in musical study and urged her having a career in music. He introduced her to the strange new genius of Wagner. Papa broke this friendship; he disliked musicians and all artists; but the stimulus endured, and the dream of a career became reality after a strenuous fight. Acts of rebellion included going up to town by herself, to hear Joachim play, and hear Brahms' *Liebeslieder* sung at the 'Saturday Pops'. This was in the 1870's and 'in those days no decent girl travelled alone; third class and omnibuses were unheard of in our world'—but they were the only way of hearing music. She used to borrow her fare from the village tradesmen and have it put down to Papa's account. After one concert she forced her way into the artistes' room to do homage to the singers, Fräulein Friedländer and Fräulein Redeker, who were kind and expansive and introduced her to a Bohemian world, at once delightful and shocking, in which one drank port out of egg-cups. At home Papa stormed, and Ethel began strike tactics by staying away from church and from parties, and none could say which was the more deplorable abstention. People talked, Papa capitulated, and in 1877, aged nineteen, the youngest Miss Smyth went to Leipzig, to that 'lingering bit of the dear old Germany of Heine and Goethe' and a world, splendid beyond her dreams, of music. It was all very proper although so adventurous: she went escorted by a brother-in-law, and lived under the strict care of a respectable lady, an aunt of Fräulein Friedländer. She was 'in deep disgrace but too madly happy to mind'.

Every detail of daily life was exciting: the food, the furniture, even the sanitary arrangements. Above all, this life of real music among real musicians was bliss. She worked extremely hard, practising the piano for five hours a day and taking classes in theory, composition and counterpoint; there were concerts, opera and theatre to attend, and presently the privilege of playing in an orchestra: in a performance of Bach's *St. Matthew Passion,* a high and holy privilege, a revelation of beauty beyond any yet discovered. She would have agreed with the description of that music as 'The Fifth Gospel'. There was no Wagner, yet, in Leipzig, but there was Brahms.

The chaperon was as prominent in Germany as in England, and it would have been most improper for her to go to concerts unattended; but once, when her hostess could not go, she disguised herself in one of that lady's gowns, padded to give a matronly contour, and a grey wig and a pair of spectacles. With knitting in her hands she sat at a table, ordered beer and a ham sandwich and in true German fashion listened to the music, happy and respectable. She loved the mingled homeliness and seriousness of the musical life. The German *Hausfrau* could literally pass from stove to piano. In the Röntgen home all the family played some instrument, the mother being the pianist. She would sometimes bid a daughter take her place, rush to the kitchen to begin or superintend the cooking of dinner and as soon as that was safely under way rush back to her instrument.

There was a wonderful holiday when her first friends, Fräulein Friedländer and Fräulein Redeker came back from England, and with them, and the aunt as chaperon, and a young Englishman called George Henschel, she went walking in the Thuringian Forest. They sang as they walked. 'Thrice in my life for a brief space I have been in Heaven and the first time was in Thuringia.' The things she most loved—music, freedom and friendship— were given her in abundance.

There were other friendships—passionate and ecstatic, with two women of the musical aristocracy of Leipzig: Lily Wachs, born Mendelssohn, and Elisabeth von Herzogenberg. This latter friendship filled even her emotional depths beyond capacity, and it was to end in grief and in separation when she was just over twenty. While it lasted it was ecstasy, and when it ended it left a wound that did not heal. A turbulent creature this young genius and gentlewoman of the seventies, she is the most dazzling proof that personality controls even a fixed pattern of life and behaviour, an exciting counterpart to any conception of the 'typical' Victorian girl.

She has some kinship with an Irish girl of the same decade, in whom there was the same love of country life, and especially of horses and hunting, and who was also born with great artistic gifts. Edith Oenone Somerville was also the daughter of a soldier and of precisely the same class as the Smyths. There was a difference in the Irish background, but the Ireland of the Protestant gentry was not far apart from that of the English; the religion was much the same for the church of the gentry was the Church of Ireland. There was the same love of sport, and this Irish girl recalled that 'I cannot remember a time when I had not a pony and a pencil'. She too was educated by governesses, though not inadequately, and had two terms at Alexandra College, Dublin, and a course of classes at the Kensington School of Art. She was gifted with both pen and pencil, the pencil coming first, the pen bringing her to the verge of genius.

This girl was little if anything of a rebel, in spite of the limits and conventions of her upbringing, partly because these were less strict for her than for Ethel Smyth, partly because the writer and the artist is less dependent on circumstances than the musician. As a writer she did not begin or develop by herself, but in a collaboration as close as was humanly possible between two separate and definite personalities, with her cousin Violet Martin. At Violet's birth, an eleventh daughter, one of the country folk remarked: 'I'm glad the misthress is well but I'm sorry for the other news.' The regret was not general and was unjustified.

Violet's youth was as full of dogs and books as her cousin's of horses and pencils, and between reading and drawing, riding and walking and discovery of the humours and intricacies of Irish life, these girls prepared themselves for the creation of *The Irish R.M.* and his friends, of *The Real Charlotte* and other immortals. Of Violet who died first, by many years, her cousin wrote that she was the embodiment of refinement, with 'an intellectual and mental refinement that rejected inevitably the phrase or sentiment that had a tinge of commonness; personal refinement in her dress' and physical refinement in the delicacy of her complexion, in her small hands and feet, and 'above all, the

refinement of sentiment'—to all of which was added a robust
and irrepressible humour.

These Irish girls had no need to rebel or to force their way
into a larger world than that of home. Like Jane Austen with
whom they have many affinities, they fulfilled themselves completely in the scenes and among the people they knew. They
had all they needed at hand.

II

*NO ORDINARY SCHOOLGIRL*

The North London Collegiate School was well established
when Molly Vivian entered in 1883. Four years earlier her mother
had told her: 'Your father is always anxious about you and afraid
of your becoming an ordinary schoolgirl with an ordinary schoolgirl's tricks and mannerisms'—on which Molly commented:
'What he meant by "ordinary" was the silly attempt to be
"extraordinary".... He wanted me to be as simple and straight-
forward as possible.'

Now this father of a singularly happy family was dead, and
Molly was offered the choice between staying at home, reading
with her mother and keeping up her French, and going to school
to be trained as a teacher. She chose the latter and went to Miss
Buss. On her first day at school she asked 'a little, white-haired
old woman, cap on head and dressed in black rather the worse for
the wear: "I say, am I going right for the Upper Fourth, do
you happen to know?" "Do you know who I am?" asked the
little old woman in awful tones. It was Miss Buss! "Oh, then
you are sure to know the way to the Upper Fourth."' This
imperturbable logic was irresistible. Miss Buss laughed and told
her the way. Molly perceived on this first encounter many
characteristics of her famous headmistress: her insignificance of
stature, like that of the most formidable ruler of all, the Queen,
her pomposity when she desired to impress, her essential kindness
and her 'instantaneous and delighted recognition of anyone who
was quite at ease with her'.

The keynote of the school was 'No nonsense here' and there was certainly no nonsense about dress, no affectation of gentility, no snobbery; the rules however were so numerous as to approach absurdity. 'One felt that if a girl were to knock over a blackboard by mistake there would be a rule about it next day.' Noise was a major sin; the girls had to sign a confession of faults and one of the most recurrent was: 'I spoke in class.' Others were —leaving a book at home, arriving wet at school, running downstairs, and walking more than three in a row. 'The iron discipline . . . made things easy for those in authority. Every moment, almost every movement was ordered.' At home, a time-table of preparation had to be filled in and signed by a parent; too much time given to any subject indicated lack of concentration and was reprimanded.

For an accumulation of confessions or 'signatures' there might be an imposition but there was more often a 'jaw' by the Head, and 'it needed Miss Buss to give a full content to the term'. There was no harshness or unkindness, but to a girl fresh from a free and happy home life, the tone was rigid. 'Marks were the life-blood of the school.' The teaching was sound and thorough, but too often dull: Shakespeare was read with footnotes which mattered more for examination than the text; French was learned from grammars and some dull reading, but rarely spoken. The old training of memory continued: some poetry had to be learned by heart for every day: a psalm on Monday, English verse on Tuesday, French on Wednesday, German on Thursday and Latin on Friday. Religious teaching was equally uninspiring. The girls were prepared for confirmation by an old, white-bearded cleric who made them repeat the catechism word for word, both question and answer, so that they found themselves addressing him: 'My good child, know this . . .'

The girl Molly saw the absurdities of the régime, the grown woman, herself a teacher, looking back recognized the difficulties: 'five hundred girls, all to be trained along Victorian lines of good behaviour' at a new and high intellectual level. It was essential that these new schools should be irreproachable.

Morals and decorum were strictly enjoined but there was a lack of the little graces and accomplishments, perhaps in reaction against the old futilities. The danger was in becoming 'a feeble imitation of what the boys were doing' without recognizing the difference between boys and girls and without the three essentials of masculine education: 'games, effective punishment and respectable learning'—respectable in the old sense of worthy of respect and honour. The standard of scholarship among these earnest women teachers was not high enough and they brought none of the tradition of ancient schools and colleges with them. The staff were, by this time, mostly 'old girls' imbued with the ethos of the school, and they were not encouraged to have outside interests.

On the other hand the freedom from snobbery was most wholesome. Poverty was no stigma, old clothes no disgrace provided they were immaculately clean and neat. There was a great deal of sense in practical matters—in regard to meals and dress. Domestic economy was taught, in theory, and Molly learned all about 'food stuffs' and 'carbohydrates' to the amusement of her mother, an excellent cook, who taught her 'to make a rice-pudding blindfold' and many another dish. There was no class in needlework but 'Miss Buss encouraged both plain sewing and Christianity by ordaining a Dorcas meeting once a month' when 'for two hours we sewed horribly coarse cotton of a dull biscuit colour and a queer smell' into garments for the long-suffering poor. The 'Dorcas' was not unpopular, for talking was allowed part of the time and for the rest an entertaining book was read aloud. Molly remembered *The Autocrat of the Breakfast Table*. Occasional lantern lectures on science and on travel helped to lighten school life. Miss Buss did not deliberately enforce dullness, she merely failed to perceive it. There were even theatricals and At Homes and the high lights of the year were Foundation Day and Prize Day. On one of these that most genial royal lady, the Duchess of Teck presented the prizes and was unanimously pronounced 'a dear'.

In spite of the rules this school time was happy and Molly

advanced rapidly into the Sixth where discipline relaxed and the
teaching was infinitely better. French was taught by a Frenchwoman, classics by 'a mental aristocrat', Miss Bryant, who was
to succeed Miss Buss as headmistress, and a certain amount of
discussion in class was permitted. Molly passed the Matriculation
and won a scholarship for the training college at Cambridge, in
1885, when she was eighteen. For this new life she was provided
with three new dresses: 'highum' for evenings and parties,
'tightum' for Sunday, and 'scrub' for every day: all of them
close-fitting, with many buttons and long skirts drawn back over
a 'crinolette', the survivor of the crinoline, 'a kind of gathering
up behind'.

The training college in Crofton Cottages was small but large
enough to give each student her own room which she could
furnish in part with her own possessions and curtains. Molly
hung hers with bright rose muslin. She enjoyed the dignity of
being 'Miss Vivian' and the variety of acquaintances. One girl
was an aesthete and free-thinker and 'dressed in dull green velvet',
another had had a mysterious romance and 'would play on the
piano and sing at any odd moment', a third professed herself a
Russian aristocrat and a vegetarian. Among such exotic types
the ordinary girl 'shone forth as original by her very common-
placeness'. The college being so tiny could allow a good deal
of freedom. The Principal, Miss Hughes, gave most fascinating
lectures on the hitherto unknown subjects of psychology, method,
hygiene and speech production. The students practised lecturing
on method to each other, with much mutual criticism. They
had few books and learned chiefly by listening and by discussion.
They were young, happy and adventurous, and teaching was still
too new a profession for women to have made a mould for them.
'The worst blight in the teaching profession is the woman who
can think and talk nothing but shop. . . . The disease was not so
rife in the eighties' and precautions were taken against it by for-
bidding 'shop' at meals and by inviting distinguished visitors to
talk to the girls. They were also taken to visit Newnham where
Molly fell in love with Miss Clough and met the brilliant Miss

Ramsay who had been First in the Classical Tripos and had inspired a cartoon in *Punch*. She was shown entering a railway carriage labelled: 'First Class: Ladies Only'.

There were parties in college; Miss Hughes gave coffee-parties, and Molly celebrated her nineteenth birthday with a feast of saffron buns and cream sent by her aunt in Cornwall; and once Miss Buss came to Cambridge and gave a ball for her 'old girls' and their brothers and masculine friends. She had warned them that Cambridge was 'a hot-bed of infidelity' but they were all, except the free-thinker in green velvet, very devout, going regularly to church, usually to King's College Chapel.

In 1886 Molly left college and went to her first post in a Yorkshire school where some of her pupils were nearly as old as her nineteen-year-old self. Her mother came with her and the last years of girlhood were peacefully busy, leading to the full happiness of her womanhood and marriage.

A near contemporary Janet Hogarth knew more of the old-fashioned domestic schoolroom before she entered college and the new ways. She was of the class for whom *The Monthly Packet* was written but did not altogether conform to type: 'It is a real disadvantage from the point of view of spiritual religion to be born a parson's daughter' as she was. Religion was thrust upon her, and its active form began, as soon as she entered her teens, with teaching a Sunday School class: 'I was never in my life so absolutely floored as I was when my Sunday School class of thirty or more little boys under seven quite got the upper hand of me and proceeded to sing and shout and generally disport themselves.' Between Sunday School, church and good books, Sunday was a weariness to the clerical young, and the worst quarrels invariably occurred that evening. Otherwise this childhood in a vicarage was happy though uneventful, with few parties or visits, and church decorating at Christmas, Easter and Harvest Thanksgiving a major excitement. They were a clever family and books were abundant. Janet and her sister had a governess and Janet went to school for a time and passed the Cambridge Local. Between seventeen and nineteen she read solidly at home,

o

studying languages and philosophy, taking a correspondence course and being coached in mathematics by an old Senior Wrangler. It was as thorough as domestic education could be, but 'I have often been sorry I did not spend more of my youth in the kitchen.... We had servants enough, though often very bad ones, to excuse us from cooking and housework' except a little dusting. The girls did plenty of sewing and 'a lot of useless fancywork'.

Part of her girlhood was spent in Lincoln. 'Never, I think, can any Cathedral city have contained such a crowd of dutiful daughters demurely dressed in bonnets with veils to the tips of their noses, as used to trip into the Cathedral, morning and evening, on Sundays and week-days'—carrying little muffs and looking very elegant in a subdued manner.

In 1884 Janet sat for Responsions and in 1885 went up to Lady Margaret Hall. Oxford was considered safer than Cambridge and Lady Margaret was impeccably High Church whereas Girton and Newnham were 'advanced'. At Lady Margaret and Somerville the students were 'shepherded by ladies of unexceptionable antecedents' which satisfied the conventions and did not greatly hamper the girls. College even with chaperons was a wide place after the confines of home. They might walk alone on the outskirts of the town but not in the High or in Broad Street, and they must always be accompanied to the Cathedral or to St. Mary's, and of course to an undergraduate's rooms. Janet was allowed to visit her brother unchaperoned, but had to enter by the Fellows' private gate.

It was permissible to go to parties in a bath-chair, the chairman being accepted as a proper substitute for a chaperon in a cab. There were balls at the men's colleges; at Magdalen Janet danced with the President and then with one of the tutors, William Courteney, whom she was to marry. Among her fellow-students was Gertrude Bell, 'a vivid, rather untidy, auburn-haired girl of seventeen who took our hearts by storm with her brilliant talk and her youthful confidence in herself and her belongings'. She would clinch any argument with the statement: 'Well you know, my father says . . .'

Another was Eleanor Jourdain, 'a psychological egoist, absorbed in her own mental and emotional processes'; a third Edith Langridge who became Mother Superior of the Sisters of the Epiphany in India, and who, like a good religious, 'did everything well and taught me to do my hair and put my frocks on better'.

From Oxford Janet went to teach at Cheltenham. Miss Beale, she found, had a wonderful insight into her pupils' minds. 'I think you have something to tell me,' she said to a child, beckoning her out from among six hundred others; and there was a fault to be confessed. From Cheltenham Janet moved to one of the new day schools in London, into a new world, a new atmosphere. Reviewing the course of nineteenth-century education for girls, she wrote afterwards that there were three periods: 'the elegant, the serious, the athletic . . . Elegance was declining even in the sixties, by the seventies it was moribund, by the eighties it was dead'. The era of Miss Buss and Miss Beale had been 'very serious indeed'; and then came the public school girl, to take the place of the young lady. Teaching had now become a profession. The curriculum of the new schools was wide; games were as important as at any public school. Most of the pupils looked forward to college and a career; the old, domestic graces faded into the background.

Much had been gained, but something lost. Janet found the girls in this high school undisciplined and unmannerly. On the other hand Church schools tended to be repressive and narrow. 'If I wanted to train a girl for normal home life, not merely as a recruit for the professions, I think I would still send her to a convent or else educate her at home. The public school girl has gained public spirit but has lost delicacy and charm; she has acquired a multitude of occupations but has forfeited the great gift of a spirit of leisure. There is something still to be said for the old ideal of home training and free access to a library; something also for the motherly influence of the convent's Mother Superior.' The staff of the new high schools had 'too much spinsterliness and even too much schoolgirlishness' than which nothing can be more tedious after eighteen.

This girl, educated in the old schoolroom and the new college, saw in her womanhood the high schools and the modern schoolgirl and mistress. She had something to do, also, with another career for girls, in the Civil Service. She became Superintendent of Women Clerks in the Bank of England. The typewriter had arrived and was one of the main instruments in the emancipation of young women. Typing was poorly paid, at 10s. to £1 a week, but the typist had an independence and leisure beyond that of most teachers, and certainly all dressmakers. It was almost a profession. If a girl chose to enter the Civil Service she went from school into a cramming establishment to learn typing, shorthand, book-keeping and other commercial subjects. She might earn only from £60 to £110 a year but she had security and professional status, and after all very few women earned much.

The business girl appeared as heroine, probably for the first time, in a novel, *The Carbridges,* by Mary Bramston, a contributor to the later *Monthly Packet.* It is a pleasant tale, presenting a type of family hardly yet known in fiction: that of a wealthy business man, living in a large and luxurious house on the outskirts of London. When the family fortunes fail, one of the daughters enters the firm as clerk. It could not have been contemplated if she had thought of seeking employment in any other house; but her career, begun in filial duty and guarded by paternal care, is shown as most admirable.

# XXII

# ROYAL YOUTH AND YOUTH OF
# LEADERS

DISCIPLINE ruled Victorian youth even at the most exalted level, and the young Prince Albert Victor and Prince George of Wales were not reared in softness. They did not know, certainly, the repression, harshness and parental antipathy that their father had suffered; that father was affectionate and benevolent, and their mother intensely loving and beloved. Their home life was happy, but their education was strict.

Lessons with their tutor Mr. Dalton began before breakfast and continued all morning; they rode in the afternoon and had more lessons in the evening. The Queen, their grandmother, would have liked them to go to Wellington as day boys, staying in a private house: 'I have a great fear of young and carefully-brought-up boys mixing with older boys and indeed with any boys in general for the mischief done by bad boys and the things they may hear and learn from them cannot be overrated. . . . Care should also be taken to prevent them merely from associating with some of the Aristocracy; good boys of whatever birth should equally be allowed to associate with them to prevent the early notions of pride and superiority of position which is detrimental to young Princes.'

Such notions were effectively prevented by the Princes' being sent into the Navy as cadets, in 1877, when Prince George was only twelve. The Queen was displeased: 'The very rough sort of life to which our boys are exposed on board ship is the very thing not calculated to make a refined and amiable Prince. . . . Will a nautical education not engender and encourage national prejudices and make them think their own country is superior to any other'—which indeed the future King did believe, with the full sympathy of his people. Naval discipline was harsh, and far from being relaxed in favour of royalty it was intensified by the attitude of the other cadets.

'It never did me any good to be a Prince, I can tell you,' King George asserted in later years. 'Many was the time I wished I hadn't been. It was a pretty tough place' with the others 'taking it out of us on the grounds that they'd never be able to do it later on'. Mr. Dalton was also on board to supervise their behaviour. They passed out in 1879 and were sent on a world cruise on the *Bacchante,* still with the industrious Mr. Dalton in attendance, who compiled two large and solemn tomes: *The Cruise of H.M.S. Bacchante.* He followed those classical historians who freely compose speeches for their heroes and made Prince George say in Athens: 'There was much to remind us of Aristophanes'—than which nothing could bear less verisimilitude to his probable remarks.

He was the livelier of the two, 'never addicted to reticence' in the phrase of his biographer, Harold Nicolson, and these years at sea enriched and enlivened his vocabulary. His naval training, as cadet, middy and lieutenant made the future King what he continued to be all his life. 'Not being an intellectual he was never variable' but was 'an integrated personality' at nineteen with the integrity that strengthened the throne in his good reign. He was affectionate, bound by strong ties to his family, he was lively and vigorous, disciplined and dutiful. When he was confirmed, at seventeen, the Queen bade Archbishop Tait point out to him and his brother 'their duty to their sovereign and grandmother as well as to their parents, and how responsible as Princes as well as youths their positions are'.

Even her highest hopes came short of the fulfilment this grandson showed in manhood and kingship.

After the first cruise there was a tour of Switzerland, to learn French. They stayed at Ouchy near Lausanne. It was not altogether gay, this life of Princes. 'Then we all took a good walk out by the cemetery and round by the town' is one entry in Prince George's Journal. Home again, he returned to the Navy as a midshipman, and cruised to Canada; then, as a sub-lieutenant he went to the Naval College at Greenwich, and to Dartmouth for a course in gunnery. He passed out with an excellent report and was lieutenant at the age of twenty; and so went along a royal way that was also one of duty and service.

It is probable that he would have acquitted himself well at school for he had the qualities that, according to Lord Baden-Powell, were the chief gifts of public school life: 'It supplies common sense, manners and guts even if it does not supply knowledge.' Robert Baden-Powell went to Charterhouse at thirteen and left it at nineteen to enter the Hussars. 'I was not a clever boy, nor, I regret to say, was I as industrious a boy as I ought to have been. According to the school reports I began fairly well in my conduct but deteriorated as time went on.'

His headmaster, Dr. Haig-Brown, took a less dismal view and reported himself satisfied; and in one activity young Baden-Powell showed both industry and talent—in amateur acting. The Head encouraged theatricals 'as a useful means of education for certain intellects' and this boy played many parts. He prepared himself for one, that of a plumber, by buying clothes from a working-man's tailor and abstaining slightly from ablutions; in this outfit he had the good fortune to meet and make friends with a pleasant young carpenter who took him home to tea and, unknowingly, coached him for a realistic performance.

He taught himself to draw; as a school subject it was an extra which his mother, the widow of a learned but poor cleric, could not afford. He was musical and played the violin in the school orchestra, the bugle in the cadet corps. Above all, he began scouting. In The Copse or woodland beyond the school playing-fields he played the trapper, creeping about, looking for 'sign', snaring an occasional rabbit, and keeping a sharp look-out for prowling enemies in the form of masters. These, fortunately, had the habit of looking on the ground and a boy on a tree was not observed. This unofficial part of his education gave a valuable training in observation and deduction—and so the Scout Movement was prepared in The Copse of Charterhouse.

At home in the holidays he shared the activities of six older brothers, in games and sport, in boat-building and sailing. They could not afford to buy a boat, so with their own hands they made one. At nineteen, in 1876, he passed into the Army. The news of his success was given him on a yachting holiday by 'the celebrated and handsome divine' Dr. Liddell, Dean of Christ Church and father of Alice who went into Wonderland.

School helped to form him and he was a happy if imperfect schoolboy; even at his least industrious, one imagines, more docile than that other great Victorian and leader, Winston Churchill, who at the age of twelve, went to Harrow and entered 'that inhospitable regions of examinations through which, for the next seven years I was destined to journey'. Had he been examined in history, poetry and essay-writing he would have done well, but the examiners preferred Latin and mathematics 'and their will prevailed'. In spite of his abstinence from Latin he was accepted by the headmaster, Welldon: 'It is very much to his credit.' He was placed at the bottom of the school where he lingered peacefully for a year, and with others of his rank was taught only English—to his immense delight and advantage. The Lower Fourth were not thought worthy of Latin and Greek, but 'I got into my bones the essential structure of the ordinary British sentences. . . . I am biased in favour of boys learning English . . . I would let the clever ones learn Latin as an honour and Greek as a treat. But the only thing I would whip them for is not knowing English'.

In his lowly position he achieved two distinctions: he won a prize for reciting twelve hundred lines of Macaulay's *Lays* without one mistake, and he passed the Army Preliminary Examination by virtue of his map-drawing.

Three of his four-and-a-half years at Harrow were then spent in the Army class, officially still in Lower School, actually working with boys of the Fifth and Sixth. With one of the latter he came to an arrangement profitable to both; this boy, a fine Latinist construed young Winston's Latin for him word by word; in return, Winston wrote his essays. The headmaster gave him the heavy privilege of special tuition, but no amount of teaching could lure him into Latinity and Greek. 'They told me how Mr. Gladstone read Homer for fun which I thought served him right.' Unhappily, a certain amount of Latin as of mathematics was necessary for Sandhurst. He compelled himself to learn enough of the latter in six months, to pass, and then sines, cosines and tangents 'passed away like the phantasmagoria of a fevered dream'. He entered Sandhurst in 1894.

'I was happy as a child. . . . I have been happier every year since I became a man. But the interlude of school was . . . a time of discomfort, restriction and purposeless monotony.'

The sternest discipline could not have crushed or repressed this dominant personality, and there were phases of happiness. Best of all experiences was his friendship with Jack Milbanke who, without being a scholar, had a poise and maturity that made him a good companion and sound influence. Then the Harrow songs were a joy: 'the greatest treasure that Harrow possesses. There is certainly nothing like them at Eton' which has only a Boating Song— 'poor sport and poorer poetry'. Most of the songs were Edward Bowen's, who also delighted the boys with a lecture on Waterloo. There were other lectures, one by Edward Whymper on climbing the Alps. Had such lectures been regular and frequent and the boys set to write a précis of them, 'Harrow would not have stultified itself by keeping me at the bottom of the school, and I should have had a much jollier time'.

The young Churchill was neither a scholar, in the academic way, nor a sport in the schoolboy's understanding of that word. Games bored him: 'I would rather have been apprenticed as a bricklayer's mate, or run errands as a messenger boy, or helped my father to dress the front windows of a grocer's shop. . . . I should have done it much better. Also I should have got to know my father which would have been a great joy to me.'

The long separation of sons from their fathers during their school years, the gulf between education and action seemed to him wrong and unnatural. This cadet of a ducal family, himself an aristocrat to the bone, and one of the great eighteenth-century mould, might in some ways have been happier in a middle-class household sharing the everyday life and interests of his parents.

Sandhurst was a new world. There was still discipline and there were still long hours of study, but there was a purpose in both, a vital interest in every aspect of military life. Games were not compulsory and there was plenty of scope otherwise. Riding was a joy. 'No one ever came to grief, except honourable grief, through riding horses. No hour of life is lost that is spent in the saddle.'

He was an adult now, and achieved his dearest desire, in comradeship with his father. The discipline of college was relieved by courtesy and an occasional tactful blindness. On one occasion Winston forgot to enter his name in the leave book before going out of bounds. Outside, he met his commander; and on his return found that that officer had himself written in his name in the book, and so given official leave for the outing.

There were, naturally, escapades, the largest being the organizing of a campaign against a campaign: a Purity stunt by a Mrs. Ormiston Chant against London music-halls. A group of Sandhurst cadets took part in a riot in the Empire when the crowd tore down the canvas screen supposed to separate the bar from that other path of vice, the promenade. There was a heartsatisfying row and young Winston made a speech in praise of freedom. Then the cadets caught the last train from Waterloo to Frimley, and there knocked up an innkeeper and obtained a conveyance, and so arrived at Sandhurst in time for morning parade.

His youth ended at his father's death—when he himself was in his twenty-first year—and in the same year he was gazetted to the Fourth Hussars and so began one of the careers of his manhood.

# XXIII

## THE HILL AND THE PLAIN: HARROW AND ETON

'IF a boy is fit mentally and physically to go to a public school . . . let him be sent to it as soon as possible, let him remain as long as he can . . . then he may absorb the *genius loci*.' The Harrovian of the 1870's, Horace Annesley Vachell, who wrote these words, himself went too late, so he thought. He was fifteen, and he left at seventeen for Sandhurst. Yet he absorbed the genius of The Hill and looked back on his schooldays with affection, translating his memories into one of the classic tales of school life, *The Hill*.

In his time there was not only a distinct school tone, but a definite tone in each house, and a strong house loyalty. There were Harrovian families—Hamiltons, Fortescues, Ansons, Vachells—just as there were families of Liberal or Conservative politics or High or Low Church traditions. The Harrovian father who was seduced by an Etonian wife into sending their sons to the school on the Plain instead of that on the Hill was regarded much as a Free Kirk Scot would be who let his family attend the Established Church.

The school had its own language: as 'teek' for arithmetic, 'teek-beak' for mathematics master, and the Fifth in its three divisions of third, second and first was called, progressively, Paradise, Paradise Lost, and Paradise Regained. Games were a cult although Dr. Butler, the headmaster, deplored their being so exalted. There was a high standard of cleanliness, maintained by a daily tub and change of linen. 'Good form rather than good manners' was inculcated and the boys had their own strict code. The political tone was Tory, and Disraeli was a school hero; so when Gladstone came to address the boys the Head thought it necessary to announce that: 'The Headmaster hopes that Harrovians will not forget that Mr. Gladstone is our guest.' This was resented by the Fifth: 'We shall behave like gentlemen, I hope, but I'm damned if I'll cheer the beast.' In the event 'the golden-tongued orator captivated us in five minutes'—whether or not his golden words were understood or remembered.

'What did I learn on the Hill? Precious little of scholarship though tiny seeds of that bloomed and blossomed later on.' Most of the boys shuffled through the classics. Cribs were freely used; the boys used to work in groups, each member preparing some thirteen lines of translation, then co-ordinating the results. Crib-bing was permissible, theft unpardonable, lying to save others from punishment was honourable. 'The ordinary boy is a-moral' but 'smutty talk was reckoned to be bad form'. In chapel the Head's sermons were good but not greatly appreciated; ritual had more appeal.

Twenty years on from his own schooldays Vachell made one of the boys in his novel express the school sentiment of honour.

'We're not sent here at enormous expense to learn only Latin and Greek. At Harrow and Eton one is licked into shape for the big things: diplomacy, politics, the services. One is taught manners.' He found the same ethos at Sandhurst. Cadets from Harrow and Eton brought their tone with them. Others, from Wellington and Cheltenham were many of them poor, and worked seriously; but the Hill and the Plain made Sandhurst.

Eton in the seventies was a happier place than Eton in the forties, and Gilbert Coleridge found himself more comfortable than his kinsman had done, thirty years earlier. It was still, perhaps even more a world by itself, with its own language, laws and values.

'The most remarkable day in a boy's life is that on which he goes to a public school'; a good preparatory school taught him something of what to expect but he must come prepared to learn more, much more, than book work, and to obey more than the official masters.

By this time there was very little bullying and a fag's duties were mainly culinary and useful: 'I take it that the man who can poach an egg without breaking it, is a more complete being

than the one who cannot.' It was all part of a liberal education.
'This slight grounding in the culinary art has been of great value
to Etonians in wild districts.'

The masters were awe-inspiring—'gods or tyrants'; the fag-
masters were even more important and Lower House boys
walked delicately as if on the eggs destined for poaching. The
penalty for wrong-doing was either a swishing or a *poena* in
lines, and the former was preferable, being quickly over: 'It
seems a pity that the rich should monopolize this element in
education'—which was not approved in State schools—for 'of
all methods of punishment that of compelling boys to write
out Georgics and the like was the most senseless that could possibly be devised', leading to bad handwriting and a distaste for
the classics.

To reach Upper School was to approach the zenith of worldly
grandeur; that prospect was the light which shone through the
encircling gloom of Lower School, leading onward and upward.
The very zenith, the ultimate peak of glory was to be elected to
'Pop', named from 'Popina' or cook-shop because it had been
instituted in a room above a 'sock-shop'. It was 'the most select
club in the world' with only twenty-eight members. 'Once
inside that charmed circle a man became a different being.'
Hardly less select was the Literary Society 'that inner brotherhood of learning which met in the Old Library and heard lectures
from the most eminent men of the day. Gladstone with his fine
and fiery presence made a tremendous impact: 'but I remember
wondering how it was possible one should not be able afterwards
to recall a single word of a discourse which, at the time, seemed
the most important communication ever vouchsafed to the world'
—so A. C. Benson, an Eton master wrote of it.

The Sixth appeared in majesty in chapel, entering in godlike
procession, followed by the choir and clergy as ordinary mortals.
Services were long and dull, relieved only by the heartiness of
the singing. Coleridge remembered a terrific rendering of Psalm
136, the choir chanting the verses, the school shouting the
refrain: 'For His mercy endureth for ever.' The service was

choral matins with an anthem and ante-Communion and a
sermon lasting at least half an hour. The Provost once, after
going on and on and on, began a new paragraph with the words:
'And now.' The school chose to take this as the ascription of
praise at the end, and rose joyfully to its collective feet. The
hint was taken:

> At the magic words 'And now'
> Runs a tremor through the hall,
> Joy awakes on every brow,
> Sleep is cast from all.

Few of the boys waited for Holy Communion, which did not
imply lack of devotion; many of them had received the Sacrament at the early Celebration in the parish church, and some
went to Clewer for High Mass. Canon Carter there was one of
the leaders in the Anglo-Catholic revival, and some of the boys
went to him for Confession. 'He would have been a bold person
who asked the Provost to confess him, and would have caused
the good man no little perturbation.'

Sunday afternoon brought 'Sunday Questions'—on Scripture
—but sometimes the boys went to Stoke Poges to read Gray's
*Elegy* in the churchyard of its setting, and to realize the *genius loci*
and a new serenity. 'For a short time Sunday Questions, dull
sermons and even cricket and the river would be forgotten, and
we strayed like wide-eyed children into the garden of the
immensities.'

It was in Coleridge's time that the Eton Mission was begun as
'a wholesome and sympathetic tie between the sons of the rich
and the poor of Hackney Wick.' The awakening of the public
conscience was beginning to be felt by the public schools as well
as by the girls' colleges and the domestic schoolroom.

The world of Eton, seen through the retrospective gaze of its
sons, appears a wider place than that of most schools; even more
than Harrow, perhaps, it prepared those sons for large destinies.
The high seriousness of Rugby was neither achieved nor desired,

the fastidious scholarship of Winchester possibly not quite equalled. More, much more was taught than the classics or any other book-lore, and much of it indirectly. The large amount of self-government, the freedom for self-development, for private reading, the following of the byways of scholarship all helped to prepare Etonians to enter the adult world with an ease which could become 'the Eton swagger' but which did give confidence and style, even *panache*. 'There are few things in conduct that an Etonian should have to learn after he leaves school.'

The perfect schoolboy should be a conformist, and one equally good at games and at the classics. Maurice Baring did not fulfil or try to fulfil that ideal, yet he was a perfectly, even blissfully happy schoolboy at Eton in the eighties: 'The surprise and relief at finding one was treated like a grown-up person . . . were inexpressibly great' after the fuss and uncertainty of a private school. The other boys carried on reasonable conversation instead of asking silly questions, and making fun of any information vouchsafed them. There was no bullying; fagging was, as Coleridge had found, merely a matter of making tea and toast and poaching eggs, and the masters, if outspoken, were without malice. 'Do you ever waken up in the middle of the night and think what a ghastly fool you are' was a question answered cheerfully in the affirmative.

Maurice was discovered by the French master Monsieur Hua (late tutor in French to the young Princes of Wales) really to know French. He had been taught from early childhood by an adored French governess, Chérie, and had been taken to France for a long holiday by his parents. The young Barings not only learned and read French, they spoke it, almost thought in it. Maurice, by one of those arrangements popular among schoolboys 'did' French exercises for his friends, one of whom in return 'did' the weekly Latin verses for the group, being adroit enough to vary their quality according to the capacity of each boy.

'There were two sorts of master at Eton, those who could keep order and those who couldn't'—and who suffered many things from that subtle fiend the boy. Those who could were reasonable, not tyrannical. The teaching was not always inspiring, but there was ample opportunity for reading and discovery. Punishment was in three degrees: a yellow ticket which had to be signed by the tutor and meant a written imposition; a white ticket which was reported to the headmaster and involved loss of leave for a week and a sort of remand: a second white ticket during that week meant a flogging. A certain amount of work was expected, but it was possible to evade overwork and extra classes by pleading a headache. 'Me Dame' in charge of the House (in that boarding system peculiar to Victorian Eton) was convinced, by the faintest hint, of an ailment 'and we sat in her sitting-room reading a novel till the crisis was over'. The tutor was no less careful of their fragile health; at the first of a cold they were packed off to bed and allowed to read bound volumes of the *Illustrated London News* and other delectable matter.

French was naturally Maurice's favourite subject; science was exciting; mathematics an obscurity. But even the darkest horrors of learning could not dim the radiance of his first summer half, said to be the happiest phase of Eton life, and proved to be all it should be: 'rows up to Surley every afternoon and ginger beer in the garden there, bathes in the evening at Cuckoo Weir, tea at Little Brown's'—with salmon and cucumber, or new peas, potatoes and asparagus, and raspberries and cream—and a reasonable amount of work. He remembered reading Greek and translating into Greek a particularly charming collection of short stories in English.

Privately he read an enormous amount of fiction, keeping a list of novels with his comments in red ink. *The Count of Monte Cristo* was pronounced a 'perfect book' and made him miss afternoon school, mercifully undetected. The list ranged from such classics as *Jane Eyre, Romola, Silas Marner, The Master of Ballantrae* and *The New Arabian Nights* through the novels of Marion Crawford (which he greatly admired) the thrillers of Wilkie Collins and of Rider Haggard, and some minor and now forgotten tales.

Certainly no boy can ever have been happier at Eton, and no writer has been more evocative in his description; for this boy it was only part of an intensely happy youth. He was the youngest but one of a large family, his elders brothers grown up and his elder sisters married by the time he went to Eton. His domestic world was one of tradition and culture; he had absorbed these riches from infancy. Leaves were spent in London, mostly at the house of one sister, going to the theatre with her and Chérie; one holiday was spent in Paris with much sightseeing and play-going. The two worlds, of home and of school, intersected. The headmaster used to invite him and his younger brother Hugo to breakfast, talk about public affairs, ask about their elder brothers. 'It was an excellent breakfast with lots of sausages.' Other masters also invited the boys, to their great pleasure, and A. C. Benson held poetry readings in his room, to which young poets might bring their work for criticism. Maurice was writing the libretto of an opera, for music by a friend, and produced a Fairies' Chorus which won tepid praise: 'I don't like those galloping metres but I see you have a good vocabulary.' He also wrote a novel, *Elvira,* of which the sole manuscript had to be destroyed when the author had measles, and a volume of poems privately printed. Benson was an immense stimulus, his own range of reading so wide, his opinions original, even heterodox.

Religion was taken calmly, and even before confirmation there was little teaching or preparation. 'I may say I had no religious instruction at school during all my school time, for which I have always been profoundly grateful.' At least it meant his having no doctrinal baggage, no burden of tradition to discard when he made his spiritual journey to Rome.

There was a good deal of music: organ lessons which he scamped probably because they were lessons; a musical society and a choir in which he sang at concerts. The boys sang Parry's setting of Swinburne's *Ode to Eton,* and the Captain of the Boats sang the solo in the *Eton Boating Song,* and the whole school joined in the *Carmen Etonense*—with no sense that Harrow might be their superior in this.

P

Maurice Baring had few scholastic ambitions, and so was all the more disposed to enjoy life as it came. In one of those few he was disappointed; he had hoped to get into the Boats, and he was admitted to Novice Eights. But during a trial he caught a crab so violently that he swamped the boat. Another, so great that he hardly dared cherish it, was fulfilled. He won the Prince Consort's Prize for French, after a stiff test in reading, translation and essay-writing. It was a moment of supreme, unforgettable happiness, shared by his family and by the beloved Chérie, and it lightened the shadow of family misfortunes (in the near failure of Baring Brothers) that might have darkened his last half. 'Nothing in after life could touch the rapture of the moment' of being told he had won the prize.

All the joys of Eton had to be captured and distilled in the last few days of the Christmas half, for it had been decided that in the New Year he would go to Germany to learn the language and begin preparing himself for the Diplomatic Service.

'Good-bye to the School Library' where he had read and written so much, discussed life and literature, and steeplechased over the tables. 'Good-bye to the playing-fields . . . good-bye to all the reaches of the river . . . to Windsor and Norman Tower' where his uncle, Sir Henry Ponsonby, Private Secretary to the Queen, had his home and which had been second home for Maurice. The last days passed, and he found himself in the train for London: 'I realized in that last fleeting glimpse of the trees, the river and the grey Castle all that Eton life had meant, and what it was in leaving Eton I was saying good-bye to.'

It had been a golden boyhood but the gold did not fade from the years that followed. He was still living in a world of ample privilege and he had an infinite capacity for enjoyment. At his christening the bad fairy must have been safely absent or entirely mollified. He went to Germany, to Hildesheim where he lived happily in a kind, academic household, studying German, learning the German way of life at its most delightful. It was still the Germany discovered by Ethel Smyth and Acton, though much more gay than anything that serious young man had known. In summer there were tours, to Dresden, Leipzig, Cologne and the Rhine, to Bayreuth to hear Wagner for the first time with a mind unbiased by any reports or discussion, best of all to Heidelberg which enchanted him. In Berlin he was enrolled as a student of the University. Back in England for Christmas he met Ethel Smyth and was caught into a lifelong friendship by her vitality, her talk, above all her music. He heard her Mass sung at the Albert Hall, and heard herself sing Brahms' and Schubert's songs, 'and I knew at once that I had opened a window on a new and marvellous province'.

Italian was an essential language, and he went to Florence for the marvellous revelation of an Italian spring. He learned easily; very soon he was reading *The Divine Comedy* and a great deal of Ariosto and Tasso and Leopardi. At the same time he continued to read omnivorously in French and English, and he wrote another novel, but burned the manuscript.

In literature and languages his capacity approached genius, but in arithmetic, that necessary evil for examination, he stayed in the depths of ignorance. Smalls and Little Go barred his way to Oxford and Cambridge respectively; the latter proved accessible by the simple process of leaving Little Go to be tackled later, and he spent a term at Trinity. It was a brief, happy and unorthodox phase of college life, without the fret and fever of examinations, and full of friendships and reading and endless talk. There were new authors to be discovered, Francis Thompson among them, new ideas to argue. He encountered a group of intellectuals, including Bertrand Russell, and was told he ought not to attend chapel 'as it was setting a bad example', Christianity being an exploded dogma. This assertion appeared to him jejune; already life, and inborn grace had shown him otherwise, although in years he was younger than many of his companions, and although he no longer practised formal religion or held the beliefs of his childhood. In his heart he knew that if ever he were to regain faith he would become a Catholic.

In his earliest twenties he went abroad again, to Italy and Germany; then home, to Oxford, briefly, where he met Hilaire

Belloc and encountered a dogmatic belief to offset the dogmatic unbelief of the Cambridge group. A spell of intensive work at a crammer's invested him with just enough arithmetic to pass into the Diplomatic Service, and he was admitted into the Foreign Office.

His college life belongs to the twenties rather than to the earlier decade of his life. Eton and Germany were his training ground up to the verge of full manhood. His youth was spent in three happy worlds: that of home, in London, at Membland in Devon, in a world of wealth and still more of beauty and kindness; that of Eton, remembered with such deep affection; and that of the old, lost Germany which no one has known who did not live before 1914.

This boyhood may be taken as the essence, the epitome of privileged youth in a golden age. He saw the Queen's Jubilee in the year he went to Eton, her Diamond Jubilee when he entered the Diplomatic Service, boyhood ended. His youth belongs to an England that seemed impregnable, to a world which, its inhabitants believed, would endure almost to the end of time.

# XXIV

## THE NOT VERY NAUGHTY NINETIES

THERE were still girls at home, passing from the schoolroom to the drawing-room which was quite as marked a progress as that from school to college; indeed to enter the schoolroom from the nursery was to begin a new life. This was the progress of Sybil Cuffe (later, Lady Sybil Lubbock) and her sister Joan who, at the age of eleven and thirteen respectively left their much-loved nurse for a governess, Miss Cutting—'Scutty'—who was to become hardly less beloved. She was kind, just, and reserved, three excellent qualities, and respected reserve in her pupils, making no attempt to invade their emotional life, and so, all the more readily winning their trust and affection.

Her teaching was excellent, especially in French and German; she had been educated in Germany and to her the language was that of her youth and that of poetry. French was 'the language of civilization'. She used to read French and German books, the French classics and German fairy-tales, aloud to her pupils as they rested on the backboard. History she made fascinating with much detail of the daily life of each period. This teaching was supplemented by classes and lectures; one class in geography was much liked because it was in the evening and meant late dinner and meeting celebrities. A course in English literature was even more stimulating for Sybil. The lecturer, Dr. Heath of London University, made his students write essays and was both critical and encouraging.

When Joan 'came out' Sybil alone in the schoolroom knew a considerable relaxation of rules and a closer intimacy with Scutty. She read solidly, and continued to attend classes: one in Italian at King's College, and one in drawing which gave her access to the Students' Room at the British Museum to copy illuminated

MSS. On the more frivolous side there was a dancing class where she learned the fashionable skirt-dancing in a long accordion-pleated dress.

There was a delightful holiday at Filey with some cousins where they all bathed from a machine, under the eye of the bathing-woman, and were dressed voluminously in blue serge suits trimmed with white braid. Mixed bathing was not permitted, a rope separating the masculine from the feminine part of the ocean. It was the simplest of holidays, with walking, fishing and games on the sand, and the happiest, marred only by the intrusion of an evangelical parson who held services on the beach. He held 'the entirely mistaken notion that young people enjoy informal religion with plenty of talk about St. Francis and the birds'. These particular young people were accustomed to Bible lessons and to church-going, 'but the right day for that was Sunday and the proper dress was Sunday clothes', not navy-blue serge and brown holland. 'To be caught unawares with bare legs and fishing nets, out in the open, seemed to us the grossest treachery.'

Another holiday in Belgium was more exciting though not more delightful. Belgium consisted of Brussels for sightseeing. Spa for the waters, and 'as a *bonne bouche* to finish with, the Ardennes for scenery'. Brussels was *en fête*, and Sybil, with *Villette* fresh in her mind was 'as astonished and more delighted than Lucy Snowe' and without that heroine's emotional complications. At the table d'hôte she sat by a benevolent old gentleman and was prepared to talk to him in her best French about Belgian art, like a *jeune fille bien elevée* when he shattered her by asking if she had brought her doll with her.

Spa was *en fête* too, with a battle of flowers and a race-meeting on Sunday, which at home would not have been permitted or even contemplated but which was entirely proper abroad. Paris, on the way home, was fascinating but too rich to be absorbed. For Sybil it was above all a place of literary associations and when she was taken to a café on the *Boule 'Miche'* she hoped to see the characters of *Trilby* in the flesh; but so well chosen was the café that it proved to be full of respectable bourgeois families, and as dull as any tea-shop at home.

One summer the two girls were left in London for a time, which they found delightful, for London out of season had the freedom of the countryside. Joan kept house and ordered meals in a matronly way; they painted their bedrooms, attended a swimming-club, and went cycling in the park. That vehicle of feminine emancipation, the safety bicycle, had arrived and been approved and did for girls and women what even the railway had not effected. Cycling was one of the great physical joys of the nineties; it extended enormously the range of activity, especially in the country. A group of girls could cycle—without other chaperonage—far beyond the scope of a walk, visit friends, explore the district; they were no longer dependent on a carriage. For those who could not afford carriages and horses it meant swift and easy transit. Joan and Sybil rode a good deal in the country. On one occasion Sybil and a girl cousin had a mishap to one of their bicycles; a young man came to the rescue, made the necessary repairs, then politely ecorted them to their own gate. Should they tell? Had they been indiscreet and would they be scolded? Candour won, and was rewarded. The mammas were amused.

'How pleasant, my dears, to be at the age when such incidents are beginning to occur.'

In spite of her cycling and other modern ways, it was a very serious young lady who was about to come out in society. Besides reading and learning, she had begun to write, and had contributed two articles to *The Nineteenth Century*: one on the question: 'Are Chaperons Necessary?' the other on: 'The Stage as a Profession for Women'. The mere discussion of such topics showed the advance of the age. The chaperon still functioned; majestic in satin or velvet, with tiara and 'dog-collar' she kept a benevolent or critical eye on her charge in the ballroom, awaited her return from each dance, was taken down to supper by someone of importance, was a source of authority, protection. help or interference according to her nature; but she was beginning to be criticized, her importance to be queried. The stage was becoming more and more part of correct society; no longer were the players rogues and vagabonds. There were theatrical families—like the Terrys and Kendals—of the highest reputation, and girls of irreproachable background like the Vanburghs were becoming professional actresses. Sybil was paid £5 for each article. She had printed them both herself, laboriously, on a dial machine. The typewriter had not yet been domesticated.

All the stress of authorship and overstudy, complicated by a brief phase of adolescent religious doubt, brought on an illness of sheer exhaustion. She was seventeen, and had hoped to be presented in the Diamond Jubilee year, but she was not well enough. Instead she was sent on a cycling tour of Holland with Scutty. This worked a complete cure and she came home happily ready for life in the great world.

'I *am* going to miss you so,' she told Scutty, who replied with wisdom and foresight: 'I don't think you *will* miss me very much. Your life is just beginning. But I shall miss you.'

The new life began with her presentation at Court; an occasion too formidable to be happy, one almost Chinese in its ritual. On a cold March day white chiffon with train and feathers was not the most comfortable and becoming costume, and before she entered the palace she must endure the slow drive down the Mall through an interested though friendly crowd. Just as Sybil entered the Throne Room the tired old Queen decided to leave: 'All I saw of her was the small round back in the opposite doorway'—and the Princess of Wales took her place.

'I still think the conditions of a girl's first season at the end of the last century were such as to daunt all but the most assured.' At balls and house-parties the young married women and the smart set generally made formidable critics and few girls could compete with them. Still, it was fun to go to parties and have new clothes: three new evening gowns all at once, a dust-coat in biscuit colour, a quantity of white blouses, and for a fancy-dress ball a china shepherdess costume in satin and brocade with powder and patches. It was a delightful ball and Sybil was exhilarated by overhearing a compliment and even more by drinking a glass of champagne: 'How much gayer the party seemed after drinking that little golden draught!' Gradually this serious young girl was learning to chatter a little. Women she found critical, men on the whole kinder to a shy young creature. Her father took her to a rather grand house-party. She felt rather grand herself with one new ball dress, another home-made, and a third altered for her from one of Joan's, but at tea she felt a little of a sparrow in her navy-blue travelling coat and skirt among the birds of paradise in the new, fashionable tea-gowns. Subsequently all went well. After dinner she helped to make bunches of artificial flowers for the *cotillon* at the ball which was to be given in the house. In the flow of work and chatter she found her exquisitely dressed and sophisticated fellow-girls become less formidable, even friendly; her own simple white frock had been well chosen, making her look young and harmless and no rival. For the ball she wore pale pink tulle over silk, had her hair waved and was allowed a light dusting of powder. She was very happy, danced every dance though not too often with any one partner, and at the end reflected: 'I even think I see how one does flirt, although I can't do it myself yet.' Some time later she accompanied her father to the South of France where he had been sent in convalescence. 'I have learned to flirt,' she reported. 'And really, considering how enchanting the voyage has been, I don't think I have behaved badly'—perhaps almost too well, for: 'I don't think I like it very much or that I shall ever do it well. It was almost impossible to be quite sincere and that makes me uncomfortable.'

Her maid, on this first visit, was deeply impressed: 'A very nice house, miss, I call it, and the housekeeper and her ladyship's maid most affable.' The servants' hall had its table of precedence, a duchess's maid ranking first, the housekeeper and butler presiding in majesty. 'We change for supper almost as you do, only her ladyship won't have low necks among the maids.' After supper, coffee and fruit were served in the housekeeper's room 'and a young man to wait on us, all as elegant as can be'.

There was godliness as well as grandeur in this house as in many another Victorian mansion. A Bible and a pamphlet on Foreign Missions lay on the writing-table in every bedroom. Sybil's own parents were among the well-doing and well-thinking section of the aristocracy. It was 'the Marcella period' influenced by the heroine of Mrs. Humphrey Ward's novel who was given to good works. The more serious girls helped in settlements and clubs in the East End. Mrs. Humphry Ward herself had started play centres for children, a charming flower from the root of Victorian philanthropy. These encouraged the natural gaiety of the young Cockneys; Sybil found them tough but happy and responsive and enjoyed teaching them traditional games and songs.

She tried to befriend some working girls, inviting them to tea and lending them books, with less success than the play with the children. There was still a gulf between the young lady and the young person; these girls did not talk the same language, could not read the same books as their young hostess. Utterly devoid of the culture she had absorbed since babyhood, they knew infinitely more than she did of the ways of life. A group of girls of her own sort was formed to attend lectures, hold discussions and write essays on the problems of the day and a variety of profound subjects. They were very far from naughty or even frivolous, some of these girls of the nineties; in spite of the bicycle and all the new freedom, Charlotte Yonge's heroines could still be found in the flesh.

If she did not become an accomplished flirt, Sybil did advance in worldly grace: 'I could now enter or leave a room, talk to any of the party, and even select my neighbour at meals without embarrassment.' The house-party was for girls coming out in society very much what college was for their brothers—a training in worldliness.

At the end of her girlhood Sybil became 'Lady Sybil' when her father succeeded to the title of Earl of Desart and to an estate in Ireland: the Ireland of *The Irish R.M.*, as she found to her delight.

Sybil's awareness of the unimportance of the débutante was shared by a contemporary: 'Girls indeed were an incident only at balls in those days' was the memory of Barbara Lister. 'It was the young married women who . . . carried all before them' and sometimes the chaperons. Her own mother, Lady Ribblesdale, 'did not spend a minute on the chaperons' bench. She was as much in request as her daughter' but sometimes she would tire, and depart early, leaving Barbara to the casual care of her father. He too would depart when it seemed good to him, leaving his daughter with 'half a crown and a latch-key' to bring herself home in a cab. This was no longer unthinkable; some lively but perfectly nice girls had been known to sit a dance out in a four-wheeler in the square, or to drive round the park in a hansom with a partner.

Barbara in her first season was watched by the loving, admiring and anxious eyes of her German governess 'Zellie', now transferred to the young Asquiths. In the earlier nineties she had taught Barbara in the schoolroom of the house in Manchester Square that knew the company of 'The Souls' in the drawing-room and dining-room downstairs. 'The lady Souls,' it occurred to Zellie, terrified by her own daring thought, 'were only a reincarnation of *Les Précieuses Ridicules*.' Yet they made a brilliant background to the schoolroom where she taught Barbara French and German so carefully, and left so much else untaught that Lady Ribblesdale sent her daughter to the classes of Monsieur Roche. These were conducted in French and included many things: History, Grammar, Literature, Mythology, Mathematics and the use of the globes. The pupils, all daughters of great families, came escorted by their governesses, and sat round a long table. After the lesson, Monsieur Roche used to fire off questions, and the girls fired back answers as correctly and as quickly as they could, the governesses in the background watching like trainers of race-horses. For a correct answer a poker chip was dropped into a box in front of each girl, and she who collected the greatest number was given a *présidence* or card of merit; the girl who at the end of term had most *présidences* was declared first in her class. The pace was terrific; formidable to Barbara and often mortifying to Zellie when her pupil 'also ran'.

In spite of this training Barbara's ignorance shocked her future uncle, Mr. Asquith; and a product of Girton, Miss Worthington was engaged to improve her education. The parting with Zellie was agony, and Barbara was rebellious—hating Miss Worthington, hating 'to have her feeble compositions called "papers"' and closing 'her mind stubbornly to Adam Smith' and Justin MacCarthy's history. Zellie's teaching helped her in the end: not the careful drilling in French and German syntax and in the recital of poems, but the spiritual influence of the governess's own quiet philosophy and that of the German hymns she had taught. Gradually the girl built for herself a stronghold of quietness, and knew something of 'the spirit of wisdom and understanding' and all the other gifts of the spirit invoked upon her at her confirmation.

She 'came out' in the brilliant world of the late nineties, the world of which she already had glimpses when her parents' house was full of guests, and when she was taken to stay at The Glen—the home of the Tennants, her mother's family, in Peeblesshire, and when she was bridesmaid to her aunt Margot Tennant at her wedding to Mr. Asquith. Like Sybil Cuffe she made her curtsy to the Prince and Princess of Wales, the old Queen having left the drawing-room. After the presentation her mother gave a tea-party for her to which ladies came in 'their tails and veils' from the drawing-room. Zellie looked on, and she sat very often with Barbara while she dressed for a ball, wishing again the things she had wished for her in the schoolroom: 'a sound knowledge of French and German syntax . . . and a good husband.' She was concentrating now on the second wish, and questioned Barbara about partners and *partis* and proposals.

This girlhood was lived gaily although under darkening skies.

The Boer War grew from a small cloud to a great storm; yet social life went on very much as usual, even when disasters came and defeat seemed near. The valiant old Queen who was not interested in defeat was to die before peace came; and the new century was to be five years old before Zellie's wish for her pupil was fulfilled and she saw Barbara happily married.

Another girl passed the boundary between the centuries in her youth—Susan Grosvenor who became Susan Buchan, later Lady Tweedsmuir. Her memories show little difference between the late nineties and the early nineteen hundreds although the tide of freedom was flowing in. She too found a ball not entirely blissful. A girl felt uncertain of herself, and the row of chaperons was formidable. House-parties too were something of an ordeal. Society was very adult, very sophisticated: 'a girl was expected to sit silently while her elders talked'—consoled by the brilliance of the talk, very often, and the beauty of the setting in some great house. In her recollection only the married women changed into the glamorous tea-gown; girls wore a 'best dress' and it was an era of best dresses as distinct from every day. For everyday wear in the country there were tweeds, heavy in weave and usually dull in colour, and the change in the afternoon was complete. Then of course there was the change to evening dress, and even the simplest outfit for a country-house visit would fill a large, domed trunk, to which were added hat-box, dressing-case and a bundle of rugs and umbrellas.

Susan, like Sybil, came under the influence of Mrs. Humphrey Ward. The Grosvenors were lent, for a time, a cottage on the Ward's country estate in Hertfordshire and there Susan and her sister met a host of men and women eminent in literature, scholarship and social work. The distinguished hostess 'worked all the time and was never interrupted while she was working', a devoted daughter acting as housekeeper and protector. Among the guests were Gertrude Bell, Vernon Lee, who was alarmingly brilliant and seemed to expect others to be equally so, and Elizabeth Robins, novelist and actress, 'the most vivid, even exotic person who ever came and stirred the air in our rather dull schoolroom'.

The schoolroom was ruled by a kind but uninspiring governess. 'I progressed somewhat in history and in English subjects, having a natural bent that way, but my arithmetic was non-existent, and in fact I never knew what the whole thing was about.' In London the girls attended lectures and classes, less happily than Sybil Cuffe, for they found it 'all very unrelated and un-coordinated. Looking back it seems to me that few people then grasped the importance of good teaching'.

The transition into the great world was all the more alarming though exciting. Society was still rigid 'with hard edges on which human beings can cut themselves' especially when young and shy. Sometimes the girl would 'thankfully have bartered the chance of enjoyment at a ball for a schoolroom supper and early bed and quiet time reading *Vanity Fair*'. Society was discipline as well as delight. 'We early learnt the useful lesson of just how kind or unkind people can be. All young people have to learn this lesson. Boys, and now girls have to learn it at school, but we had to learn it when we grew up.' On the whole people were kind rather than unkind, and it was a good world for the young; but it was still better for boys than for girls.

The dress of these girls coming from the schoolroom to the drawing-room and ballroom was still simple though pretty and graceful: white or pink or pale-blue tulle or silk or other delicate fabric for parties, the new modish coat and skirt in tweed or serge for day wear. The new activity of life for women was influencing fashion, although the long skirts, high neck-bands, full sleeves and general elaboration continued only slightly modified from the eighties. Paris still led the vogue but in one style England was pioneer—in the tailor-made. No one could cut and make a coat and skirt like an English tailor. Sometimes it was of fine cloth and trimmed with satin revers or with embroidery, but more and more it was becoming a severe though elegant dress, in tweed or serge, sometimes worn with a waistcoat, and nearly always with a plain shirt blouse and a mannish hat: a

Tyrolese or Homburg felt or a straw 'basher'. Collar and tie were worn, and a fashion article in one magazine of the period suggested a set of collar and cuffs as a most acceptable gift for any lady or grown-up girl. Sybil Cuffe admired her elder cousins in their new tailor-mades, and Edith Somerville adopted this costume when she left the schoolroom, and wore it with distinction.

Blouses were in vogue, of every type from the frilly and lacy to the shirt with collar and tie, and this enlarged a girl's wardrobe at little expense. Even the college student of moderate means need not be limited to Molly Vivian's three dresses, 'Highum', 'Tightum' and 'Scrub'. Perhaps the greatest change from previous decades was in the popularity of rougher woollen materials, that were warm and that wore well, and were suitable for travelling and walking and every kind of activity. For all that, simplicity came very slowly, and slowest of all were the discarding of layers of underwear, the shortening of skirts and lowering of collars. Even into the new century a tennis frock would be designed with a high neck, long sleeves and skirt only just clearing the ground; and a print of a tennis blouse in 1892 made a large concession by having a turn-down shirt collar, coming half-way up the throat but not starched or boned, and turn-back cuffs. What more could a girl ask?

In their serge frocks or tailor-made coats and skirts the more studious girls of the nineties went to high school and college. Life was real and earnest but still adventurous and not altogether without worldliness. In some of the schools the staff realized the fears of such critics as Molly Vivian and Janet Courtney in being spinsterish or schoolgirlish and addicted to 'shop'; but in others they were women of the world. Neither Miss Lumsden, the first headmistress of St. Leonards, nor Miss Dove, her assistant and successor, lacked this mellow worldliness; still less did Miss Sandys who was a notable personality. She 'dressed well, talked well, had perfect society manners, and a pretty taste in furniture, food and wine'. She also played bridge well, and was said to smoke during the holidays. Could feminine sophistication and daring go further within the bounds of perfect breeding?

A great woman of our own day—Lady Rhondda who (as Margaret Haig Thomas) was one of her pupils—remembered her with gratitude for her integrity, her wisdom, her kindness. Her rules must be kept but they were few. 'We were never children to her, always people.' There was no coddling; games were played with increasing skill and there was plenty of fresh air. Minor ailments like colds were not encouraged and did not persist, once a guileless matron had discovered the unwisdom of sending the patient to bed with a posset of hot blackcurrant tea. Miss Sandys herself had 'the three necessary attributes of happiness: courage, self-discipline and unselfishness', and tried to inculcate them in her girls.

St. Leonards was very much a public school for girls, with the cult of games, with an ethos of wholesome morality tinged with Victorian reticence—'we did not discuss sex and religion'— a truly Victorian and public-school coupling, and with Sunday discipline. The girls read approved books in the afternoon for an hour known as 'Stale' but by no means boring or unpopular. Novels were allowed. One of this girl's favourite authors was Anthony Hope whom she compared in an essay with Shakespeare. The English mistress was not impressed.

St. Leonards was fortunate in its setting in that old grey city by the sea, and there were memories of walking round the play-ground on a winter night, wrapped in the hooded cloak that was part of the uniform, with the tang of the sea in one's nostrils and the sight of the ruined Cathedral walls in one's eyes.

Margaret was a happy schoolgirl and a somewhat reluctant débutante.

'Already the shades of the drawing-room were beginning to close around me', and she went home for her first season 'to be a young lady' for 'in those days a young lady *was* a young lady'. It might serve as title for a period piece. 'It was a long time before I was so happy again as I had been at school'— certainly not when she went to college, to Somerville, at twenty-one. Perhaps the interlude of social life had jarred the rhythm; she was a little too old for a resumption of community life, and she found less, not more, freedom at college than at school. Somerville was dowdy, St. Leonards, with all its discipline and austerity, was beautiful.

In the south, St. Leonards had a counterpart at Roedean, founded in 1885 by three sisters, the Misses Penelope, Millicent and Dorothy Laurence. By the late nineties it had grown to be a great school, in four houses, each with its regent and separate staff, and even more of the cult of games and the public school atmosphere than its northern sister. World affairs were part of the teaching, and it was as near as possible a feminine Eton.

The cult of games was taken also to Wycombe Abbey, founded by Miss Dove who left St. Leonards for that, her own school. In 1898 she contributed a chapter on 'Cultivation of the Body' to a volume, *Work and Play in Girls' Schools* edited by Miss Beale.

'We do not desire girls to be brainless athletes any more than we wish that they should be delicate or stunted blue-stockings'— and games were not played merely for fun. 'The mind must receive much of its training through the exercise of faculties other than the intellectual' and games taught self-control, self-discipline, the team-spirit, loyalty.

'I think I do not speak too strongly when I say that games . . . are essential to a healthy existence, and that most of the qualities if not all that conduce to the supremacy of our country in so many quarters of the globe' (but can there be more than four quarters?) 'are fostered if not solely developed by means of games.' The far-flung bounds of Empire radiated from the playing-fields and the *memsahib* was bred at Wycombe Abbey.

Miss Dove did not encourage intellectual forcing; three to four hours' study were enough up to the age of fourteen, after that, five hours with six as maximum. Nor did she advocate austerity. The school itself must be spacious and comfortable, beautiful if possible in setting; the food generous.

Miss Beale herself contributed more than one chapter to this

Q

volume: one on history, her own favourite subject: 'History and biography show the Divine Government adapting itself, so to speak, to the necessities of man ... History corrects the judgment of the world . . . reverses the pernicious teaching which puts before the young success as the main object of life. . . . The heroes of history are those who endured hardness and lived and died for others. . . . The villains are those who lived for self in ease and splendour.'

Her own ideas had grown enlarged and she urged the teaching of political economy. Girls, unlike boys, could not hope to become lawgivers but they should be trained in citizenship and public morality: 'A selfish, wasteful citizen is a disgrace, a sort of moral caterpillar.'

Miss Alice Anderson wrote about the teaching of modern history, recommending historical novels. 'Nothing makes history more real.' Scott's came first, Charlotte Yonge's a close second, and then a host of others: Emma Marshall, Anne Manning, Sarah Tytler, Edna Lyall and Conan Doyle and A. E. W. Mason, though not for Sherlock Holmes or Hanaud.

Miss Beale wrote also about philosophy which she would have liked to see taught in schools: 'The school is the link between infancy and mature life, between the home and the world, the secular and the spiritual.' Girls must be prepared for life, taught to 'know the truth, feel nobly and hence act rightly'. There is an echo of Dr. Arnold here, as there is of Old Brooke in Miss Dove.

School was now the norm, and it was necessary to link school life and home life so that the discipline of one might not be lost by the ease of the other. There must be relaxation at home, in the holidays, but it should not be an utter abandonment: there should still be fixed hours for study and serious reading, and parties, theatricals and bazaars should be allowed only in moderation. The bazaar was still a worldly gaiety!

The new headmistresses were encouraging new ways; some of them in study, others in games, all or nearly all in dress. Simplicity was an ideal; high heels, tight lacing, all extremes of fashion were deprecated when they were not actually forbidden. Realism was creeping in. Refinement of mind, reticence and decorum were still admired and inculcated, but delicacy of body was deplored, cured if possible, while affected delicacy was discouraged. We are a long way from Miss Pinkerton's Academy.

# EPILOGUE

*I saw the new moon late yestreen*
*Wi' the auld moon in her arms.*

THE new century which was to bring more than its share of changes and chances carried the old in its arms for at least a decade. The Victorian security lasted through King Edward's reign, the gaiety of the nineties continued, the comfort and sweetness of life pervaded an increasing portion of society.

In the world of youth there was a gradual amelioration as there had been since the middle of the old century. For boys there was still the way of their fathers at school and college; masculine values did not greatly alter. The public school at the end of the reign of Queen Victoria was a better place than it had been at her accession, but the spirit so largely influenced by Dr. Arnold, endured. In two classic tales of school life, one describing the 1830's, the other the 1890's, there is far more likeness than contrast.

One of the high lights of *Tom Brown's Schooldays* is Tom's first rugby match. The climax of H. A. Vachell's *The Hill* is the Eton and Harrow match at Lord's, played in the serene and splendid afternoon of the Victorian aristrocracy. In both, loyalty to school, even to house, is intense. The emotional height of *Tom Brown* is reached in the last chapter when Tom, kneeling in chapel, recalls his beloved headmaster; that of *The Hill* is in the letter which John Verney receives from his friend and hero Desmond, fighting in the Boer War. Desmond writes on the eve of the battle of Spion Kop where he is killed.

'The sight of the Hill brings back our Hill. . . . I have the absurd conviction . . . that tomorrow I shall get up the hill faster and easier than the other fellows because you and I have so often run up our Hill together.'

The loyalty has deepened into self-oblation, the public-school spirit has developed a heroism without heroics. The emotional

233

Englishman who flourished up to the beginning of the Queen's reign has given place to the laconic master of understatement, to the hero who will go down to the river of death as if to row for his school, and enter the last conflict as if it were a school match. This schoolboy lived until 1914 when he died in his thousands on the plains of France and in Gallipoli and on the bitter North Sea.

As for his sister—her world had known a peaceful revolution, begun in the schools, continued in the colleges, in offices, even in surgeries. There were still some headmistresses and heads of colleges who had been bred in the old domestic ways, but the modern woman, product of a high school and of Girton or Newnham, Lady Margaret Hall or Somerville, was more and more guiding and educating the girls who were young in the last years of the old century. For over thirty years, now, since the valiant combat fought by Elizabeth Blackwell, Elizabeth Garrett and Sophia Jex-Blake it had been possible for women to qualify and practise as doctors.

At the beginning of the new century Anne Thackeray Ritchie, that most charming of Victorians, born in the year of the Queen's crowning, visited St. Andrews and was captivated by the spell of the past and the brightness of the present: 'All day long the University lads and lasses, in their quaint red gowns and trencher caps, are flitting on their way to and from the Professors' lectures.'

In the other three university cities of Scotland, Glasgow, Aberdeen and Edinburgh, girls of the new century were wearing the scarlet gown of the undergraduate and would soon exchange it for the black gown and coloured hood of the graduate. In Glasgow, Queen Margaret College had received her students since 1883, and since 1894 they had been taking their degrees in medicine, arts and science.

Many doors were open for them now, and the way of new freedom branched out into many ways of new service. In that dawn many found it bliss to be alive, and to be young and a girl, very heaven.

# BIBLIOGRAPHY

*Prologue*

*The Training of a Sovereign,* by Lord Esher (John Murray).

*The Grveille Memoirs* (Longmans).

PART I—*Early Victorian*

*Life of Frances Power Cobbe,* by Herself (Allen & Unwin).

*Memories of Ninety Years,* by Mrs. E. M. Ward, edited by Isabel McAllister (Hutchinson).

*Diary of Lady Frederick Cavendish,* edited by John Bailey (John Murray).

*Charlotte Mary Yonge: Life and Letters,* by Christabel Coleridge (Macmillan).

*Charlotte Mary Yonge,* by Ethel Romanes (Mowbray).

*Charlotte Mary Yonge,* by Georgiana Battiscombe (Constable).

*Victorian Best-Seller,* by Margaret Mare and Alicia Percival (Harrap).

*Tom Brown's Schooldays, Tom Brown at Oxford* and *Memoir of A Brother,* by Thomas Hughes (Macmillan).

*Eton in the Forties,* by an Old Colleger (Arthur Duke Coleridge); (Bentley).

*What I Remember,* by Thomas Adolphus Trollope (Bentley).

*Memories of Two Cities,* by David Masson (Oliphant, Anderson & Ferrier).

*Winchester College 1393–1893* (Edward Arnold).

*Memoir of Anne Jemima Clough,* by Blanche Clough (Edward Arnold).

*Frances Mary Buss,* by Sara Burstall (S.P.C.K.).

*Frances Mary Buss,* by Annie Ridley (Longmans).

*Dorothea Beale,* by Elizabeth Shillito (S.P.C.K.).

*Emily Davies and Girton College,* by Barbara Stephens (Constable).

PART II—*Mid-Victorian*

The Novels of Charlotte Yonge (Macmillan).

*The Monthly Packet.*

*Glimpses of the Past,* by Elizabeth Wordsworth (Mowbray).

*Yellow Leaves,* by Louisa Lumsden (Blackwood).

*North London Collegiate School 1850–1950* (Oxford University Press).

*Mary Gladstone: Her Diaries and Letters,* edited by Lucy Masterman (Methuen).

*From Friend to Friend,* by Anne Thackeray Ritchie (John Murray).

*Recollections of a Scottish Novelist,* by L. B. Walford (Williams & Norgate).

*Dulce Domum,* by C. A. E. Moberly (John Murray).

*The English Miss Today and Yesterday,* by Alicia Percival (Harrap).

*Victorian Working Women,* by Wanda Fraiken Neff (Allen & Unwin).

*Pages From the Diary of an Oxford Lady* (Mrs. Jeune), edited by Margaret Jeune Gifford (Basil Blackwell).

*My Way of Faith,* by Maude Petre (Dent).

*Directions for Novices of the Ursuline Order* (Burns, Oates & Washbourne).

*Early Reminiscences,* by Sabine Baring Gould (John Lane).

*The Story of My Life,* by Augustus Hare (George Allen).

*Memorials of Edward Burne-Jones,* by Lady Burne-Jones (Macmillan).

*William Morris,* by J. W. Mackail (Longmans).

*Robert Louis Stevenson,* by Graham Balfour (Methuen).

*Robert Louis Stevenson,* by J. A. Steuart (Sampson Low).

*Memories and Portraits,* by Robert Louis Stevenson.

*The Man Who Made a School: Thring of Uppingham,* by Geoffrey Hoyland (S.C.M. Press).

*Edward Thring: Life, Diary and Letters,* by G. R. Parkin (Macmillan).

*Six Great Schoolmasters,* by F. D. How (Methuen).

*Edward White Benson,* by A. C. Benson (Macmillan).

*Almond of Loretto,* by R. J. Mackenzie (Constable).

*Edward Bowen,* by W. E. Bowen (Longmans).

*History of Glenalmond,* by G. St. Quentin.

*Alexander Whyte,* by G. F. Barbour (Hodder & Stoughton).

*William Robertson Nicoll,* by G. H. Darlow (Hodder & Stoughton).

Parliamentary Papers: *Reports on Employment of Women,* 1843 and 1863.

*The Village Schoolmistress's Assistant,* 1852.

*Reports on Elementary Schools 1852–58,* by Matthew Arnold (Macmillan).

Pamphlets:

*The Religious Teaching of Church Training Schools.*

*Report on Prevention and Reformatory Schools.*

*Practical Suggestions to the Founders of Reformatory Schools.*

*Juvenile Crime,* by John Horsley.

*Report on Parish Schools 1858.*

*Position and Prospects of Catholic Liberal Education,* by Hon. and Rev. William Petre (Lord Petre).

*Memories and Adventures,* by Arthur Conan Doyle (Hodder & Stoughton).

*Downside By and Large,* by Hubert van Zeller (Sheed & Ward).

PART III—*Late Victorian*

*Englishwomen's Clothing in the Nineteenth Century,* by C. W. Connington (Faber).

'*And Gladly Wolde He Lerne and Gladly Teche*', by Frances R. Grey (Sampson Low).

*Reminiscences of a Student's Life,* by Jane Ellen Harrison (Hogarth Press).

*Recollected in Tranquillity,* by Janet Courtney (Heinemann).

*The Women of My Time,* by Janet Courtney (Dickson).

*Work and Play in Girls' Schools*, by Dorothea Beale, Jane Frances Dove and Others, 1898.

*Impressions that Remained*, by Ethel Smyth (Longmans).

*E. OE. Somerville*, by Geraldine Cummings (Andrew Dakers).

*Irish Memories*, by E. OE. Somerville and Martin Ross (Longmans).

*The Girlhood of Our Queen*, by Mrs. Herbert Strang (Hodder & Stoughton).

*Blackstick Paper*, by Anne Thackeray Ritchie (Smith Elder).

*This Was My World*, by Viscountess Rhondda (Macmillan).

*A London Girl of the Eighties*, by M. Vivian Hughes (Oxford University Press).

*The Child in the Crystal*, by Lady Sybil Lubbock (Jonathan Cape).

*The Lilac and the Rose*, by Susan Buchan (Lady Tweedsmuir); (Duckworth).

*The Call to the Cloister*, by Peter Anson (S.P.C.K.).

*King George the Fifth*, by Harold Nicolson (Constable).

*Lessons From the 'Varsity of Life*, by R. S. Baden-Powell (Lord Baden-Powell); (Pearson).

*My Early Life: A Roving Commission*, by Winston Churchill (Thornton Butterworth).

*Distant Fields*, by H. A. Vachell (Cassell).

*The Hill*, by H. A. Vachell (John Murray).

*The Story of J.M.B.* (Sir J. M. Barrie), by Denis Mackail (Peter Davies).

*The Puppet Show of Memory*, by Maurice Baring (Heinemann).

*Dear Youth*, by Barbara Wilson (Macmillan).

Also of interest to students of the period is:
*How Different from Us*, by Josephine Kamm (The Bodley Head).

# INDEX